The Innocent Anthropologist
A Plague of Caterpillars
Not a Hazardous Sport
Native Land
The Coast

Nigel Barley

The Duke of Puddle Dock

Travels in the footsteps of
Stamford Raffles

VIKING

VIKING

Published by the Penguin Group
Penguin Books Ltd, 27 Wrights Lane, London W8 5TZ, England
Penguin Books USA Inc. 375 Hudson Street, New York, New York 10014, USA
Penguin Books Australia Ltd, Ringwood, Victoria, Australia
Penguin Books Canada Ltd, 10 Alcorn Avenue, Toronto, Ontario, Canada M4V 3B2
Penguin Books (NZ) Ltd, 182–190 Wairau Road, Auckland 10, New Zealand

Penguin Books Ltd, Registered Offices: Harmondsworth, Middlesex, England

First published 1991
1 3 5 7 9 10 8 6 4 2

Set in 12/14½ pt Lasercomp Sabon
Printed in England by Clays Ltd, St Ives plc

A CIP catalogue record for this book is available from the British Library

ISBN 0–670–83642–7

Contents

Map vi

Acknowledgements viii

List of Illustrations ix

1. Footprints 1
2. Names 10
3. All Good Friends and Jolly Good Company 25
4. Spice Invaders 42
5. Scenes of Old Batavia 57
6. The Great Garden 71
7. Noblesse Oblige 90
8. White Elephants and Other Beasts 110
9. Hope and Glory 131
10. Arise, Sir Stamford 145
11. This Other Elba 158
12. Empires of the Imagination 182
13. Flotsam and Jetsam 196
14. Founding Father 210
15. Leaps and Bounds 215
16. Dust to Dust 227
17. Almost My Only Child 236
18. Fame 253

A Bibliographical Note 268
Important Dates in the Life of Stamford Raffles 271
Index 272

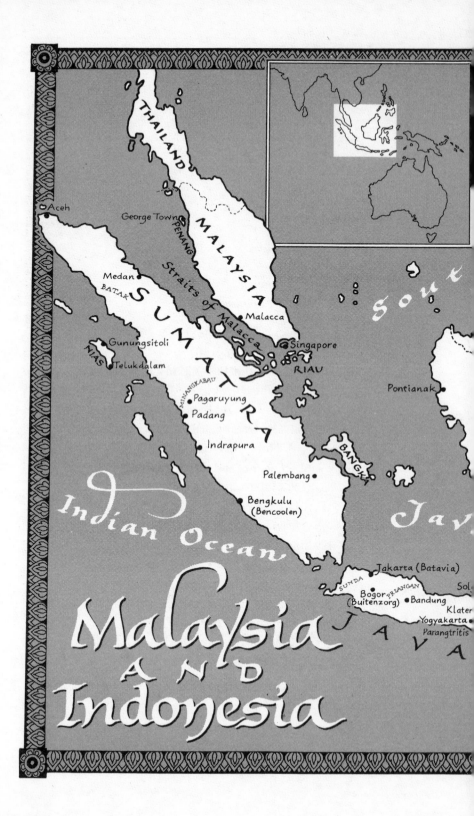

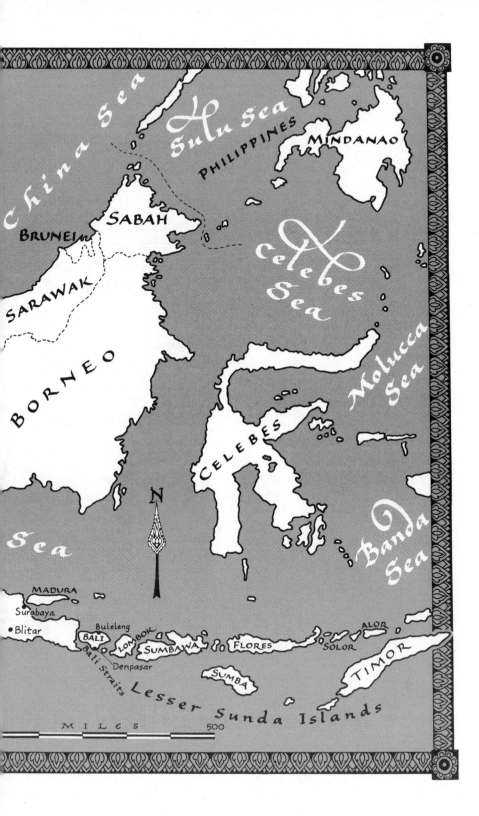

Acknowledgements

The author and publishers would like to thank the following publisher and literary representatives for permission to quote copyright material:

Cindy Adams: to Macmillan Publishing Company, and Mrs Carlton Cole for extracts from *Sukarno: An Autobiography* (Bobbs-Merrill, 1965), copyright © 1965 by Cindy Adams.

Emily Hahn: to Aitken & Stone Ltd. for extracts from *Raffles of Singapore* (Doubleday, 1946).

Every effort has been made to trace copyright holders; any omissions brought to our attention will, of course, be remedied in future editions.

List of Illustrations

Frontispiece. Memorial statue to Sir Thomas Stamford Raffles by Sir Francis Chantry in Westminster Abbey, by courtesy of the Dean and Chapter of Westminster.

1. Penang harbour. Photo: National Maritime Museum.
2. A Dutch judge and dignitaries witnessing the execution of criminals. Photo: British Library.
3 Surveying Prambanang Temple. Photo: British Library.
4 The tomb of Olivia Raffles, Jakarta. Photo: S. B. Sani.
5 View of Gunong Salak, near Buitenzorg. Photo: British Library.
6. The Palace at Bogor. Photo: S. B. Sani.
7. The memorial to Olivia Raffles, Bogor. Photo: Nigel Barley.
8. Borobodur Temple, central Java. Photo: S. B. Sani.
9. A Javan of the lower class, reproduced in *The History of Java*, by T. S. Raffles, 1817.
10. A *gender*, a musical instrument from the Raffles Collection. Photo: British Museum, Museum of Mankind.
11. Portrait of T. S. Raffles by G. E. Joseph now hanging in the National Portrait Gallery, London.
12. Fort Marlborough, Bengkulu. Photo: Nigel Barley.
13. An obelisk tomb in the British Cemetery, Bengkulu. Photo: Nigel Barley.
14. Raffles House, Bengkulu. Photo: Nigel Barley.
15. Hamilton Monument, Bengkulu. Photo: Nigel Barley.
16. Raffles' country house, Bengkulu. Photo: British Library.
17. A flower of the species *Rafflesia arnoldi*. Photo: British Library.

18. The Palace at Pagaruyung, Minangkabau. Photo: S. B. Sani.
19. Bawamakaluo, Nias. Photo: Nigel Barley.
20. The Raffles Statue, Singapore. Photo: Nigel Barley.
21. The Raffles Institution, Singapore. Photo: Nigel Barley.

'I have chalked out for myself a very varied and diversified course; but what is life without variety? and what is existence without occupation?' – T. S. Raffles

1. Footprints

'Raff-lesh,' said the Javanese noodle-seller, making two syllables of it. The final 's' was wet and slushy, a Javanese 's'.

He leaned over the wobbly wooden counter and took the Raffles cigarette packet in a slim, brown hand, cupping it tenderly in a gesture of respect as one would the frail skull of a baby. His fingertips ran lightly over the embossed, phoney crest like braille. The nails were carefully tended. That on the little finger was foppishly long. He had just used it to test my fried noodles.

'Raff-lesh,' he read again. 'He was here, you know – in Bogor.' He indicated the street around our roadside stall. 'They called it Buitenzorg then – "no worries" in Dutch.' A horse-cart rattled past, the little horse's iron shoes slipping and sparking on the steep hillside. The driver wore the sort of peaked cap favoured by American astronauts. His face suggested he at least had worries. Round the brim was written 'Two children are enough', the slogan of the family-planning campaign. Perhaps that was the nature of his worries. Behind us, mountains towered up with lofty indifference into the swirls of fog where they grew tea.

'His wife's grave is there. He made the garden here – the palace garden.' That, I thought, was untrue. It was – well – some Dutchman or German, after his time. Then, reading the packet again, 'Virginia. Raff-lesh was an American?'

'No. He was English like me . . . But I think this is another

Raffles. This one was a –' 'Cat burglar' would never go literally into Indonesian '– he was a thief.'

The stall-owner pursed his lips sagaciously. For all his twenty-odd years, he was a man of the world. 'Are not all colonialists thieves? But perhaps the English were not such big thieves as the Dutch. But I think every great family has naughty children – Raff-lesh too. So it is not strange another of the family should steal. Why, here in Indonesia, there was the case of . . .'

He left the sentence unfinished, thinking better of it as a policeman strolled past, paunch and buttocks straining against the buttons of his uniform, ears visibly apout. I offered a cigarette across the hot wok and, non-smoker that I was, lit one myself and let it smoke untasted into the wind. Most Indonesian males smoke. Not to carry cigarettes is to be without the small change of friendship.

He waved his token of friendship happily, scattering Rafflesian ash over the noodles, pluming smoke from healthy mountain lungs.

'It is good to name cigarettes after big men.' A toothy grin crept out shyly from under his moustache. 'We should have a Bung Karno cigarette. That would be great. You know Bung Karno?'

I threw up a hand into the air, fingers spread, the way children do on Independence Day, five fingers for Pancasila, the five pillars of the nation. '*Merdeka*! Freedom!' The stall rocked dangerously. We both grabbed it. 'Sukarno?' I asked. 'Father of the revolution? First President? Would that be respectful?'

He giggled and spooned out more noodles on to my plate. 'Eat some more. It would be no problem as long as they were the finest brand. If they made people sick, *that* would be bad. But he would not mind. He was a friend of the people. My father *adored* Bung Karno. He had his picture in every room of the house. He, too, was here.'

'Your father?'

'Nooo.' He swatted at me playfully with the spatula. 'Bung Karno.' His voice dropped to a whisper. 'After the problem with the Communists when Pak Harto took over, they kept him in the palace here – the same place Raff-lesh lived. Bung Karno, Raff-lesh, perhaps it is all the same. That is history.'

'Perhaps.'

'It would have a Garuda bird with big claws and Bung Karno's head like on the banknotes when I was small – wearing his *songkok* hat.'

'What? Oh, I see. The cigarettes. But Raffles – Raff-lesh – what did *he* do?'

The noodle-seller shrugged and screwed up his face as if staring into a bright light. 'All I remember from school is he sold government land but got caught. In those days, if you sold land, everything went with it, cattle, people, women.' He laughed and shook his head at the absurdity of it, tasting the word 'women' on his lips, reluctant to let it go.

'He sold them as slaves?'

'Yes. I suppose so.' He frowned in thought, then raised his clotted spatula in token of swearing an oath. 'Yes, Raff-lesh sold off the land and made our people slaves. He *was* a thief.' It seemed like the solemn verdict of Indonesia. After all, history is not what happened. It is what you remember.

He was not giggling now. A shadow had fallen over the wok. The ghost of Raffles had come between us, abruptly chilling the noodles, filming them with fat. Was it true? Raffles a slaver, an embezzler? I did not know. I knew nothing about Raffles. But my curiosity was smouldering. I would look him up as soon as I got back to London – well, one day.

I paid for my noodles and we shook hands. I would walk up the hill and have a look at the palace gardens.

'Red and white!' he called after me. 'Red on top, white at the bottom, like the Indonesian flag.'

What? Oh God. He was talking about Bung Karno cigarette packets again.

'. . . and king-size. Bung Karno was small but he was king-size.' There was satisfaction in the thought.

*

'Raff-lesh.' The minister beamed delightedly and folded his arms with composure. He was on a flying visit to London from America on his way back to Jakarta. The real business was to talk about coffee prices but, in a free hour, he had come to the British Museum to promote general interest in Indonesian culture. As someone who attempted to speak the language, I had been wheeled out to receive him.

Reporters milled around. He flashed an even-handed smile at them, as at unruly children. They flashed back with cameras. In the showcase before him stood a *gender*, a sort of traditional xylophone, shipped by Raffles from Java in 1817. The keys glowed softly with the sheen of ancient tempered metal, soaked in the dulcet tones of tinkling, classical music. The base was artfully carved and gilded with the outspread wings and rearing beak of a huge Garuda bird. In the minister's lapel, a discreeter gold Garuda with sharp claws offered defiance back. On his watchface, even more discreetly, gleamed the symbol of the ruling party.

'Raff-lesh,' he said authoritatively. 'A name that recalls the enduring link between our two great countries. Raff-lesh admired the beauties of Indonesian culture. While he was Governor of Java, the Indonesian people came, in turn, to know something of that concern for liberty and progress that are characteristic of the English. Though a colonialist, he is remembered as a reformer and pioneer of social justice.'

He flashed another ravishing smile and posed deftly on terms of equality with the Garuda, a mythical beast humbled by his personality to a mere pet. He hailed some reporters familiarly by name, rained sincere handshakes upon them and rapped out a suitably risqué joke in Indonesian and idiomatic American.

As the laughter died down, he observed, 'Raff-lesh, himself, promoted coffee in Java. He owned a plantation, you know. Is that no so?' The question was addressed to me.

'Er . . . well.'

'Quite so,' he resumed smoothly. 'Raff-lesh *means* coffee.'

Then the talk seemed to turn all by itself to the price of beans and the reasonableness of Indonesian hopes that it would rise at a forthcoming meeting. The reporters, entranced, wrote down everything he said with panting fervour. It would appear in a dozen newpapers the next day. Suddenly he was gone, trailing an after-whiff of devastating charm, as the Devil is said to move in fumes of sulphur.

*

'Hrraffle.' It was like a clearing of the throat or the noise of disapprobation made by retired colonels in comic strips. We had paid our entry fee to Westminster Abbey and the man from Guinea was determined to have his money's worth of the infidel faith. It was his first visit outside his Marxist-oriented homeland, and I was his guide. He stared at each statue in turn, read the inscription, checked its significance with me. He had not liked the excessive praise heaped on William Wilber-force and the abolitionist movement by the monument next door. He would not like Raffles.

He pouted peevishly. 'Hraffle was the man who instituted the fascist, racist clique in Zimbabwe.'

'No. I think you must mean Rhodes. This is Raffles – Asia,' I added vaguely. 'Quite different.'

A group of tiny, be-denimed Japanese waited politely behind us to take their photographs. He glared at them. He had not finished. He wanted to read the inscription. He was no mere tourist; he had serious work to do.

'*Selected at an early age to conduct the government of the British conquests in the Indian Ocean, by wisdom, vigour and philanthropy, he raised Java to happiness and prosperity unknown under former rulers.*' His voice became increasingly sneering as he progressed.

'How can people write such nonsense? *After the surrender of that island to the Dutch and during his government in Sumatra, he founded an emporium at Singapore.*

'What is an emporium? Is it a polite word for imperialist exploitation?'

'No. It's more a place of trade, a sort of big shop.'

'Capitalism?'

'Yes . . . sort of.'

'Exploitation, as I said.'

The Japanese had despaired of our moving and were trying to sneak their lenses under his armpits.

'Go away,' he said loudly in French and waved his floppy raincoat at them. The label read 'Fabriqué en URSS'.

They cowered back. He bent to read further. 'Ha! Listen to this . . . *where he established freedom of person as the right of the soil and freedom of trade as the right of the port.* Nothing but bourgeois false consciousness of the self.

'*He secured to the British flag the maritime supremacy of the Eastern seas.* Imperialist mystification.

'*Ardently attached to science, he laboured successfully to add to the knowledge and enrich the museums of his native land.* That, surely, is social reproduction through ideological suppression.

'*In promoting the welfare of the people committed to his charge, he sought the good of his country and the glory of God.*' That was beyond all comment.

He straightened and stared triumphantly up at Raffles, content at having seen through the lies of convention in which national heroes are wrapped. Raffles looked back, serenely but not unkindly, the whisper of a smile upon his lips, one finger raised pensively to his brow. He looked about to speak. Just so, he must have regarded the natives 'committed to his charge'.

I wondered, not for the first time, what he was like, what he must have thought and felt, straining to insert myself into the inert stone and see through those blank sockets. A colonialist, be himself had been colonized by so many others – *appropriated*, the Guinean would say. He was cigarettes, coffee, a thief, an oppressor, a champion of freedom. In my own childhood he must surely have been included in those pre-Mao, pious little red books we had read on the founding fathers of the Empire. He was great, therefore good.

We were not here by chance. I had been reading about Raffles recently and felt a need to sidestep the shortcomings of the literature by some sort of direct, personal experience. The literature was not impressive.

There was stolid, patriotic Boulger, who bristled with rage when his sources criticized Raffles, come to the subject after a semi-mystical encounter with a Raffles relative in a London fever hospital. There was the dourly self-effacing *Memoir* of Sophia, second wife and widow, who doggedly referred to herself as 'the Editor' and mentioned the first wife, only once and in a footnote, as one of her husband's 'dearest and closest connections'. Many of the expressions of the Abbey inscription echoed hers. Perhaps she had written it herself. Then there was Hahn, slaphappy-American-wisecracky, and Wurtzburg, studiously archivistic. There were many, many others all drawing on the same few primary sources, quoting and repeating each other in a false, antique-dealers' economy that lent a spurious solidity to a rickety framework of knowledge, resting on firm ground at a few points only.

'Marble,' said the Guinean looking down the line of ossified white figures that constituted the British national past.

Crowded together, they formed one of those absurd crowds you saw in paintings of the French Revolution, each person totally irrelevant to the pose and bearing of his neighbour, gesturing emptily into space, expending untold benevolence and mute eloquence upon walls and ceilings.

'Marble,' he announced with finality, 'was taken from Africa.'

'Surely not. Italy. Other places as well. Anyway, it's not all marble. It's too white for that.'

'No. Marble from Africa. I have seen it. It is – ' he drew a deep breath and flapped his francophone raincoat in frustration – 'a . . . a *scandale géologique!*'

Raffles looked on unmoved. About his feet lay scrolls in stone – not marble. That would be his *adding to the knowledge of his native land*. Or perhaps he was trampling on them, engaging in *social reproduction through ideological suppression*. At this distance in time it was hard to tell.

As we moved away, the Japanese swarmed in, the children of the Rising Sun filling the void of another abandoned outpost of Empire and automatically forming grinning groups of five in front of the statue, obliterating Raffles's inscription in a production-line of souvenirs. Maybe winners never have self-doubt. They are too busy being winners to worry about the value of what they are creating and destroying. They live happily in the present and the future, not the past. But Raffles had *not* been like that.

He would have been surprised by the Japanese, having *had views* about them. I recalled that he once wrote a paper about their national character. But for him they were primarily a natural market for British woollies. They just needed to be opened up. Well, they had been.

In common with all those muted, pigeon-spotted statues that stand about – like flashers – unregarded and embarrassed in the parks and piazzas of the world, Raffles looked as though he still had something to say, as though he was straining against an imposed silence. It was hard not to feel a sort of pity for him. It was a good face, open, eager to learn, humane, wryly optimistic. There was no veneer of prettiness. It was a face with the certain strength of mahogany furniture with solid brass fittings. It would always be comfortable and reliable, a face that would wear well and take on the patina of age without shoddiness. But he had had no chance to age – dead in his forties. And it was only a public face.

In that instant, I knew what I would do. Perhaps there was still one way to put myself in his skin. I would go to the places that were important to him, the places that he had invented or transformed. I would look for his traces in the stones and the memories of the East, follow his tracks from Penang to Singapore. Then, I would come back and see him again.

2. Names

It is Captain Francis Light, founder of Penang, and not Raffles, whose statue was made to stand on the waterfront of the town that brought him fame. Originally, Light pointed his plump behind at this small island – Prince of Wales Island as the British would have it – off the western coast of Malaysia. His face stared with manic vision out on an empty sea, declaring the immutability of history through the permanence of stone. But in the East, the permanence of stone, like the facts of history, has always been precarious and negotiable. During the war, the Japanese prised him loose, dumped him contemptuously in a warehouse and, with blatant symbolism, stole his sword. Nowadays he stands outside the museum amongst a red pillar-box, a defunct carriage from the funicular railway and a pot of ferns, a relic of potent Empire reduced to a harmless item of garden furniture. The Malaysians have never been moved to give him his sword back.

Penang does not, of course, mean 'Prince of Wales', it means 'areca nut', the chewing-gum of the East. But nations come together only to misunderstand each other. The Malays have always named islands by what they look like on a map rather than by what they produce. So there is little areca nut grown here and this was just the first of many misunderstandings that marked the relationship between the East India Company and the natives.

*

I slumped at the airport, having forgotten it was Independence Day and, a foolish virgin, my wick untrimmed, I would have to pay the price. Independence celebrations in Singapore, Malaysia, Indonesia, you can hit them all, one after the other, like a month of Sundays.

'No taxis,' said the man at the information desk to a small but actively resentful crowd of foreigners. 'It's closed. *I'm* closed.' Even worse, the banks were closed and I had no Malaysian money.

'Look,' said the man cheerfully, 'there's a bus in ten minutes. Go to some hotel where you can charge everything. The banks open in the morning. You've got Singapore money? Well, there you are. They take Singapore money on the bus, at par. Yes I know it's worth twice as much as Malaysian money but it's not profiteering. It's a matter of national pride. One for one. It *is* Independence Day.'

The crowd muttered. He was being helpful. Therefore he had accepted responsibility. Therefore it was all his fault. He grinned a ravishing Malay smile, the best defence he could have chosen, a better barrier than the counter.

'You all sit down and I'll tell you a story.'

It was an absurd thing to say to Europeans. We should have all bridled at the childishness of it. Yet somehow it tapped into deep currents of memory, nursery school, a treat from teacher, a story before going home to tea. We obeyed without murmur, settling down, brassy women, pushy executives, a dotty blue-rinsed lady. Mouths gaped, arms were crossed. We sat up straight.

'Right,' said the man, 'I'll tell you where Penang came from.'

*

Penang was a botched rehearsal for Singapore, the city that Raffles would later found. There had been several such rehearsals. Penang was simply in the wrong place, believed to be useful in the trade between India and China, which it was not. It was expected to grow opulent on the commerce of Thailand and Burma, gain aromatic wealth from the spices of the Moluccas. It was to have had a mighty shipyard building East Indiamen of Asian teak to replace scarce British oak. It was to help in this enterprise that Raffles, after ten years' service in London, was recruited to the 'absurd and extravagant' Penang government in 1805. But only one frigate was ever slid down the slipway and the wood had to be brought from India at crippling cost. All his life, Raffles would feel contempt for the government of Penang.

*

'It all started with love. We Malays,' the man on the information desk almost crooned, 'believe in love.' A woman at the back snuffled. She, too, clearly was a believer.

'Francis Light came in search of land in 1786. The Malays were very fierce. Oooh, we were so fierce we used to frighten *each other*! We were all pirates and warriors.' He eyed one of the brassy women boldly to show the old skills had not been lost. 'To be in business then was a terrible thing. Men's business was killing and robbing.'

Not knowing what else to do, some of the tourists took photographs.

'Well, Francis Light landed but they would not listen. They seized him and took him to the chief. "Wah!" shouted the chief. "Cut off his head! And all his men." The Malay sailors they would make into slaves.' He paced up and down behind his counter, a caged tiger. 'They took him and tore off his coat. One of the men took his dagger and held it to his throat.' He seized a pamphlet on tourist facilities in the north and rammed it, trembling, against the imagined throat of Francis Light. His lip quivered with rage and contempt. 'But just as he was about to strike, there came a cry. It was the princess. She had seen the stranger and fallen in love with his fair hair and pale skin. She rushed out weeping, and begged her father to spare his life.'

He crouched behind the desk and wrung the pamphlet in agony between his hands.

Hang on. Wasn't this a remake of the Pocahontas–John Smith story? Never mind. He had the audience in the palm of his hand.

'Oh, Father,' he intoned piteously, 'spare this beautiful man so I may marry him.'

'Very well, my daughter,' he exclaimed back in manly gruffness. 'You may have him and I give you' – exultantly – 'the island of Penang as a wedding present!'

A woman cried. A man clapped. A wheezy, broken-down vehicle appeared on cue and coughed black smoke.

'And now your bus is here. Have a good journey!'

*

It is the best sort of myth, flying in the face of every known ethnographic and historical fact. There is a more pedestrian version. It says that the Company came looking for a convenient staging-post on the way to China and offered to pay rent in cash. The Sultan of Kedah needed the money and hoped to use the Company's presence to keep the Siamese at bay. Later, the unintimidated Siamese invaded and the Company got behind with the rent. That version has the ring of truth. For it is unfulfilled expectations and crazy optimism that sum up John Company in the eastern archipelago.

Having acquired a jungle-covered island, Francis Light had to develop it, for, in that first wave of enterprise culture, it was the rise in property values that was to pay for the establishment that did not yet exist. The solid facts of imperialism rested on a mirage. The cheapest expedient – he realized with brilliant originality – was to load the Company's cannon with silver dollars and fire them off into the bush. The acquisitive Malays swarmed out with machetes, hacked and trampled down the undergrowth to recover the coins and so cleared the island, free of charge, for the British. That, too, is myth. Paul Theroux would later re-use it, shifted to the setting of an African school, in one of his stories. Writers are like slow-chewing termites that reduce literary leaves to a timeless humus and Raffles, too, was a writer. The history of trade is perhaps that men meet to exchange things and end up exchanging ideas and stories. Raffles was unusual in that, for him, the ideas were more important than the things. This had been so since his childhood and the child holds the key to the man.

*

'Where to?'

'Love Lane.' The rickshaw-driver behind me was Indian, very black, with thick, ponderous legs and splayed toes, leathery knees like calluses. Raffles would have called him a Chuliah. We cycled through needling rain, for it was the rainy season in Penang.

'Love Lane,' he repeated. The name seemed to strike a chord. He leaned forward and brought his mouth level with my ear.

'You want fuck?' he hissed. I thought at first this must be a personal invitation, then he added, 'Schoolgirls?' I had a vision of fat, Chinese matrons with ring-covered fingers squeezing themselves into school-uniform blouses. 'Tourist not know difference lah!'

It was a shock to the system, like spooning in your morning cornflakes and finding whisky had been substituted for milk.

'No, I most definitely do not want fuck. For one thing, it's only ten in the morning.'

A woman crossing the road clutching a child and dressed in the long Malay dress and headscarf gave me a dirty look, annoyed at such language.

For all sorts of cultural reasons that was probably not a clinching rejoinder anyway. Few things vary as much from place to place as what is known to be universally true about sex. From student days, I recalled a Malaysian engineer incredulous at college rules that sought to prevent fornication by excluding ladies from rooms after two in the afternoon but not in the morning. But then he had firmly believed in the aphrodisiac properties of cocoa, having observed White Men to drink it before going to bed.

*

The Javanese noodle-seller was right. To read of Raffles is to read of Sukarno. Yet there is a paradox in this. While I was being taught at school to see Raffles as a benefactor of humanity through empire, Sukarno was emerging as one of the demons of the third world, his very opposite. He had led his nation in a successful struggle for independence from the Dutch in the thirties and forties, overcoming regionalism and religious factions. He was vilified in the Western press, depicted as endlessly anti-democratic, difficult and tiresome in international affairs, a military enemy in the semi-official war over Sabah and Sarawak, a President of Indonesia who delighted in undermining the conventional certainties that constituted international order. Ultimately, in the sixties, his playing off of one group against another would end in an avowedly anti-Communist military coup and he would find himself penned up, a powerless figurehead, in his own palace. How then could his life and that of Raffles possibly intersect?

Perhaps this is the proof that what we have is not the truth about such men but something already structured in advance. Beneath the exigencies of time and place, they are incarnations

15

of the great archetypes by which we can approach the bare facts of history by pressing them into a known mould. They are Poor Boy Makes Good, Triumphant Patriot and ultimately both are Wronged Hero. Their footsteps constantly cross, their words intermingle. A passage written about one always seems to recall something about the other. Their lives inform each other, a mass of dots that can be joined to form a dozen different pictures.

But where to start with a man? Perhaps with the name that recognizes his separate existence. Bung Karno, for instance.

> 'According to Ibu Wardoyo, when he was small, Soekarno was called Koesno. But because he was constantly ill, his name was changed to Soekarno. The name Karno is full of meaning to Javanese. Adipati Karno from Ngawonggo in the old shadow-puppet plays is a symbol of the hero who is outstandingly loyal to his country until the end of his days.' – R. Rahim, *Bung Karno Masa Muda*

It is a common belief in the eastern archipelago that the name of a child is important. A name that is too 'heavy' may weigh upon a child and make it ill. So a sickly child may have to be renamed. In the West, names are not without their burden of class and affectation, but Christian names are given once and for all at christening. Yet in defiance of the dictates of the Church of England, Raffles too seems to have been christened twice.

The circumstances of his birth were unusual. He was born in Jamaica in 1781 on the West Indiaman of which his father was master. The vessel was named *Ann* after his mother. On this first occasion he was dubbed Thomas Stamford Bingley. Bingley was a shadowy, even shady, godfather who turned up later in Java during Raffles's years as Governor. Raffles for some reason then denied his relationship to Bingley. Stamford was a merchant in the West India trade, otherwise unknown. From the point of view of posterity, he is named after Raffles. Three years later, Raffles was christened again as plain Thomas after his grandfather and thus he would remain until his knighthood when the name Stamford re-emerged. The history of those early years may be seen as the passage from plain Thomas to Sir Stamford, the passage from a 'light' name to a 'heavy' one.

*

The rickshaw-driver's response to Love Lane was an argument for historical continuity, evidence that, after more than two hundred years, it was still in business. It was here that the young bachelors – the 'writers' of the Company – lived in Flowerpot Hall. The cost, I recalled irrelevantly, had been one and a half dollars a day, which included a bottle of wine among four. Their amorous needs had given the street its name but their generous donations of genetic material had not marked Penang. For Penang is a ramshackle Chinese city, laced with Indians. Malays seemed in a decided minority. They only appeared at night to throng the seafront food stalls and show off their flashy motorbikes.

*

At the age of fourteen, Raffles joined the East India Company as the lowest form of clerk. Initially, he is an unattractive hero. He is a swot. He isn't even good at games.

> 'My leisure hours, however, still continued to be devoted to favourite studies; and with the little aid my allowance afforded, I contrived to make myself master of the French language, and to prosecute enquiries into some of the branches of literature and science; this was, however, in stolen moments, either before the office hours in the morning, or after them in the

evening ... I shall never forget the mortification I felt when the penury of my family once induced my mother to complain of my extravagance in burning a candle in my room.' – T. S. Raffles

Bung Karno was marginally luckier.

'Actually, Soekarno's room already had electricity. However, since he did not have the price of a light bulb, he preferred to read and study with an oil lamp.' – R. Rahim, *Bung Karno Masa Muda*

Raffles's childhood sings a song of poverty and, like Sukarno, his principal friends were books. The precise cause of his father's lack of substance has never been established – illness, drink, gambling? Raffles always wrote as if he had no father at all, though he seems to have lived until 1797. Raffles only had two years of proper schooling and all his life would feel the lack of it. He described himself in later years as being 'as ignorant as a Hottentot'. Like many who lack formal education, he saw it as the panacea for all human ills and yearned with missionary zeal to give it to others. That is a major theme of his life. Themes, of course, are constructed retrospectively and beloved of biographers who usually like to make their characters move in straight lines.

Given the straitened circumstances of his youth, it is small wonder that Raffles kept quiet about that pretentious 'Stamford' and 'Bingley' of his first fonting. His aunt twitted his intimations of gentility with the nickname 'The Duke of Puddle Dock', a poor area in Wapping. He was comparatively lucky in this. In later days, he might have ended up as 'Bing'. The English poor have always been merciless to members of their own class who attempt to rise. During my own boyhood, in those same London localities, 'The Duke of Puddle Dock' had yielded to a coarser peer. Anyone showing such a frustrated sense of position as Raffles was typically rewarded with the name 'Lord Muck from Turd Hill'.

*

We turned down a narrow side street. There it was, Love Lane, proclaiming itself upon the wall but not as I had pictured it in my imagination. The houses were too similar to Catford dwellings to be exotic, and evoked rising damp and the difficulties of sanitation rather than romance. A few sleazy Chinese hotels stood dankly about on slick asphalt, exuding hard-edged discomfort. A thin old man in a vest emerged from one of the houses, worked his chest briefly and projected a mouthful of phlegm neatly into the street in front of us. It was probably not a personal comment.

The ground floors of the buildings provided a sort of covered walkway as prescribed by Raffles in his designs for the houses of Singapore. Perhaps he had taken the design from here – but then there is a uniform Portuguese–Chinese–European architectural style that is much the same from Macao to Timor. Motorbikes had been wheeled out of the rain and effectively barred access to pedestrians so that they were forced into the seeping gutters.

'The Chinese do that!' snarled the driver. It was the sort of petty resentment that racial feuds are built of.

I tried to think of Raffles here, stalking around in knee-breeches, probing this, inquiring into that, making endless notes, but could detect no answering resonance from the past. It was like shouting down a well and hearing no echo. But then, Raffles had not been a bachelor on arrival in Penang. Perhaps he had never lived in Flowerpot Hall.

'Where to?' the driver called again.

*

19

'Mr Raffles went out to India in an inferior capacity, through the interest of Mr Ramsay, Secretary to The Company, and in consequence of his marrying a lady connected with that gentleman.' – H. Colburn, *Biographical Dictionary of the Living Authors of Great Britain and Ireland*

It was through his marriage that scandal first touched the life of Raffles. In an age of patronage, he seems to have gained promotion by merit alone, rising in a single bound from London clerk at £70 a year to Penang Assistant Secretary at £1,500. His contemporaries might have chosen to believe that this was the recognition of his sheer ability and ten years' hard work. Instead, they looked for a less creditable and more plausible reason.

They found it in his wife. Five days after his appointment, Raffles was married to Olivia, the widow of an Indian surgeon and some ten years his senior. The acquisition of a ready-made Company wife might be seen merely as completing his tropical outfitting, or be the result of sudden passion invading the arid, industrious life of young Thomas. But rumour wanted it otherwise. The 120 white residents of Penang were hungry for gossip and needed someone to disapprove of. It was said – almost certainly libellously – that Ramsay, Raffles's boss, had needed to dispose of an importunate mistress. Raffles had got her out of the way in return for promotion.

'". . . Utari is now motherless. Tjokro worries much about her future and who will watch over her and give her love. This is a deep concern on his mind. I think, possibly, if you were to ask my niece to marry you it would relieve some little bit of pressure from Tjokro."

'. . . "Well," I explained slowly, "I owe Tjokro much gratitude and . . . I love Utari . . . But not very much. However, if you think I should ask for her hand because this may make the burden lighter for my idol, then I will do so.”’ – C. Adams, *Soekarno: An Autobiography*

I could hear the sea at the bottom of the road. 'The fort,' I said, a little peevishly. 'Take me to the fort.' Perhaps I would find him there.

*

It was Penang that was Raffles's introduction to the East. By the time the six-month outward voyage was over, Raffles could speak Malay, something most of his seasoned colleagues would never learn to do. For them it was a language to be quarantined within the interpreter's domain. His career at Penang has more than a touch of unconscious comedy about it. His office must have been like that small cabin in the Marx Brothers' movie which ends up containing the entire ship's population. One by one, he assumes all the important jobs of the colony. He keeps the minutes of the Council, oversees the newspaper, produces the dispatches for home, acts as Recorder to the law court, discovers that the official translator cannot, in fact, speak Malay and takes over the job himself. In his spare time, he researches the history and customs of the Malays. And here he begins to form about him 'the Family', a clique of intelligent and slightly hungry men who look to him as their guiding light and will stick with him throughout his career.

*

'Being of a cheerful lively disposition and very fond of Society it was surprising how he [Raffles] was able to entertain so hospitably as he did and yet labour so much as he was known to do at the time, not only in his official capacity but in acquiring a general knowledge of the history, Government and local interests of the neighbouring states; and this he was

21

greatly aided in doing by conversing freely with the natives who were constantly visiting Penang at this period, many of whom were often found to be sensible, intelligent men and greatly pleased to find a man holding Mr Raffles's station able and anxious to converse with them in their own language. – Captain T. Travers, *Journal*

Again and again, writers comment on the extraordinary fact that Raffles actually *liked* the peoples of the East and treated them with *respect*. Raffles's love-affair with the Malay nation had begun.

*

The rickshaw swung round towards the waterfront. A clutch of white, classical buildings stood out against the sea, their fancy-pastry fronts compromised by roofs of asbestos sheeting. Raffles might well have seen those, peeling in the damp heat. At night nowadays they are lit up with fairy-lights.

The driver gestured towards the museum, another white-pillared pile.

'You go there. They got the Rolls-Royce from when the Communists shot the Governor but they washed off the blood and filled up all the bulletholes. No fun any more.'

'That was certainly a mistake. But I've already been.'

'They got old British uniforms.'

I had seen them, worn by white-faced mannequins with long Beatle haircuts fit to give a sergeant-major apoplexy.

'I've been.'

'They've got old *Japanese* uniforms . . .'

'The fort,' I said. 'Just take me to the fort.'

*

It is in Penang that Raffles begins to be able to discharge patronage, slipping a commission to a friend here, easing

22

another into an office there. The immediate, personal result of this is that his three sisters – two later to be certified dowdy by Lord Minto – emerge from the shadows and become marriageable. Henceforth, there will usually be one of them in the wings of Raffles's life. In succession to his new brother-in-law, Raffles becomes the Naval Agent, bringing down official displeasure on his head by combining offices of Company and military. But the last laugh is his. When, in 1807, he briefly leaves the colony for the sake of his shattered health – destroyed by malaria and overwork – the Council are forced to send a longboat after him begging him to return. In his absence, no one even knows how to send an official dispatch back to London.

*

An air of failure still hangs over Penang. In the nineteenth century, the great wonder of the place was a Chinese bakery powered by water. That has now gone.

The fort remains a self-conscious tourist attraction. In front of it stands an unremarkable bungalow, as at Eastbourne, owned by the Malaysian navy. It is made glamorous only by stern warnings against the perils of photography contrary to the Official Secrets Act.

Fort Cornwallis was begun in 1805 and almost immediately began to fall apart. The Company was endemically incapable of building forts in the Far East. It was the same at Bengkulu, where the tower fell down.

The rain had mitigated to a fine mist like steam, encouraging the lichen sprouting among the cannon. That day, Fort Cornwallis was attracting few tourists. A legend claims that the cannon are frequented by barren women hoping to be cured by the sheer phallic potency of ordnance. None was apparent. The interior was haunted by feral cats and raucous crows that stalked each other among the ramparts. Obviously effete

Chinese youths trailed their scarves and struck advantageous postures against the skyline – a trysting place of sorts, then. Rounding the corner of a pillbox, I came across a panting young man and giggling girl at grips in the damp grass and thought it best to stare into space like Francis Light and keep walking as if towards some celestial vision. The path was a dead end, and the only alternative to retracing my steps was to climb down some twenty feet on to sharp railings that ripped my trousers.

'All here is dull stupidity,' Olivia had written tartly of Penang. It was still an unexciting town, ramshackle but not mysterious. Raffles had never given himself to Penang. It was an upstart place. An upstart himself, Raffles was curiously in awe of history and could not wait to leave it for the ancient city of Malacca. There was nothing for me here. I decided I would hurry after him.

3. All Good Friends and Jolly Good Company

'For forty days the Portuguese ships traded at Malacca; but still the Portuguese commander remained on shore, presenting dollars by the chest and gold; and how many beautiful cloths did they present to the illustrious Shah Ahmed Shah, so that the Sultan was most happy!

After this Sultan Ahmed Shah said to the commanders of the Portuguese, "What more do you require from us, that you present us such rich presents?" To this the commander replied, "We only request one thing of our friend, should he be well inclined towards the white men ... We wish to request a small piece of ground, to the extent of what the skin of a beast may cover" ... The commander then took the skin of the beast, and having rent it into cords, measured out therewith four sides, within which the Portuguese built a store-house of very considerable dimensions, leaving large square apertures in the wall for guns; and when the people of Malacca enquired the reason of the apertures being left, the Portuguese returned for answer, "These are the apertures that the white men require for windows."' – T. S. Raffles, 'On the Malayu Nation'

That any fortifications are still there in modern Malacca is due entirely to Raffles. The Dutch succeeded the Portuguese. Then the British, at war with Napoleon, had seized the city from the Dutch in a sort of uneasy trusteeship that was half military occupation, half smooth civilian face. By the time

Raffles arrived in 1808, the normally dilatory East India Company had decided on a bold stroke. They would demolish the entire city and forcibly disperse its mixture of European, Arab, Chinese, Malay and Indian inhabitants in the hope of diverting its trade to Penang. The fort was already gone. They had blown it up.

> 'The Fort was the glory of the town of Malacca, and when the fort was destroyed, the town lost its glory like a woman whose husband is dead. Her face no longer has its glory.' – Munchi Abdullah, *Hikayat Abdullah*

*

In the course of his life, Raffles wrote many reports lauding the resources, prospects and potential of the parts of the world he wanted to grab. They are in the bland and soft-edged language that one nowadays recognizes as the domain of the estate agent. Areas 'abound in' game and fish, are 'enbosomed' in verdure, resources are 'virtually limitless'. He wrote one on Malacca arguing that it was a valuable possession and should be retained, that the policy of destruction would work no magic for ailing Penang. It should have got him fired. Instead, it convinced the Council, saved the city and made him an important friend in Lord Minto, Governor-General of India. All his life, he would try to catch the tone of such a report again, writing on Java, Nias, the Philippines, Singapore. He never did. One suspects that the Malacca document carried conviction by showing that the city paid its way. It still does.

*

> 'The prejudices of the inhabitants are too well known to require comment here; and it is no common advantage that will induce them to quit the tombs of their ancestors, their temples sacred to their Deity, their independence and estates on which they depend for their livelihood and respectability.'
> – T. S. Raffles, Report to the Governor and Council at Penang

I sat in the small stall at the base of Bukit China, where the Chinese still bury their dead. The air is heavy with the cloying scent of frangipani. The Malays call it 'dead Chinaman flower' because it grows in profusion in their cemeteries. Herds of tourists are led around by Indian guides disgorging pointless information.

'The Portuguese arrived in 1511 and built the fort at the bottom of the hill . . . the largest Chinese graveyard in South-East Asia . . . The Chinese build their graves in the form of wombs . . .' A woman squawks, 'Did he say *moons?*' 'No dear, *tombs.*'

Across the road, with the relaxed logic of the East, stands a traditional Chinese temple dedicated to a man who was actually a Muslim. Serried ranks of bespectacled faces stare back at the worshipper, each photograph glued to a piece of wood.

'They've just put the rent up,' a man complains, tumbling bundles of counterfeit money into the flames. 'My father is costing me a fortune.' We both look blankly at the heavenly money now transferred to his father's divine account, a way of cheating, really. 'No, not *this* sort of money, the money – the *real* money – I pay to keep his picture here.'

Elsewhere people are reading fortunes, leaning over into the future. A young woman lies back sluttishly against a shrine with her hand out.

'What sort of shrine is this?' She looks blank. 'Buddhist, Taoist?' She shrugs.

'Don't ask me. I just kill devils.'

Inside, a child sits at a table before a glass of water, its meniscus brimming like a tearful eye. He slips coins into the water. The water does not overflow.

'Magic,' he says happily.

A line of skinny Chinese joggers appear in designer sportswear and labour up the hill on hairless legs, dripping with sweat, pausing to do limp step-ups on a convenient womb-tomb. I am shocked at this domestication of death, or perhaps I have absorbed Eastern notions of the uncleanliness of feet. The stall-holder laughs at my expression.

'No, no. It is not the young misbehaving. These athletes are our heroes. This is politics. We are fighting for our heritage. It is a protest against the government plans to demolish our cemetery and build a housing estate for the Malays. The Malays have too many children. Too many. They have put our leaders in jail, so we show our solidarity with our ancestors by jogging on their graves. They can't touch us for that.'

*

In Malacca, there seem to be none of those small, informal hotels you find in Indonesian towns and large hotels belong to nowhere. The lift wishes me good morning in a robot voice with a Japanese–American lilt. Downstairs is a continuous buffet called 'hi-T', a cornucopia of food from three conti-nents, with, at the end, a dish to bring tears to an ex-pat's eyes – bread-and-butter pudding, slimy with eggy goodness, dusted with brown sugar. Suddenly there is a gust of sniggers. A gaggle of Chinese schoolgirls enter, simpering in sailor suits, and descend on the bread-and-butter pudding with flailing spoons. They chop it up with little cries and eat it with boiled squid. Then they sit with their hands neatly folded in their laps and sing to one of their number: 'Happy birthday to you/ You belong in a zoo.'

*

It is time to give Raffles a face. What did he look like? You grope for a reliable icon. The statues are inaccurate. Some of the artists had never seen him. The portraits all show him pensive, bowed in thought. A sketch of him made from life in Bengkulu suggests this to be flattery: he is virtually a hunch-

28

back. Fortunately, Raffles would return to Malacca in 1810 and meet another writer. Munchi Abdullah, then a boy of about twelve, would, as befits a child of mixed Arab and Indian descent, become one of the founding fathers of Malay literature. It is typical of Raffles that he bothered to be kind to a small, native boy of no importance, to encourage him in his studies. Unlike many Europeans of that age, he could always see himself in the troubled people he ruled. Abdullah's candid eye leaves us a description of Raffles and Olivia that disarms by its simplicity and sets the portraits in their context.

'And when I first saw Mr Raffles, he struck me as being of middle stature, neither too short nor too tall. His brow was broad, the sign of large-heartedness; his head betokened his good understanding; his hair being fair betokened courage; his ears being large betokened quick hearing: his eyebrows were thick, and his left eye squinted a little; his nose was high; his cheeks a little hollow; his lips narrow, the sign of oratory and persuasiveness; his mouth was wide; his neck was long, and the colour of his body was not purely white; his breast was well-formed; his waist slender; his legs to proportion and he walked with a stoop . . .

'. . . I observed his habit was to be always in deep thought. He was most courteous in his intercourse with all men. He always had a sweet expression towards Europeans as well as native gentlemen. He was extremely affable and liberal, always commanding one's best attention. He spoke in smiles. He was also an earnest enquirer into past history and gave up nothing till he had probed it to the bottom. He loved most to sit in quietude, when he did nothing else but write or read . . . He had a time set apart for each duty, nor would he mingle one with another. Further, in the evenings, after tea, he would take ink, pen and paper, after the candles had been lighted, reclining with closed eyes in a manner that I often took to be sleep; but in an instant he would be up and write for a while until he went to recline again. Thus, he would pass the night, till twelve or one . . . He kept four persons on wages, each in their peculiar departments; one to go to the forests in search of various kinds of leaves, flowers, fungi, pulp and such like products. Another he sent to collect all kinds of flies, grasshoppers, bees, in all their varieties, as well as scorpions, centipedes and such like, giving him needles as well as pins with a box to stick the creatures therein. Another he sent with a basket to seek for coral, shells, oysters . . . and another to collect animals such as birds, jungle fowl, stags, mousedeer and so forth . . . Further, people brought books on Malay history to the number of many hundreds, so as to nearly finish the national literature . . . Now Mr Raffles' disposition was anything but covetous, for, in whatever undertakings or projects he had in view, he grudged no expense so that they were accomplished . . . Thus loads of money came out of his chest daily, in buying things, or in paying wages. I also perceived that he hated the habit of the Dutch who lived in Malacca of running down the Malays and they detested him in return; so much so that they would not sit down beside him. But Mr Raffles loved always to be on good terms with the Malays, the poorest could speak to him . . .' – Munchi Abdullah, *Hikayat Abdullah*

*

There is an odd lopsided look about Malacca. It takes a while to realize why. They have moved the sea, pushing hills into it in reclamation projects. It no longer laps pensively at the hill with its Portuguese fort, like a child at an ice-cream. The fortifications stick up bare and embarrassed like men unexpectedly caught with their trousers down. In the church on the hill is a statue of St Francis Xavier, who brought the

Catholic faith to the East and died here for his pains. The locals, whatever the name of their God, rub his back for luck. The statue lacks a hand. They tell you how the Pope demanded that a hand should be hacked off the corpse of St Francis and sent to Rome as a relic. When severed, it gushed fresh blood. The statue was erected in atonement. That night a falling tree sheared off the hand of the statue. Malays like stories like that.

The church is bathed in the sound of Viennese waltzes, blowing across from a 'song and lumier' show in the football stadium.

'Does it have Raffles in it?'

'Yes, yes. Laffers, orl history of Maracca. You buy ticket.' The Chinese ticket-seller tried to push one into my hand.

'Who plays Raffles?'

He grinned. 'Is my brother, thin man, have wig.'

I pictured a Chinese Raffles, powdered and perruqued, shouting, 'You no destloy Maracca-lah!'

No. I did not yet have a firm enough grip on Raffles to deal with caricature. I passed on.

Round the back of the hill is the reconstruction of the royal palace, executed in wood. Rickshaw-drivers congregate in front of it to play Malay pop music on their radios. Here, absurdly, above the blare of a song about hens and cockerels, a thinly veiled treatment of Malay marital relations, I bump into a colleague from England. We perform a dance of very English embarrassment in the middle of the road, both feeling like matter out of place. He is led off by Malay friends to the museum of the independence struggle and joyfully photographed under a label, 'the beginnings of British interference'. There is hardly any mention of Raffles in there, just an adulatory story of the endless bickering of second-rate modern politicians.

I sidle off and find a damp, small British cemetery, tucked

away behind the hill, fitting really, a bit of an English garden awash with the same Malay pop music but full of Madras soldiery. The British of that time regarded all of South-East Asia as a mere offshoot of India. Raffles had been one of the first, in his paper 'On the Malayu Nation', to recognize the Malays as a separate people.

The white monuments are like loaves set aside to rise, pocked and buckled with time. One reads:

'Frances Anne died age 5, 1862. Early piety, affection and precocious talent were her distinguishing and endearing characteristics.

> Too sweet a blossom for a tainted earth,
> She blooms transplanted in the courts of heaven.
> The stone, despairing to describe her worth,
> Tells but of blighted hopes and bosoms riven.'

There would be plenty of riven bosoms for Raffles later on, but for the moment he was in his element, for the first time in his life fully alive, released from the purdah of his office – he was going to war with an army brought for him from India.

*

The British were on the move in the East. The veto on expansion had been lifted in the struggle against Napoleon. They had seized the French islands of Réunion and Mauritius with embarrassing ease and a Dutch force in the Moluccas had most inconveniently surrendered. Now they looked to the threat of a French fleet using the Dutch colony of Java. In those long, dreamy writing sessions of the night, Raffles created paper empires of the imagination and plotted the annexation of islands and brown, friendly peoples. He yearned for Java. For once Company policy was in agreement with his own designs. He was transferred to Malacca, the personal protégé of Lord Minto, to gather intelligence about Java, make friends with the local princes and help plan its invasion. He was like a bird released from its cage. The Penang government were furious.

*

'The Portuguese arrived in 1511. We have been here ever since.'

It was one of those breathtakingly simple statements that required dismantling and holding up to the light. The Portuguese of Malacca are a fiction that has become a fact.

Alfonso Alvarez lived in the Portuguese Square, an ancient colonial structure built a few years ago by the government. The walls were decorated with 'Come to Malaysia Year, 1989' stickers. Beneath them could be seen, confusingly, 'Come back to Malaysia in '87' stickers. He was nineteen years old. During the day he worked in the museum, selling postcards of the traditional Portuguese wedding display to tourists. In South-East Asia if you want to have a regional identity you have to have a wedding ritual and a local costume. The costume here was something like the outfits worn by the fake Mexican folk-singers who haunt Jakarta hotels.

At night he worked in the Lusitanian restaurant, across the square, selling Portuguese food. The menu included something which after lengthy interpretation turned out to be meat pie. A popular alternative was 'Kentucky Fried Chicken – Portuguese Style'.

He spoke English, Malay, Chinese and – most importantly – Papia Kristen, a pidgin of Portuguese and Malay, once the lingua franca of the whole vast archipelago, now shrunk down to this small enclave in the way that Latin has become the language of chemists.

Alfonso and his friends Diego and Rodrigo were the most

untypically friendly people I had met in Malacca. They were attractive, relaxed, easy-going with the slow, open-handed gestures of fishermen. Physically they were Indians. When the Dutch threw the Portuguese out of the East, there were great tidal migrations back and forth between Malacca, Timor and Goa. Many empires have risen and collapsed in these islands, leaving their ethnic debris. Raffles had used such 'Black Portuguese' troops in Bengkulu. I remembered they had been called Topazes.

'We are Catholics. Yes, yes, we all go to church every Sunday – even the young. We are fishermen. It is hard, dangerous work. We need God's protection. We cannot marry Malays, they are Muslims. But we can marry the Indians and the Chinese.' Alfonso executed a groin-writhing movement. 'Wah! I shall marry a Chinese. They are pale-skinned – beautiful.'

I got out a word-list. This was a Rafflesque windfall for pedantry. I had a colleague who was researching pidgins. It would be useful thesis-fodder, an opportunity not to be missed. We were halfway through the list when a fat, slightly threatening man appeared. The lads leapt up and proffered chairs with respectful gestures, made room for him to sit, fell silent.

'Garcia,' he said, stabbing out a hand like a swordthrust. 'I own the restaurant here. If you want to ask about the Portuguese, you must ask me.'

We had to start the word-list again. This was clearly the official version. The answers were different.

'These are children. They know nothing. See, they give you Malay words. I have been to Portugal. I know the proper words, so I correct them all the time.' Music started up and drowned his correct words. In an unthinking gesture, he reached out frowning and slapped the nearest boy sharply round the ear as if it were his fault. 'The folk-songs too. I

34

have fetched the records from Lisbon, so we get the words right.'

'How long have you been here?'

'The Portuguese arrived in Malacca in 1511 . . .'

'No,' I amended, 'how long have you been *here*? In the square.'

'It was a priest who moved us here in the thirties. He said it was the only way to keep the language. We have the Bible in Papia Kristen but now we use English. Maybe you don't think we look Portuguese?'

'Well . . .'

'I tell you. We are a mixture. Indians, Malays, Europeans but. . .' he eyed me shrewdly, 'we have *become* Portuguese. It is important our children stay Portuguese.'

I could see his point. Instead of being the odds and ends, the racial dandruff, the result of three centuries' playing the genetic fruit-machine, they were now the original Portuguese, not the upshot but the source of it all. It is too simple to say that tourism destroys a people's identity. By selling the Portuguese identity to tourists, they had come to feel it themselves.

We chatted on. When the owner left, the boys whispered together in their doubtless faulty Portuguese, then quietly lost my bill.

Alfonso walked me back to the gate, a rueful grin on his face.

'They don't know it yet,' he said, 'but I'm leaving. A friend's fixed a job for me in Australia. Lots of us go there. Here there's no work. And there we can marry white women. A fisherman's life's so hard, you can't imagine. I want better things. I have dreams. I've got a job in a cheese factory.'

We stood by the sea wall and, without any particular reason, looked out over the bay, the stuff that Europeans build their dreams of.

'That island,' he said. 'It looks like a pregnant woman, see there's the lump. They're developing it for tourists. There's a story that only the righteous can go there. The boats of the unrighteous would sink.' He looked at me. 'Are you righteous? We always believed the English were righteous.'

'Inhabitants of Java! . . . Your future happiness or misery, as well as that of your families, is in your hands. The English character is not unknown to you – it is for you to decide.' – T. S. Raffles, 'Proclamation to the People of Java'

'At that time, there were not yet many English in the town of Malacca and to see an Englishman was like seeing a tiger, because they were so mischievous and violent. If one or two English ships called in at Malacca, all the Malacca people would keep the doors of their houses shut, for all round the streets there would be a lot of sailors, some of whom would break in the doors of people's houses, and some would chase the women on the streets, and others would fight amongst themselves and cut one another's heads open . . . Moreover, a great number were killed owing to their falling in the river, owing to their being drunk; and all this made people afraid. At that time, I never met an Englishman who had a white face, for all of them had "mounted the green horse," that is to say, were drunk. So much so, that when children cried, their mothers would say, "Be quiet, the drunken Englishman is coming," and the children would be scared and keep quiet.' – Munchi Abdullah, *Hikayat Abdullah*

'We are now in the agony of preparation for Java; and I will whisper in your ear that I am going there myself, not to command the Army but to see all the political work done to my mind. "Modeste" is to be my state coach.' – Lord Minto

*

I walked down past the memorial to the war dead, across from the new Japanese clock. A perfectly preserved Morris Minor chugged past – thirty or forty years old, but immaculate. Its driver steered it as though driving a statue of Queen Victoria. Through the balustrade of the bridge you could see the harbour of Malacca. It is not what it once was. It no longer teems with the multifarious trade of the Indies. The rich scent of spices no longer overwhelms the stench of the water. In Raffles's time it held a vast flotilla of sixty ships crammed with British and Indian troops and a single, low, black vessel, the *Modeste*, the ship of Lord Minto commanded by his peevish, horse-faced son. The mouth of the river has silted up and been sidestepped by Raffles's other home, Singapore. Yet you can still find an exotic mix of nationalities in this narrow waterway, flat-faced Javanese, sharp-nosed Buginese, disdainful Achinese.

A rusty hulk was loading coconuts with an even rustier crane, chains rasping and jangling. The logic of coconuts in the East has always escaped me. They seem to be simultaneously imported and exported by just about everywhere. Perhaps the appropriate model is the exchange of women in marriage, since everyone ends up with the same number of coconuts but *different* coconuts.

Away from the main channel a small vessel, a *pinisi*, flying the red-and-white Indonesian flag, was being slapped from side to side by the waves as if they were trying to sober it up. A man was gutting fish into a bucket, using a dagger whose sheath lay on the deck. He looked up and caught my eye and gave that unmistakable Indonesian gesture of acknowledgement, a simultaneous raising of the eyebrows and widening of the cheekbones. In the West it could only be a sexual advance. In the East it means something like 'We do not know each other, we may never speak, but I acknowledge your presence.' I twinkled back and he smiled, threw down the fish and gestured a circuitous route with wrist and elbow by which I might come abroad. It was time to get out the cigarettes again.

He held out a hand in greeting. It was slimy with fish-scales.

'Where are you from?' I asked.

'Wah! You speak proper Indonesian. We are from Woring. You will not know it.' He picked up the fish and squeezed out the contents of its head as one would burst a boil.

I *did* know it. I had been there a couple of years before.

'It is near Maumere, Flores. Your boat was built by Habib.'

He reeled back. 'You know Habib?'

'I met him. He was building a new boat for a man from Australia.' It was true. It was their first foreign contract. Everyone in the village had been very excited. It would mean a trip to Australia for the men who delivered the boat.

They were sea-gypsies, and the government was trying to settle them and turn them into farmers and good citizens. But they could not abide living in houses. They turned sickly and died. Then a brilliant local official had worked out a compromise. He discovered houses were fine as long as they were built of coral so the people could smell the sea all around them. Even then they built them on stilts out over the water.

He gave me a fishy hug. 'My name is Dion. I have four children, all of them boys. Too much of this, I reckon.' He waggled his thumb suggestively through his fingers and laughed.

In that instant, I realized how little I had been enjoying Malaysia up till now. The people had been nice enough, but rather as Europeans are nice. They were polite. They did not disturb you. In Malacca, it would be possible to go for days without talking to anyone, like in London. But Indonesian friendliness was a powerful bear-hug that grabbed you despite yourself. It changed you, made you a warmer person.

His voice dropped to a whisper. 'We were headed for Singapore but we had problems with the navy. Last year they shot up a couple of boats. I am too old for that.'

'Navy? Which navy?'

He sighed. 'The Indonesian navy, of course. They don't like direct trade. Everything has to go through Jakarta. It's taking the rice from our children's mouths. They call us smugglers.' He leaned over the edge and slid a mouthful of bubbly saliva into the water.

I laughed, but not because of what he said. I had suddenly found Raffles. I was now quite certain he had been here and had this same conversation before me.

*

The British had sought to impose a blockade on Java. The annual Buginese fleet approaching to trade from the east had taken this very ill and it had come to a fight with casualties on both sides, as the British, eager for prize-money, fired on their ships. The Dutch meanwhile sought to uphold their own monopoly over most of the archipelago. Spice was produced by a few islands only in the Moluccas, at the eastern end of their empire. To trade illegally in spice carried the death penalty, and the Malays were caught in the middle. One Western power blockaded Java, the other channelled all trade through it. One urged the 'illegal' export of spice, the other punished it with death. The Malays were ill-disposed towards such interference and Raffles was delegated to soothe them.

Raffles had another reason to talk to the sailors. The Eastern monsoon had set in and the wind was in totally the wrong direction for the expeditionary force. In the face of an equally stiff opposing wind from the navy, who declared the route impossible, Raffles urged sailing almost directly for Batavia using night winds and currents to sail against the monsoon. The navy declared this too dangerous. They would have to pass round the whole island of Borneo and approach from the other side. Raffles took his plan from the Malay sailors in the harbour. That was what they had told him to do. It succeeded brilliantly. The navy, including Lord Minto's ratty son, George, was furious.

'When I saw the appearance and form of Lord Minto, I was very much amazed, for I had been imagining what he would look like, and how handsome he would be and big and tall, and about his clothes . . . As to his appearance, as I saw him, he was past middle age, his body was thin, and his actions gentle, and his face pleasant; it seemed to me he could hardly lift a twenty-five-pound weight, so feeble did he appear to be. I noticed he was wearing a black coat of broad-cloth and black trousers, and there was nothing else I could mention . . . I did not see the slightest sign of haughtiness or raising his head but he merely bowed with a pleasant face . . . At that moment I was deep in thought, remembering the truth of the Malay proverb, which says, "If a snake creeps along a root, it will not lose its venom": and still more the Chinese proverb which says, "Will the water shake in a full barrel? But in a barrel half full the water will shake" . . . I noticed that amongst all the numerous officials Mr Raffles was the only one who dared to approach him . . .' – Munchi Abdullah, *Hikayat Abdullah*

*

'Come back with us to Flores. There is plenty of room.' Dion was cooking the fish into a rich, peppery stew.

'I can't. I have to go to Jakarta. Anyway, the Immigration Department wouldn't like it. They'd put me in jail. They'd call me a smuggler.'

Dion mashed the fish-head against the side of the pot. The eye had gone opaque as though with cataract. 'Governments!' he cried in disgust. 'Everyone should be able to go where they want and carry cargo where they want. You come and stay with me. I bring my family to stay with you in Australia. We buy, we sell. It's no one else's business.'

'Er . . . right.'

Raffles would have agreed with that too. As he got older, he saw freedom of trade as the basis of all human freedom.

*

The man in the Singapore Airlines office was skittish.

'I can't hear you!' he had shouted smirking across the counter. 'Not until you take a number from the queuing machine!'

I had taken a number and sat down.

'There's no need to wait. There's no one else queuing.'

I hauled myself up again and went back to the desk.

'One way to Jakarta.'

'*One* ticket? Go on, buy two.'

'I'm on my own.'

He shrugged and grinned. 'If you have a spare ticket, you'll find a friend.'

'You're Indonesian,' I suggested.

'How did you guess?'

'Your vowels,' I lied.

'Tourist or Raffles?'

'. . . or *what*?' I had dropped my number. The name came at me out of the blue like a punch to the stomach.

He sighed. 'Raffles *class*. I know it's silly but it's what we call it.'

I thought of poor Raffles sleeping under a cannon on an East Indiaman, the foul water, the vomit and fever, the stink of men and horses, cockroaches running over his face.

'It means Business.'

'Yes. I suppose it does.'

4. Spice Invaders

'Now I must admit that in my youth I was so terribly handsome that I was almost girlish-looking. Because there were so few female intellectuals in those days, there weren't many girl members and when Young Java put on a play I was always given the *ingénue* role. I actually put powder on my face and red on my lips. And I will tell you something but I don't know what foreigners will think of a President who tells such things ... Anyway, I will tell it. I bought two sweet breads. Round breads. Like rolls. And I stuffed them inside my blouse. With this addition to my shapely figure, everybody said I looked absolutely beautiful. Fortunately my part didn't call for kissing any boys on stage. I couldn't waste my money so after the show I pulled the breads out of my blouse and ate them. Watching me on stage, spectators commented that I showed a definite talent for playing to audiences. I concurred wholeheartedly.' – C. Adams, *Soekarno: An Autobiography*

On top of everything else, the British forces on the way to Java had to put up with amateur theatricals starring nautical female impersonators as 'young, accomplished and generally sentimental ladies of quality'. Lord Minto adored it all. In Malacca there had been balls, comical plays and, on board ship, charades. Lord Minto had immediately set the festive tone by freeing the slaves of the Company and rebuilding the prison along humanitarian lines – acts that Raffles would not forget and would take as models for his own administration. In Minto he saw a relaxed, instinctively civilized man of spontaneous generosity, with an aristocratic contempt for calculation. Minto provided a precedent for all that was good in anxious, hard-working and repressed Thomas Raffles.

Raffles, for his part, had organized a meeting of the Malacca Asiatic Society. He was desperately anxious to impress. To 'scientifically' protect the fleet against lightning he had caused an inverted glass tumbler to be nailed to the top of each mast. Since not a single ship was lost it must have proved efficacious. The serious nature of the business could not hide the fact that this was, for both Minto and Raffles, the earl and the former office boy, an enormous jaunt.

A third figure was involved, John Leyden. Leyden was a Scot, like Minto, of peasant stock but formidably learned. By the age of nineteen he had exhausted the knowledge of his professors at Edinburgh University, studying Hebrew, Arabic, Theology and Medicine. That knowledge, it must be admitted, was probably not very great. He was a famous poet, though his verse is excruciating to the modern reader. Against all expectation he joined the Company as a medical doctor, then became Professor of Hindustani at Fort William. Minto always respected learning and it was owing to Leyden that Raffles became known 'at court'. He it was who slipped Raffles's Malacca report before the busy earl and made sure he read it.

Raffles was totally in awe of him and his official, shop-bought scholarship, and it must have been his encouragement that drove Raffles on in his own studies; for through his friendship with John Leyden, Raffles first became part of an academic community. After Leyden, Raffles's scholarship changes as if to a higher gear. One pictures Raffles with the lord and the scholar, listening all agog, learning, laying down the attitudes and principles that would guide him for life.

Leyden had met Raffles in Penang and learned Malay with

contemptuous ease. They had become close friends and, more than that, he had also fallen – poetically – in love with Olivia. Now he was to accompany the fleet to Java and was destined for high office there. The three felt like little boys whose parents were away for the weekend. Lord Minto spoke gleefully of them 'frisikfying'.

'Dr Leyden's learning is stupendous and he is also a very universal scholar. His knowledge, extreme and minute though it is, is always in his pocket at his finger's end, and on the tip of his tongue. He has made it completely his own and it is all ready money. All his talent and labour indeed, which are both excessive, could not, however, have accumulated such stores without his extraordinary memory. I begin, I fear, to look at that faculty with increasing wonder; I hope without envy, but with something like one's admiration of young eyes. It must be confessed that Leyden has occasion for all the stores which application and memory can furnish to supply his tongue, which would dissipate a common stock within a week. I do not believe that so great a reader was ever so great a talker before. You may be conceited about yourselves, my beautiful wife and daughters, but with all my partiality I must give it against you. You would appear absolutely silent in his company, as a ship under weigh seems at anchor when it is passed by a swifter sailer. Another feature of his conversation is a shrill, piercing, and at the same time grating voice . . . If he had been at Babel, he would infallibly have learned all the languages there . . .' – Lord Minto

'. . . You always said I was a strange, wild fellow, insatiable in ambition, though meek as a maiden; and perhaps there is more truth than otherwise in what you said; but with all, I will assure you this, that although, from want of self-confidence and from natural shamefacedness (for I will not call it modesty or bashfulness), I am as unhappy at times as any poor wretch need be, I have times in which I am as happy as I think it possible for man to be; and it is one of these life-inspiring moments that I now purpose passing with you à la distance ... We are now off the coast of Java, having come a-head of the fleet; but we expect them tomorrow, and the attack will be made in the course of the week ... Conquer we must.' – T. S. Raffles to William Ramsay

The breathy excitement of a young man before the battle comes across. But there was another reason for trepidation. By now he also knew that if they conquered Java, Thomas Raffles would rule it and Leyden would be his secretary.

*

When the fleet reached Java, Leyden would be the first to land at the village of Cilincing, ten miles east of modern Jakarta – Batavia as it then was. Before 11,000 baffled troops, he had rifled the costume box to appear dressed in the charade outfit of a pirate, complete with red tasselled cap. After all, Cowboys and Indians had not yet been invented as a game, being still a minor matter of distant American foreign policy. Fortunately, there was no one on the beach for him to fight with his cutlass except a very large cockerel and several hens. It was a jaunt.

*

'Cilincing? It is not there any more. It has all been improved. It is part of Ancol – you know – the pleasure park. They have dolphins and boats, a swimming pool and at night there are women who ...'

'Are you sure?' We pored over the copies of the old British campaign maps. After their unopposed landing, the British had dragged their field guns up from the ships and driven the Dutch, under their French officers, back to the new fortress at

Meester Cornelis. 'Surely it's the other side of the river nearer Tanjung Priok?'

Agus sucked on his lip. 'Mmm. Maybe. Why don't we go to Ancol? We will have a good time. Tanjung Priok is no fun.'

Could this be the Agus I had known in London? For three years he had doggedly eaten halal food, never gone to the cinema because it was wicked, made no close English friends. After gaining the worst possible degree ever seriously awarded by the University of London he had returned to work for the oil company that had sponsored him and become – overnight – exotically Westernized. He ate hamburgers, played golf, lived in a compound with security men on the gate and servants washing cars in front of the houses. The words 'When I was in London' were always on his lips and he insisted on speaking a version of English with absurdly long vowels where even the Prince of Wales has short ones. He was embarrassed because I did not have matching luggage. When I arrived he had given me his card and was upset that I did not have one to give back so he could put it in the large bowl of cards he kept on his desk. The bowl was, I noted, a hideous but expensive Asmat container of the sort in vogue in Jakarta. In Jakarta, 'primitive peoples' were a fashion accessory, like Gucci labels.

'*You* go to Ancol. *I'll* go to Tanjung Priok. How do I get there?'

'Oh, by taxi of course. No wait, I'll borrow a company car – and a driver. We have a refinery up there. We can call it work. No one goes to Tanjung Priok for *fun*. I'll lend you a tie.' It would, I knew, be a fake Christian Dior, locally made. 'I shall bring some friends. *Kita pergi main-main.*' That would have to be translated, 'It'll be a jaunt.'

*

The 11,000-strong British army was a mixture of European and battle-hardened Indian soldiers. They faced a force of some 18,000. Only a small part of these were efficient French troops. The rest were a mixture of locally recruited Dutch whose allegiance to France was doubtful and Indonesian 'volunteers' whose allegiance was so beyond all doubt they were delivered to the army in chains. Batavia swiftly surrendered, but since all Dutch males had been driven like livestock into the fortress of Cornelis, the city was wide open for the expression of popular discontent. Martial law was declared.

The British, which is to say Indian, army was furious to find the streets of the capital ankle-deep in sugar and coffee. *That* would have been valuable prize-money. Leyden, on the other hand, was interested in a different sort of booty and rushed off to rummage through the manuscripts of the archives. In the cold store-rooms he caught a chill that rapidly became a fever. His death followed shortly afterwards. It was a bitter blow to Raffles, who was devastated at his loss. Over the years he would become more inured to death. One by one he would see almost everyone to whom he grew attached picked off.

Yet Leyden's influence lived on. Amongst his papers was a translation of the *Malay Annals* that Raffles would publish as a memorial to his friend. It brought to his notice an ancient city that would later be of importance in his life – Singapore.

*

Agus's friends were recognizably drawn from the gilded youth of Jakarta, masters of the arts of leisure. They could do barroom tricks with playing cards and matches. They beat all comers at computer games and tennis. They knew the composition of fifty different cocktails. They brought with them the latest cassettes for the car, fearful lest they have to listen to something out of date, and they were vaguely 'students' of some unrevealed subject. They had names like Beni and Rudi and their lady companions giggled and wore too much makeup. I found it impossible to tell them apart. Agus had once confided to me that, as a small boy, he had lived in a village and kept goats. *That* should clearly never be mentioned again.

*

The assault on the citadel at Cornelis began with a typical fuddling of orders. People got lost, rendezvous were missed. Ultimately, only a small part of the force ended up in the middle of enemy lines with the rising sun about to give them away. They stormed on and took the fort by sheer old-fashioned heroism. The man of the day was Gillespie, a name that would one day scald Raffles's ears. Lord Minto, typically, was struck by other matters.

> 'The humanity of the men to the wounded prisoners on that day was admirable. No distinction of colour on that occasion. Our soldiers picked up English, Dutch and Malay, without distinction, in the jungle and carried them with great labour to the hospital . . . Next morning I went, before daylight, to visit all the works – our own as well as the enemy's. A field of battle seen in cold blood the day after is a horrid spectacle, but is too horrid for description. The number of the dead and the shocking variety of deaths had better not be imagined.' – Lord Minto

Raffles found himself, then, at thirty years of age almost sole ruler of a fertile, delightful island of six or seven million inhabitants whose civilization he found enchanting. The Honourable, the Lieutenant-Governor had a free hand. He was eager to made his mark, full of good intentions. What on earth should he now actually *do*?

*

The road to Tanjung Priok was one of those heartless roads,

long and straight and narrow, a metaphor of virtue. It was a hot day and the sun hit me like an iron bar. There was room for two lanes of traffic so four had formed, jostling and honking. Beni/Rudi took the wheel himself and drove with consummate ease and fashionable panache. On the back of his trousers was a large label: 'This pant was own by genuine American officer. Wearing it make you genuine American hero.'

When the Dutch built Batavia they had diverted half the river into the town to form sluggish canals and so bring malaria direct to the heart of their new city. The canals are still there as open sewers, clogged with all manner of nameless filth and, during the dry season, lying like pools of septic ink, bubbling with various gases of putrefaction. In Raffles's day this was the 'miasma', known by all to cause malaria.

Men were working by the roadside, shovelling ooze from the canals on to the verge. With the heat, the car exhaust and the stench, it would be hard for a theologian to design a vision of hell for such people that was worse than their current circumstances. Beni/Rudi was telling us about a new Japanese restaurant he had discovered. As he slowed the air-conditioned car to circumvent a particularly large heap of sludge, the men leaning panting on their shovels looked in the window, waved and smiled. Had our positions been reversed, I am not sure that would have been my instinctive reaction.

Tanjung Priok was a place of scabby warehouses and factories linked by intestinal pipes. Big ships stood off in deep water. Agus looked ill at ease. It was a place to make money in and then withdraw to sweeter climes.

'The people here are tough,' he explained. 'Whenever the government raises taxes or devalues the currency they're straight out on the streets, rioting. Usually they kill a couple of policemen.'

'Here, everybody is poor,' Rudi/Beni explained happily. 'Even the *Chinese* are poor.' In support of the assertion a Chinese rickshaw-driver cycled mournfully past in torn shorts.

His rickshaw was empty. It looked as if it was always empty, covered with dust. We drove on over a pot-bellied bridge on to a mudflat where reeds sprouted resentfully like beard stubble.

'Cilincing,' said one of the girls emphatically, as if she came there very week.

It was like the marshes around London, characterless, cheerless, unredeemable wasteland, blasted by a chemical wind. If this was where Leyden had stormed ashore and the British had trundled their heavy cannon, they had been asking for trouble. The road petered out. A faded sign said 'Access for project vehicles only'. We drove on. The only project seemed to be more mud.

We came to an unbridged river and stopped. I got out and looked over the sea. A man appeared at my elbow. He pointed to a small island.

'That's the old fort that was converted to a mosque. The people go there to fast and pray all night. There are many ghosts. They have visions.'

'What sort of visions?'

'They dream of the number that will win the state lottery. Lots of people have made money that way. You will want to see the house.'

'What house?'

'Si Pitung's house.'

'Tell me about him.'

He looked shocked, the way Beni/Rudi did when I did not know the name of a Western pop-singer they wanted to talk about.

'Si Pitung? He was a hero. He fought the Dutch and gave money to the poor people who lived here. He was betrayed by his friend who told the Company men they could kill him by shooting him with a golden bullet. They had quarrelled; it was a matter of some woman.'

He scowled at the girls as if they were to blame for all women coming between all men. Unwisely, they giggled. The story had doubtless been told with greater artistry, but I got the drift.

'When I was in London,' said Agus, 'I heard much of Robin Hood in Shakespeare's plays. Si Pitung was the same – only a Muslim. We shall go to his house.'

The man paddled us across the river to the village. The girls refused to come, afraid – cat-like – of the water, and stayed squealing on the bank. Beni or Rudi stayed to comfort them. Simple houses were constructed on stilts by the water's edge so that at every tide the water flushed under them. People stood around examining fish. It was not clear whether they were buying or selling or just comparing fish. They seemed surprised we had not brought fish too.

Si Pitung's house was a simple Malay dwelling, though with an elaborate set of bars and aged watchmen to protect it. Inside it was totally bare, but the centre of the floor was not the usual thick, dusty planks – rather a wickerwork of rattan. Sea air and a wonderful golden light were thrown up in our faces.

'Natural air-conditioning,' said the watchman with relish.

'The British,' I ventured. 'Raff-lesh – when they came to Jakarta, they landed here.'

The man shook his head. 'No,' he said, 'you've got it all wrong. It was the Dutch who were here. Si Pitung fought the Dutch. He was a friend of the people.'

'Raff-lesh too.' I insisted. 'He fought the Dutch. He too was a friend of the people.'

'No,' he insisted. 'It was the Dutch. Si Pitung fought the Dutch.'

'Right.'

*

The first thing Raffles had to learn was to disobey orders with upper-class arrogance. Lord Minto taught him. He had been clearly instructed to take the island, dismantle the Franco-Dutch defences, arm the natives and withdraw. But he had decided on the invasion *before* the orders came, while it was all still a dream to Raffles. Neither he nor Raffles had the least intention of doing as they were told, nor did they intend to return their conquest to Holland at the end of the war. Their ultimate aim was that Britain should retain Java permanently. Minto had taken to the place. He wrote to his wife explaining that the only word he could use of Java was 'civilization', a concept Raffles was to make great use of.

In those days it took seven months for a letter from England to arrive in Indonesia, longer if it were routed via India. The scope for prevarication, misunderstanding, taking-initiatives-that-regretfully-could-not-be-reversed-at-this-late-date, was enormous. Minto showed Raffles how to use all this to the full. He never looked back. He became a master of the instrument.

Java, it was discovered, could under no circumstances be simply abandoned. The whites would all be massacred, as indeed some were later in Palembang. There was no financial cause for alarm. Minto and Raffles were convinced Java would make a huge profit. The British were reluctantly forced to stay. They were sure the Company would agree.

The Company was furious.

*

'Please, we must stop here.' Beni/Rudi was pointing excitedly through the windscreen. 'It will not take long, half an hour.'

What was it? An ice-cream parlour?

'Palang Merah,' he explained, suddenly serious. 'Red Cross. I give blood every month, good Indonesian blood. You do not get paid. You do it for love of country. If you do it fifty times, you get to shake the President's hand and you get a medal. Afterwards, they give you a plate of noodles with an egg.'

*

The British forces too received a medal for their blood. Otherwise, the victory in Java passed largely unnoticed in a preoccupied Europe. The Prince Regent alone seemed petulantly enthusiastic, but this was the measure of his eccentricity. It would later be translated into a knighthood for Raffles – much later.

It is hard to know where an idea begins. That certain plans appear in the letters of Minto is no evidence that they did not originate in Raffles's head. That Raffles argues forcefully for the limitation of slavery or the reform of land-tenure is no proof that this did not come from Minto. They had been collaborating together for over a year, discussing, planning. They probably no longer knew themselves whose idea was whose. Both knew the importance of producing paper justifications to be quoted at the Company in the inevitable disputes that would follow the annexation of Java. They covered for each other.

They were intuitively in agreement – more, in sympathy. The Dutch administration was wicked, based upon vicious exploitation and corruption. In the government coffee warehouses, for example, different measures were used to weigh the coffee coming in and going out. From a delivery of 240–270 pounds the Company received merely 126 pounds, and the native grower was paid for just fourteen; the rest 'disappeared'.

The British would be humanitarian and work for the benefit of the natives. To extend British dominion over them was an act of liberation, an act of charity. Once the natives had come to understand this, they would be loyal and grateful. This was obvious to both of them. Dutch historians always accused Raffles of deviousness. In fact he was somewhat naïve, expecting human motivations to work in simple, straight, predictable lines.

For once in his life Raffles could trust the man immediately above him. He knew he could rely on him for the protection that would be essential. A caretaker, after all, is not normally expected to start a revolution in government.

*

The swimming pool at Ancol was full to bursting of Chinese, undergarments frowsily retained under frumpy swimming costumes. Indeed, we and the staff were the only people *not* Chinese. No, wait, there was a little boy and girl, very dark, very Javanese. The boy had mastered the trick of floating, perfectly still, face down with his arms limp. It made the lifeguards uneasy.

Beni and Rudi demonstrated their proficiency at diving, swimming fancy strokes, lifesaving each other. The girls withdrew under the shade of a pavilion, disdaining the water.

'They are afraid for their hair,' explained Agus, proudly. 'They are MPs' daughters.'

'What's that got to do with it?'

'Tomorrow is Independence Day. They have to go to Freedom Palace to be received by the President, so they have had their hair done.'

'Oh.' Hugh Hope, Raffles's Civil Commissioner, had lived next door to the State Palace, but that was not perhaps to the point. I forbore to mention it.

*

In a warehouse in north London the ethnography department of the British Museum has a storehouse. It is a lending library for the world's museums. Beside a fetid, English canal, in a

54

building worthy of Tanjung Priok, stands a monument to the ingenuity of the human spirit, a vast collection of material culture from city, swamp and jungle – carvings, textiles, forgotten or still-potent gods, weapons of war, everything that man has wreaked or wrought. Much of it is stored in wooden boxes known as 'coffins', fumigated in poison gas to destroy insect life, then cosseted in controlled humidity and temperature to resist the ravages of time and lay down a deposit that can be mined by generations yet unborn. Scholars from around the world come here to reconstruct the past, plan the future, pin down the elusive present. Conservationists move among the objects, dusting with brushes, mending, resetting, tending the wounded. A museum is in essence a time-machine where clocks are stopped and the moment is eternal as in Heaven and the writings of anthropologists.

At the end of one rack is an unremarkable plywood 'coffin' with an 1859 registration number, the date when it entered the museum's collection. To anyone who has worked on the material culture of Asia that means one thing only – 'Raffles Collection'. Inside is a white nest of tissue paper with lumps like in school semolina pudding. You open them to find hooped and stirruped devices of brass with heavy iron threads and bolts, instruments of torture made for the crushing and smashing of Indonesian feet and hands, carefully preserved from rust and decay. They are quite small, for the hands and feet were small. Torture was a regular part of the Dutch judicial process. It was the very first thing Minto and Raffles abolished. Torture having been stopped, its instruments were packed up and shipped far away. That unremarkable box is a memorial to their humanity.

*

'The Chinese are of a very lustful temper. They are accused of the most detestable violations of the laws of nature; and it is even said, that they keep swine in their houses, for purposes the most shameful and repugnant.' – J. Stockdale, *Sketches Civil and Military* (1812)

*

The little Javanese boy and his sister came over. He shook hands in a matter-of-fact, man-to-man way and introduced himself as Marwan.

'You will want to go and see the graveyard,' he said. 'It is full of Dutch.'

'I'm not Dutch, but why are they buried here?'

'They were killed in the fighting.'

'The fighting with the English?'

He looked at me as if I were mad. 'English? No, the Japanese. My dad says they were killed by the Japanese. Look,' he said changing tack, 'I need to borrow an adult to take us on the water-slide. I'm eight and she's six. They won't let us on alone. I can't ask the Chinese.'

'Why not?'

'They're not Indonesian.'

'I'm not Indonesian either.'

'You're a white man, a *bule*, that's different.'

'But they were born here. Chinese have been here for hundreds of years. Why aren't they Indonesian?'

Marwan thought about it. 'My dad says they take all the money from the Indonesians so we are poor and they are rich. That's why they are bad.' Inspiration suddenly struck and he gave one of those dynamite smiles that rock you on your heels with their innocence and openness. 'Yes,' he said triumphantly, 'they are Indonesians, *bad* Indonesians.'

5. Scenes of Old Batavia

'Batavia shines in the natural neatness of the Dutch. The streets are wide, not paved, but the roads formed of very fine gravel, and excellent. From the town, the roads run along canals, or streams of water, in some places quick and almost lively, mostly, however, slow, dull and *always* yellow.' – Lord Minto

'In June 1775, C. P. Thurberg dined with a party of fifteen, on the eve of his departure for Japan. On his return at the beginning of 1777, he found that eleven of the fifteen were dead. Von Wollzagen found in 1792 that all his friends had died within a period of sixteen months. Of one hundred and fifty soldiers who arrived with the ship *Morgenstern* in 1770, only fifteen were alive four months later. Dysentery, typhus, typhoid and malaria were the principal diseases.' – E. Hahn, *Raffles of Singapore*

A sign by the road says 'We are turning Jakarta into a tourist city – beautiful, clean, peaceful and cool.' They have a long way to go. It's ugly, filthy, noisy, hot and a surprisingly good place to live.

Morning comes early to the city, the imams starting up about five, calling out pious words into the world. By six the food-stalls are open, frying noodles and rice, the hiss of fat blending with that of the mosque loudspeakers. The poverty is to be seen in the boys dodging between the cars and selling

57

single cigarettes to drivers stuck in traffic jams. There is a well-organized distribution network. One day the children sell iced water, the next face-flannels, the next flashing Yo-yos. The lives of the middle class are lived to the music of those anxious to serve their every need. From morning to night, there is an endless procession of street-traders past the house – brushes, chairs, mirrors, portraits of the President – all are for sale. The range of food alone is astonishing. People want to wash your car and mend your saucepans, sell you fake Cartier watches and clothes with designer labels. When Agus loses a key to a suitcase, a man comes to the gate and just looks at the lock, works out in his head what the key would look like and carves one out of metal with a file. It works first try. It seems that there is nothing Indonesians cannot make or mend.

*

'. . . All the mischievous, deteriorating and grievous maxims of a narrow, monopolising and harsh policy are in full force and vigour in every department of affairs . . .

    While we are here, let us do as much good as we can.' – Lord Minto

Trade was to be the key to the prosperity of Britain's new colony. Both Raffles and Minto had imbibed the spirit of free trade and enterprise at the breast – as it were – of Adam Smith. The Dutch colony had been run on the contrary assumption of monopoly.

The Dutch had been concerned to acquire spices and coffee at the lowest prices possible and sell them to Europe at the highest they could command. To do this they used forced labour and forced deliveries, imposed prices and ruthlessly destroyed any surplus or interlopers who could undermine their control of the market. On one occasion this had required nothing less than genocide. They had not baulked at genocide.

Apart from controlling deliveries of tropical produce, the Dutch had little interest in the administration or welfare of Java and were content simply to manipulate local rulers.

The British were in a different position. They had powerful manufacturing industries that needed raw materials and foreign buyers. The increasing wealth of foreign dependencies would create a natural market for Britain's manufactured goods and cargoes for the outward journey. It was in Britain's interest to promote freedom of trade and wealth among its subjects. Yet the East India Company, too, was narrowly monopolistic, allowing its employees a free hand in local or 'country' trade as long as the long-distance trade with China was kept its exclusive preserve. One day the contradiction between these principles would become intolerable, but for the moment Raffles was happy to pocket up the Dutch monopoly while freeing local trade through a complete revision of the customs regulations. It was not until he saw the British being excluded from the Indies by an increasingly aggressive Dutch Empire that he would fully espouse free trade in the interests of Singapore.

There was one fatal flaw in all this. It was Raffles's misfortune that he had no market. The continent of Europe was blockaded by British ships, for the Napoleonic Wars were in full swing. The only remaining outlet was closed when hostilities began between Britain and America in 1812; but even before that there had been no vessels to carry produce. The Spice Islands, though now British, were not under Raffles's control. Forced deliveries were still extracted from the inhabitants and used to supply markets directly. Previously all spices had passed via Java. The Jakarta warehouses, now cut off from world trade, were packed with rotting cloves, nutmeg and coffee. Storage costs were just another drain on finances. The destruction of crops caused by the invasion had been a blessing. Raffles had taken over the colony at the very moment when it could not conceivably do anything but lose money.

*

Money was at the bottom of another of Raffles's problems. The Dutch authorities had issued paper money like confetti. No one trusted it: trade was being strangled by the lack of coinage. To raise more money, in 1810 the Dutch had started selling provinces to the Chinese. One of the conditions of sale had been that the Chinese should also buy up 50,000 of the new paper notes every six months and so introduce them into circulation, forcing them on a reluctant public. This became known as Probolingo currency. The public resisted accepting the valueless Probolingo money, and the Dutch had been obliged to pass a law imposing the severest penalties on anyone refusing it.

When the Chinese purchase of 50,000 Probolingo notes fell due, they joyfully paid for them in other worthless Probolingo notes, citing the government regulations that made it a crime to refuse them. The Dutch were furious.

*

It should not be thought that Raffles at this time did nothing but work. That taste he had acquired for society, coupled with a sense of his social duty as 'the Honourable, the Lieutenant-Governor', led him to revolutionize Batavian notions of hospitality. The night before Minto's return to India there was a great ball at Government House, already decorated by the French for the celebration of Napoleon's birthday but usurped by the British for their own festivity. Even the vanquished General Janssens was invited. The Dutch were shocked at the levity of the British. Raffles is said to have been borne round the room in a chair to general acclamation. One of the English innovations was drinking toasts to music, and a subversive humour matched music and text. The toast 'The Queen and Royal Family' was drunk to the tune 'Merrily Danced the Quaker's Wife and Merrily Danced the Quaker'. When it came to the toast 'The Company', they drank it to 'Money in Both Pockets'.

*

'Today an average international gathering in the Far East would probably greet with amused incredulity the statement that a *British* government, of all groups, should have had a lightening, gay effect upon any society whatever, but so it was in 1811. In those days and by comparison with the slow Dutch, the British looked like tearing, merry madcaps.' – E. Hahn, *Raffles of Singapore*

'It is impossible to give you anything like an adequate notion of the total absence of beauty in so crowded a hall. There never is a dozen women assembled in Europe without a few attractions amongst them. Here there was no difference, except in some few varieties of ugliness and ordinariness of dress and manner. The Dutch did not encourage, nor indeed allow freely, European women to go out to their colonies in India. The consequence has been, that the men lived with native women, whose daughters, gradually borrowing something from their father's [*sic*] side, and becoming a mixed breed, are now the ladies of rank and fashion in Java. The young ladies have learnt the European fashions of dress, and their carriage and manner are something like our own of an ordinary class. Their education is almost wholly neglected; or rather no means exists here to provide for it. They are attended from their cradles by numerous slaves, by whom they are trained in helplessness and laziness; and from such companions and governesses, you may conceive how much accomplishment and refinement in manner or opinions they are likely to acquire.' – Lord Minto

'In Batavia everybody drank a bottle of wine a day as a matter of course, quite apart from the beer, sake, spirits and so on which were consumed on the side. Heavy drinking was customary at parties. Visitors were given a toast with each glass of wine, principally no doubt to compensate for the lack of intelligent conversation. Official parties were punctuated with a numerous and official toast list, sometimes accompanied by cannon shots and three cheers. The widow of Governor-General van der Parra, about 1780, who according to contemporary witnesses was an exceptionally sober and strait-laced man, died long after her husband but still left forty-five hundred bottles of wine and over ten thousand bottles of beer.' – E. Hahn, *Raffles of Singapore*

'There will be games,' said Agus, 'and a whist-drive. People will eat dry crackers hung from ropes without using their hands. There will be races with balloons and water.'

'I know,' I said smugly. Earlier that morning I had won the men's race round the block carrying a bucket of water on my head. One is ill-prepared at my age to discover such un-suspected abilities.

'In the main streets there is a big march-past but here, in the back streets, the people have their own way of celebrating independence. Do you know about *pinang*?'

'It is an island,' I said. 'In Malaysia. Raffles was there, he . . .'

'No,' said Agus firmly, '*pohon pinang*, areca tree; it is a special tree like your Christmas tree I saw when I was in London. I will take you there.'

We set off through the narrow streets. A whole boiling village life teemed behind the city façades. People called out greetings and introduced their children. Officious men were pinning up bunting. Another wearing a peaked cap was draw-ing lines for the races on the street with all the aplomb of someone on official business. In the distance we could hear screams and cheers, a wail of despair, a crash, more cheers.

One bank of the canal was covered with laughing spectators in their best clothes. On the other, the young bloods of the area had gathered, flexing their muscles. In between flowed the canal, its waters deep and heavy with pollution, swirling with scum and debris. In the water, they had set up a vertical pole some twenty feet high, covered with grease. From the top hung desirable prizes – clothes, saucepans, most alluring of all a chiming clock.

'*Pohon pinang*,' said Agus, pointing, 'the areca tree.'

The only way to gain access was an oiled bamboo pole leading from the far bank like a gangplank. A line of soaked, wretched figures, their teeth chattering, testified to the difficulty of getting across. As we watched one boy missed his footing on the slippery bamboo, teetered deliciously on the brink, eyes agog, arms flailing, then slowly, inexorably, tumbled head-first into the water. The crowd hooted and cheered. There is great satisfaction in the white-linened contemplation of the filth and discomfort of others.

At the height of it all the clock chimed 'East is East and West is West and the wrong one I have chose . . .' The crowd joined in, la-la-ing happily.

*

Raffles was now on a slippery slope. He had taken over responsibility for the Probolingo currency. To pay for that failed land sale, he was obliged to sell off more government land and have a lottery. To encourage the Dutch and British to make friends, he kept open table. To pay for that, he had to appropriate the money from the government monopoly of edible birds' nests. He would never get clear of the chaos of Java's finances.

Yet in his first year Raffles brought out the new set of trade regulations, set up a programme to research the natural resources of the island, reformed the legal system, instituted health care, suppressed piracy, began a complete reform of land-tenure and the basis of taxation and completed a successful military campaign against the native rulers. In spare moments he founded a newspaper and revived the Batavia Academy of Arts and Sciences. When one speaks of Raffles doing all this, it is scarcely a figure of speech. There were almost no competent British officials. Much of the work he simply did himself; for the rest, he had to rely on the army, especially the surgeons. They, at least, could read and write. Many of the Dutch officials, corrupt and disaffected though they might be, had to be left in their positions. This sometimes led to problems. There is a, possibly apocryphal, story of Raffles writing a terse letter to one Dutchman pointing out that his assistant was hopelessly corrupt and must be immediately suspended. The Dutchman, whose command of English was wobbly, looked up the word in his dictionary, took the assistant outside and hanged him.

*

'The cannon is worshipped by barren women who come and sit astride it to be cured.' What? No, surely that was Padang, or was it Malacca? I whirled round to look at the speaker. The man was small, ferrety. The English was slick and shallow, the moustache that of a second-hand car dealer. He was clearly a tourist guide. We were in the old town square of Batavia. Here the British troops had been plied with drink by agents of the French while a Chinese tried to fire the magazine. As if in emulation, a stall-holder waved a can of Coca-Cola from across the road.

'The end of the cannon is in the form of a clenched fist. In Indonesia that is a gesture that means . . .'

'Yes. Thank you.' The universal symbolism of cannon had

been appreciated by someone. As subtitle, they had scrawled the word 'Seks' on it in chalk.

I made my way across to the old Town Hall, now a museum. The small entrance fee would put him off. From the balcony up there the Dutch judges had watched those they sentenced hanged, impaled on spikes in the hot sun, mutilated, until Raffles had put a stop to it.

It was a heavy, ungainly building, filled with heavy, ungainly furniture.

'Furnitures,' said my guide, unhelpfully pointing. Of course, I should have known better. The guards were his friends, possibly relatives; they had let him in free.

'Come,' he said, taking my hand and leading me to a row of portraits. 'I show you all Dutchmen. Here is Daendels, the Dutch Napoleon. He built the roads and the forts and killed 10,000 Indonesians in forced labour. Here is Janssens. I don't know much about him. Perhaps he didn't kill anyone.'

'Minto?' I asked. 'His portrait was brought here with salutes before he left for India.'

I was being unfair. He had never heard of him.

'Raffles, then. No Raffles?' His face lit up and he began pacing up and down wildly.

'Raffles? Yes, yes. We keep Raffles in the cellar. Wait, wait.' He rushed back to the desk. There was a long discussion. 'Ah . . . Is problem. The director has the key. He is absent. It is not known when he will return. Yesterday was independence,' he said reproachfully. 'No Raffles.'

'Olivia, then? Mrs Raffles. Is she in Bogor or here?'

'Oh, Bogor, yes. Bogor.'

'But in the thirties her grave was here in Tanah Abang. There is a photograph of it there. Isn't it just an empty memorial in Bogor?'

He looked around frantically. It had been a mistake to ask in front of the guards. He was embarrassed not to know.

65

'They move her to Bogor,' he gabbled. 'Impossible to move whole body so they cut off her head and move that.' Like poor Francis Xavier. One of the guards started to laugh.

'Oh yes,' I suggested insidiously. 'There was a story that when they cut off her head she started to bleed.'

He looked offended. 'No,' he objected. 'That's not possible. *That* would be silly.'

*

'In speaking of Mr Raffles, you will think me, perhaps, biassed by his kindness to me; but really, setting this aside, and judging impartially from what I have seen of him, and I have now seen and *marked* him closely for three months, I do not hesitate to say, that I think most highly of him. He is a superior character – perfectly the gentleman – of the most polished manners – and of a suavity of disposition that I have not seen exceeded. This, perhaps, is his foible; he is rather *too* good-natured; and as a governor, might have had a squeeze of acid mingled in his composition with advantage. He is possessed of considerable information on most subjects; and is at once the gentleman, the scholar and the man of business.' – G. Addison, *Journal*

*

When the old Tanah Abang cemetery was bulldozed, they saved a small part of it as a park, the Taman Prastasi, and shifted some of the graves there. The outside was walled round with old Dutch gravestones, deeply carved in granite with the titles of their high offices. Broken stones had been formed into a crazy paving that jumbled ages and nationalities into a symbolic expression of death's levelling effect. Reclining, mortal figures stretched out on the cool marble and granite. One returned my smile.

'Yes,' he grinned, 'at last the Dutch are doing the Indonesians some good.' He turned over and I could see his back quivering with laughter at his own wit.

The interior had been colonized by the employees, and huts had been erected among the monuments to house a flourishing domestic activity of cooking and washing. There was a cornucopia of masonry styles, solemn urns and truncated pillars, flights of steps that led nowhere, blank-faced angels – even cornucopias. One incongruous element was what I took to be a hideous plaster deer until it moved. It was *real* and cropping the grass. A cast-iron bishop glared down from a skewed plinth.

'A tree fell on him,' explained the gnarled guardian.

'Francis Xavier,' I thought again. But no mutilation for this bishop, protected as he was by the sterner technology of iron. Then, through the clutter of crosses, I glimpsed a familiar shape, the great square tomb of Olivia with its circle of stumpy pillars, left when the roof collapsed. Raffles had originally buried her next to Leyden – in an almost literal act of laying down one's wife for one's friend. I had been told he was here but there seemed to be no trace of him, the place being usurped by the grave of 'Monster Engel'.

'Leyden,' I asked the guardian. 'Is he here?'

'Dutch?'

'No, English.' It had never occurred to me before how much misunderstanding that would have caused in Java. 'He was the *pacar*, the lover, of Raffles's wife, so he buried her here.'

'English men let their wives have lovers? Did he not beat her?' He flashed wide-eyed amazement.

'No. It was different – poetry, flowers – no sex.' I wondered about that for a moment. How urbane had Thomas Raffles been?

He laughed. 'No sex? What sort of lover was that?'

'It was,' I hazarded, 'like Bung Karno with his first wife, Utari. No sex. *Kawin gantung* – a "hanging" marriage.'

'Like Bung Karno? Well in that case they have a list of names in the office.'

They were all sympathy. 'A relative? Family, maybe?' To look for a family tomb was an honourable thing, a holy thing. It would bring much virtue. The list was long and not in any particular order. Patiently they went through it with me. There were similar names, but none quite right. It seemed he had disappeared for ever beneath the bulldozers. They hugged me, offered their condolences and looked as shamefaced as though I were a freshly bereaved mourner who had seen them filching flowers from the grave. They were really very sorry.

*

The English were much amused at Dutch preoccupation with position and formality. Regulations governed the wearing of shoes and clothes and the carrying of umbrellas. When Raffles's carriage passed, as heir to the Dutch Governor-General, all other vehicles had to stop and their occupants alight. In Sukarno's day, some of the bitterest arguments of Indonesian intellectuals would be about whether they should wear hats and sarongs.

The *Java Government Gazette* best expresses the new ethos. It is a mixture of public announcements, news from Indian and British papers, law cases, descriptions of social events, advertisements for drink, novels and slaves, execrable poetry, Irish jokes and lunatic letters.

Hat Concern

'A correspondent informs me that the taking off of hats upon the public road is now become the subject of dispute in the Eastward; and that even putting on one's hat a little too soon, after taking it off, is considered as a very gross insult for which one is liable to be instantaneously brought to an account by the infliction of a dozen stripes with a horsewhip on the spot. Since, then, the taking off of hats be deemed a matter of such vast importance, and since a poor ignoramus is likely to be thus severely dealt with, for not holding his hat in his hand for a certain length of time; it would perhaps be an acceptable piece of service to the public at large, were the precise quantity of time necessary to elapse, before it is proper to put on a hat, that has once been taken off, mathematically defined and ascertained. My correspondent says that an arithmetical table should prove highly useful, in enabling the lower orders to regulate their conduct towards different ranks of Society, without the hazard of giving offence . . .' – An Enemy of Folly

*

I arrived back at the house hot and careworn. The area was awaking from its long afternoon doze. Between five and six, many people get back from work. They have a bath and begin to drift around the streets, the men changing from trousers into sarongs to mark their leisure.

If you go up a tall building in Jakarta and look down, you see the roofs and electricity cables tangled with lots of little white squares like postage stamps. They're not stamps, of course, but kites and, above all, this is the time for little boys to gather on street corners to fly kites. They're simple affairs, a square of plastic bag stretched over a springy bamboo frame. You can buy them anywhere for about 30p. The string is attached to two points on the frame so that by pulling it you can flex the whole thing and work the kite upwards on the slightest gust of wind. The other end of the string is rolled round a tin can. Fathers and big brothers hover around to give advice and take over in moments of stress. In Malaysia they have international kite-flying championships. In Thailand to 'fly one's kite' is to masturbate, but there seems to be no need to grope for sexual symbolism here.

It's all a rehearsal really for the manly pleasures of blatantly phallic cock-fighting and pigeon-racing that a boy will be expected to graduate to in maturity. But you only have to look at the fathers' faces to know that on the end of that piece of thread tied to his kite, miles away across the city, is a little boy who will *never* forget the glory of his moment of victory.

For kite-flying is a serious business, men's business. It all starts when one kite gets up above the first-floor roofs and the dangerous snagging wires to climb hundreds of feet into the evening air. It issues a silent challenge to all the other kites of Jakarta. From all over the city you see them working their way up towards it. When they are close a fight begins. The string at the tail of the kite has been dipped in glue and rolled in crushed glass or plaited with razor blades. With experience you can pick just the right point to come up below your opponent, spin your kite with a twirl of the finger around the spot where his string must be and slash downwards. The severed kite crashes back to earth and skitters down the tiles and gutters maybe miles away – adding itself to the cosmic dandruff of the rooftops. The kites whirl and dip as each tries to get the advantage of the other, plunging down towards the houses, suddenly jerking upwards to throw off pursuit. The boys know their opponents. 'That,' says one, 'is a rich part of town. That boy can afford the fancy, shop-bought thread with glass woven into it. It cuts better. It makes him more dangerous.'

Pedestrians and vehicles dodge good-naturedly under the strings across the roads. No one complains as they would in England. When their sons are locked in battle, the fathers can hardly keep their hands off the thread. When their sons win, they whoop, hug the boys, run up and down with them laughing.

As the sun begins to set the mosques send out their call again, one voice battling with another in the evening air. The kites are hauled down one by one, a victor over the other side of town holding on longest, savouring his triumph, dancing in the night sky.

6. The Great Garden

'Soon after the capture of the island, and when Lord Minto had gone to Bengal, Mr Raffles removed from Ryswick to Buitenzorg, the country residence of the former Governor, distant forty miles from Batavia and here he kept a most hospitable table. He went to Ryswick every week to attend the council, consisting of General, then Colonel, Gillespie, Commander of the forces, with Mr Muntinghe and Mr Cransen, Dutch gentlemen, who had held high situations under the former government. At Ryswick he remained a day or two, according to circumstances, and occasionally saw company there; but the climate at Buitenzorg being so far superior, he was always anxious to return, and seldom lost much time upon the road, performing the journeys in four hours. He was most attentive to members of the former government, who were constant guests at his table.' – T. Travers, *Journal*

'Buitenzorg – er, Bogor – what's the best way to get there – by train or bus?'

'By taxi,' said Agus irritatingly.

'That's a silly waste of money.' This – surprisingly – from Beni, or perhaps Rudi. 'I will give you a lift to the bus station. You catch a bus from there, two or three thousand rupiahs only. It takes just forty minutes. You can be back tonight. Lots of people who work in Jakarta live there. The bus station is very near the garage where I must take my car for *ketok magik*, "magic knocking".'

I waited until we were on the way.

'Magic knocking?'

'Yes. Do you not have it?' He looked surprised. 'If you have an accident and your bodywork is damaged, the best thing is to have it mended by magic. It started in Blitar. You know Blitar, Bung Karno's village? There is much magic there. Bung Karno was full of it. Anyway, you have to be careful. In Jakarta there are many frauds, people who pretend to repair bodywork by magic, but they use big magnets to pull out the dents.' It sounded unlikely.

'What exactly happens?' At the back of my brain, I could hear Raffles asking the same question as he strode about his new island, gathering the information he would later publish in his *History of Java*; information on how to make a knife, how to pattern a cloth or grow rice, how to extract poison from the *upas* tree. He must have been an irritating guest. He wanted to know everything. He believed everything was knowable.

'Well, I will tell you what I have experienced. When you have an accident you take the car there. He is a good man, a pious Muslim, so you have to be careful what you say. It is demons who do the work. He has control over them.' He blushed and laughed. 'You put the car in a shed, or maybe you just cover it with a tarpaulin. Then the man prays and you hear this banging, right away. After an hour your car is repaired and it's not like a normal garage. The paint is still good. You don't need to paint the repair. It's just as if nothing ever happened. But they can't mend broken bits, lamps or glass. You have to buy a new one.'

'It must be expensive.'

'No! That's the point. It's much cheaper than going to an ordinary garage. But they give you a precise price. 2,479 rupiahs, say, and you have to pay that, not one rupiah more, not one rupiah less. You can imagine. Nowadays, you can't easily get less than a fifty-rupiah coin, so you have to go round the antique stalls in Jalan Surabaya looking for old money. It's a bore. Then there's the business of the conditions.'

'Conditions?'

'Yeees.' He bobbed and ducked to see round me. I shrank back in my seat, thinking I was blocking his view of the road but it was only the backside of a woman he wanted to appraise as she gyrated down the street.

'Wah! Nice! There are some things you're not allowed to do if a car's been repaired with magic. Often, you can't take it out on your birthday. If you do, you have an accident with exactly the same damage as before. That's what happened here. I took it out on my birthday. Two days later – this.' He nodded at a dent in the wing. 'That's why you have to be careful buying a second-hand car in Indonesia. You don't know whether there are conditions attached to it.'

There was a crackle of automatic gunfire. I looked out and saw soldiers, crouched in a field, firing at targets, an officer shouting at them with empty rage after the fashion of officers. One stood up and hung his head. Shame. The Malays are sensitive to shame, Raffles had noted like a proud father, and should never be humiliated. In the nineteenth century shame was an important element of the claim to full humanity. The black races, it was believed, were congenitally incapable of shame, since black skin did not allow them to blush. Malays could. They were proper people.

We drove round a military base and up to a gate. A sign said 'Ketok Magik'. At the end of a dirt road was a cluster of buildings with several wounded army trucks parked in front, leaning over at angles. Even the vehicles showed shame. Beni went off to find someone. On the wall were sets of 'before' and 'after' pictures showing twisted wrecks restored to wholeness by the power of magic.

A man in a hat and a sarong came out and looked at the crumpled wing of Beni's car. He sucked air noisily between his lips in the manner of mechanics all round the world and shook his head. In England he would have said, 'You're in dead trouble there, mate.' He touched the car gently, as a doctor would a sensitive wound. A look of pain crossed his own face, a look of sympathy with the machine.

'I can't help,' he said. 'Look, I've got this contract with the army. A big truck takes a lot of prayer and army trucks are extra tough. You have to pray harder. I'm busy all week.'

I offered a cigarette.

'Tell me about *ketok magik*,' I said. 'Who does the work? Is it demons?'

Beni groaned and blushed. The man looked at me sharply.

'I'm a good Muslim,' he said bridling. 'I just pray to God. I don't know anything about demons. If God wants to use demons, that's up to Him. But it works so it must be His will. This is genuine. I'm from Blitar, Bung Karno's village.'

I tried to look impressed. 'How long would it take to mend this car?'

He appraised carefully. 'Maybe one hour, maybe two. It depends . . .'

'I'd love to see it,' I said. 'We don't have things like this in my country. We don't know how to do this.' He wavered. 'Could you show me? I'd be really interested.'

'Weeell . . . Let me think . . .'

'Go on.'

'Well . . .' He rubbed his chin and blew out air. 'No, sorry. Look I'd like to help but there's a truck in the shed now. I've got more waiting. I can't do this till tonight. Come back then. I'll let you see everything.'

But when we returned that night, pockets tinkling with ancient coinage, the car was already fixed. The demons, it seemed, had knocked off early. The mechanic had gone to the mosque to recharge his divine batteries. Beni/Rudi shrugged and laughed.

'These are Javanese demons. Like Javanese people, they are lazy. It is not enough to pray to them. They have to be whipped.'

*

'The official documents, already published, give a full, clear and satisfactory account of the zeal and ability evinced by Mr Raffles in the administration of Java, whilst few, perhaps, are aware of the application and attention which he devoted to his public duties. With a constitution already impaired by climate, everyone was astonished at the exertion and fatigue he underwent; and the Dutch, who were altogether unaccustomed to witness such activity of mind and body, were unable to keep pace with him.

... His mild, conciliating, and unassuming manners, obtained for him the respect and confidence of the Dutch, whilst the natives, who had been led to form the highest possible opinion of his character, looked with anxious hope for that amelioration in their condition which they afterwards experienced, and which will make his memory adored on the island of Java for ages to come.' – T. Travers, *Journal*

*

The National Palace of Bogor is a large, white, somewhat homespun classical building. Raffles tinkered with it to suit his own solid tastes, adding an upper storey. In prints of the period it looks topheavy and ungainly. After his time, the Dutch rebuilt it. There was a fire, further revision. Then, Sukarno, erstwhile architect, made another attempt on its virtue. It ended up looking confused.

It stands now in a large, well-ordered park ruminant with deer and statuary. Next door is the Kebun Raya, the Great Garden that is the home of botany in Java.

Raffles installed himself here with a small staff, his wife, his books and ruled as a benevolent autocrat, a country squire running his colony as a large estate, always the style that suited Raffles best. He could seldom get away from the idea that the whole of Java was just a bigger version of his own garden. Just as, years after he moved against slavery, slaves were still labouring in the plantations, so he had been unable to free the men who worked in the grounds of his own house. The Dutch, of course, would later see this as the ultimate proof of his sinister hypocrisy.

His authority gave him powers to overrule the other members of the Council, powers he would shortly need in order to push through his own vision of Java. Yet Raffles always naïvely expected to be loved for the goodness of his intentions.

It is recorded that he required three scribes to keep up with his own output of government work at Bogor. Sometimes he even dictated to two while writing a third letter himself, yet he never forgot his scholastic mission:

> 'My present situation, and our new conquest, afford such a wide and unparalleled field for research, that I should be worse than a Goth or Vandal if I allowed it to remain untried even in the literary way.'

*

The ideal of the philosopher-king, though unknown in the East, is one of the most tenacious ideas of the West.

> 'It was the kind of life lived by Raffles and Olivia at Buitenzorg that probably did more than anything else to set a standard of dignity and decency for social relations in Java. In that charming and well-ordered house, there was no place for vulgar ostentation, bad manners or slovenly dress. Not that life was at all formal. If Raffles on official occasions could act as every

76

inch a Governor, at home at Buitenzorg he was the perfect host, ready, with his own charming manners, to put everyone at his ease, to discuss affairs of state with one and fine points of language or science with another, or to play cards or promote theatricals, if that was the general desire. Off duty he loved gaiety and happy guests.' – C. Wurtzburg, *Raffles of the Eastern Isles*

*

The girl in the Head of Protocol's office inspected my letter from the Tourist Ministry with exactly the same facial expression the magic mechanic had used. I wondered if she weren't perhaps his sister.

'I'm sorry,' she said. 'You cannot come into the State Palace of Bogor. Without the right letter, even a minister cannot come in. We need two weeks' notice.' She might have added, 'In Raffles's time anyone could come here, but now we are a democracy.' I went into protracted displays of disappointment, mimed my desolation. Anger, I knew, would get me nowhere. Exciting pity might. A man appeared and they went into a huddle. I looked downcast and tearful. After a certain age, it is hard to look endearing.

'It is all right,' she said, soothingly. 'We can change the date on the letter. My friend is willing to take you round. You have a camera?'

'No camera. Is it not forbidden?'

'It is forbidden to take photographs *inside*, but not *outside*.' She swayed her hands from side to side as in a Javanese dance. '"Inside the palace" does not mean "inside the garden of the palace". Also making movie films is forbidden. You do not intend to make movie films? Outside are the deer, many fine statues. It is a pity you have no camera. The soldiers too are very smart.'

'Yes, a pity. I did not know.'

We set off through a series of tall, carpeted rooms, furnished in heavy, bourgeois style. The thick carpet sucked at our feet. Great swags of red velvet hung at the windows. In the heat of Jakarta, this would be unbearable. Up here in the mountains it was cooler. There was dew on the grass.

The furniture was an uncomfortable mix of modern and traditional, spindly forms of solid, expensive wood. Suddenly I realized where I had seen it before. It is the stuff with which the senior common rooms of redbrick universities are furnished. In England, those cupboards would be full of sherry glasses and the minutes of the last meeting.

'There was a famous Englishman who lived in Bogor before,' twinkled the guide. 'He was called Raffles.'

'Is anything left of what he built? There was a fire, an earthquake . . .'

'No. The Dutch tore it all down. But all that was just an excuse. The Dutch wanted to rub *him* out. When *they* moved out, they took everything. All they left were those mirrors that were too heavy to shift.'

We moved through another room, full of the flags of the unaligned nations and out on to an airy veranda with marble flags of a different sort, cane chairs, potted palms. Cooling views of the high mountains flaunted themselves through low cloud. Raffles wrote somewhere of the beauty of the views from his office. His wife revealed they could move him to tears. He had doubtless sat, snuffling, on this spot.

'I know what you're thinking. You're thinking how nice it would be to be an old colonist and sit here watching your gardeners working in the hot sun.'

'How did you know?'

He laughed and ushered me back inside.

'Everyone thinks that here. Bung Karno was the last to really live in Bogor. Everyone else is afraid to come here because of ghosts. This was his bedroom.'

There was a polished wood bed, looking vaguely foolish as beds do when unoccupied. All you can do is stare at them and imagine people in them, in itself a voyeuristic act. On the wall, scenes from the *Mahabharata* by Indonesian painters, nasty, over-busy productions that seemed desperately to be working up to the invention of the authentically Indonesian cherub.

We walked on down a long corridor, being scrubbed by a team of workers with such enthusiasm it looked as if cleaning it were something they had wanted to do all their lives. He flung open another door.

'This too was Bung Karno's bedroom.' As we moved round the palace, it became clear that Bung Karno had needed many bedrooms as he acquired and shed wives. The complexity of his marital life had finally led to the construction of bungalows in the grounds.

'Aren't *you* afraid of ghosts?'

'No. I was born in Bogor. When I was a little boy, there were no railings around the palace and the garden wasn't separate like now. But none of us dared come in. I used to stand and look in and one day Bung Karno saw me and waved to me. What other president would bother to wave to a little boy?'

I thought of Raffles and Muchi Abdullah.

'. . . So ghosts here never bother me. They are friendly ghosts. This was Bung Karno's office.'

It was cordoned off. I peered round to try to look at the books on the shelves, seeing titles in Russian and German snarling across the spines. 'Go on,' he gave me a nudge. 'You can go in if you like. I won't tell.'

We stepped over the rope. A security man came up but said nothing, only grinned. There were silver-framed portraits of Nehru and others, now forgotten, with illegible scrawled dedications, a big desk with a fresh blotter, a complex paraphernalia of pens.

'If you like,' he whispered, 'you can sit at Bung Karno's desk. Go on. It's all right.' I perched demurely.

'No, put your feet up, like he did.' I tipped the chair back and swivelled tentatively. It took only a small act of the imagination to see not Bung Karno but Raffles – but he would have had no stylish desk, but a stout, workmanlike table, paper wedged under one corner to stop it wobbling, and all the books would have been scattered about the room in constant use. No pen holder, quills rather – and half the geese on the pond slaughtered to make more pens for ever-scribbling Raffles.

They looked at me eagerly, seeming to expect something more. I couldn't think of a single thing to say or do. Perhaps Bung Karno had felt the same, sitting there in the 1950s with all Indonesia looking at him. Then the sun shifted and hit me full in the face. Sweat streamed down my forehead. I wiped it theatrically away. I got up.

'Bung Karno's chair is too hot, too heavy for me.' It hit the culturally right note of total insincerity. They were pleased.

As we passed on, the percentage of representations of naked women increased steeply. They were everywhere, sprawled languorously along the tops of bureaux, standing in bowls of water. Somewhere, Bung Karno remarked that near the ballroom in Bogor was a plaque showing the birth of Hercules surrounded by no less than fourteen beautiful women. At his own birth there was only one extremely old man present. I commented on it.

'I think it is normal for men to like to look on women,' the guide replied a little frostily. 'This is Sarinah – a lady Bung Karno greatly . . . admired. You have heard of the chain of shops called Sarinah . . . named after her.'

She was demurely beautiful, a slim, fair-skinned woman with a Javanese hairstyle. It was an accomplished painting that captured an impression of lightness and freshness. I looked at the signature. 'Soekarno.'

In Indonesia, every child learns that Sukarno was a gifted painter, but you always doubt such adulation. Politicians who are great artists are so the way Hitler was a great artist – by self-definition, daring others to disagree with them. Here was evidence Sukarno really could paint.

The guide seemed to think so too. He came up very close and looked over my shoulder. I could smell clove cigarettes on the breath that tickled my ear. He spoke very quietly.

'After the . . . New Order . . . When Bung Karno no longer really ran the country, they brought him here. He used to walk in the garden, but most of all paint. He always thought they would call him back – to take over, but he always saw himself as an artist. That's what he *really* wanted to be. He wanted to have exhibitions. He liked artists. He told stories. If you ever heard him speak . . . He could hold a crowd . . . Politics wasn't enough for a man gifted like that. He was an artist.'

*

Land was for Raffles the ultimate reality. His whole administration stands or falls on the question of land. He had read Adam Smith, the political economist, and believed in the naturalness and therefore goodness of unfettered trade, though himself obliged to operate within Company monopolies. Adam Smith made political liberality respectable by showing it was good for business. Petty despotism became the horror of the trading classes. It was these unexamined assumptions that moulded Raffles's whole policy on land and the native rulers.

One of the first acts of his administration was to set up an inquiry into landholding to discover precisely who had what rights in land. His aim was to give the peasants control over their own labour and the fruits of their labour, to free them from arbitrary taxation and rapacious officials. Raffles firmly believed in human nature and the natural good sense of his subjects. If it was in their own interests to be honest and industrious, then that is what they would become. It is this belief that makes Raffles a natural optimist and an attractive personality. It was, at that time, a revolutionary doctrine.

A more generally held view of the nineteenth century, that Raffles too never quite shakes off, is that native peoples have innate characteristics, like breeds of dogs. According to the Dutch, South-East Asians were idle, perfidious and untrustworthy. Raffles's own committee, appointed to look into land reform, declared unreservedly that Javanese would never work unless compelled to. Luckily, he had the arrogance of his optimism and began his great experiment regardless. He believed in redemption through good works.

*

Many years later Raffles would observe the peasants of France and write:

> '. . . When I see every man cultivating his own field, I cannot but think him happier far than when he is cultivating the field of another; even if he labours more, that labour is still lighter which is his pride and pleasure, than that which is his burden and sorrow.'

Yet, over a hundred years later, Sukarno would have the same insight, believing it to be a wholly original and Indonesian revelation, and make it the basis of a lifelong political philosophy:

> 'On our islands are labourers poorer even than church rats – too pitiful financially to ever rise socially, politically, or economically – yet each is his own boss, beholden to no one. He is the horse-cart driver who owns his own horse and cart and employs no other manpower. And the self-employed fisherman whose total equipment including the rod, hook, line

and proa [boat] is all his. And the farmer who is the sole owner and consumer of his product . . .

Pedalling around aimlessly on my bicycle – thinking – I found myself in the southern part of Bandung, a compact agricultural area where you see many farmers in their little fields, each of which is less than a third of a hectare. My attention, for some reason, was captured by a peasant hoeing his property. He was alone. His clothes were shabby. This typical scene struck me as being symbolic of my people. I stood there a while contemplating it silently. We Indonesians being a warm, friendly sort, I approached him. In the regional Sundanese, I asked, "Who is the owner of this lot on which you are now working?"

He said to me, "Why, I am, sir."

I said, "Tell me, does anyone own this with you?"

"Oh, no, sir. I own it all by myself."

"Did you buy it?"

"No. It was handed down from father to son for generations."

. . . "The crop on which you are working, for whom is it?"

"For me, sir."

. . . "Do you sell any of your produce?" I asked.

"There is barely enough to keep us alive. There is no extra to sell."

I then asked this young farmer his name. And he told me, Marhaen. Marhaen is a common name like Smith or Jones. At that moment, the light of inspiration flooded my brain. I would use that name for all Indonesians with the same miserable lot. From then on I would call my people Marhaenists . . . Marhaenism is Indonesian Socialism in operation.' – C. Adams, *Soekarno: An Autobiography*

*

'Development News' appeared on the TV screen accompanied by a vague thud of drums and shots of pipelines as at Tanjung Priok. Wheels of industry whirred for the camera and some vile pollutant squirted into the landscape as lean-jawed young men in hard hats stared towards a better future like poor old Francis Light at Penang. On the table before them lay plans of some great enterprise on which they tapped with authoritative brown fingers.

'I always mean to tell this programme about my grand-mother and the telephone,' said Agus, sipping at his whisky.

'Mmm?'

'You know I'm not from this island? Well, when I got this job, I paid for my parents to have the telephone. It was horribly expensive, but I have a friend who works for the company and my father is now village head ... Anyway, whenever my grandmother answered the phone, she just shouted in it, "I can't understand you!" and slammed it down.' He giggled. 'But it came in useful for the witchcraft, last year. There had been all sorts of things going wrong and finally she sent for the *dukun*, the old man who knew about such things, and he dug around and found something buried under the house. It was neighbours who had done it, of course. I don't know what it was. We had to get rid of it in the sea.' He preened his moustache thoughtfully, seeing the nameless horror in his mind. He shuddered.

'The *dukun* said it was beyond him and my granny wanted me to get a proper Jakarta *dukun*, but I couldn't afford to send him all the way to my village and you know their powers won't work over water. So we used the telephone. He came here and talked down the phone and the words went out to the satellite and back to the village.' He looked pleased with himself. 'It was my idea.'

'Did it work?'

'Oh yes.' He preened his moustache again.

'So your granny isn't frightened of the phone any more?'

'Oh yes she is. She's terrified when it rings, it could be some *dukun* who'll start whispering in her ear. She won't answer it at all now.'

*

Before he left, Lord Minto did more than lay down the general political lines Raffles was to follow, he engaged in a very paternal action that showed his close personal relationship to Raffles. He sponsored him as a Mason.

Freemasonry was rife in both the English and Dutch trading companies. Daendels, Raffles's predecessor, had been so worried by the possibility of Masonic conspiracies that he decided to build a new club, the Harmonie, where expatriates would meet openly. In an attempt to encourage Dutch and British to mix, Raffles completed it with public funds.

The list of Masons is inevitably incomplete, and the role of Freemasonry in empire is a huge book that remains to be written, but we do know that *all* Raffles's immediate associates were members. He eschewed both the Batavia lodges at that time and joined a small lodge called 'Virtutis et Artis Amici' on the Pondok–Gedeh coffee plantations near Bogor. A fellow initiate was his Dutch ally, Muntinghe, and a fellow member his future arch-enemy, General Gillespie. Raffles never mentions his Masonic activities, but accounts of Freemasonry in India and London dot the pages of his *Java Government Gazette*. From the records, we know that he took it seriously enough to rise to the third degree of Freemasonry during an overnight stay in Surabaya in 1813. Shortly before leaving Java he 'received Perfection in the Rose Croix Chapter "La Vertueuse" in Batavia', in the company of his secretary and his banker.

The Masonic meeting house 'Star of the East' still stands in modern Jakarta, just round the corner from the street where the Harmonie embraced both Dutch and English. It is the area where Raffles and the other prominent members of the English

85

community lived. The building was apparently known as 'the house of demons'. In the square in front of it, Daendels had drilled his troops; the British used it for horse-racing.

It is impossible to know for sure what attracted Raffles to Freemasonry. As an endemic outsider, he may well have appreciated the opportunity to really 'belong' to the ruling clique of the Company. As a practical man, he may well have pined for some sort of ethical organization that would cross-cut national lines so the Dutch and British could be true 'brothers'. From a religious point of view, Raffles occasionally gives sign of that moderate and functional eighteenth-century faith that left no room for enthusiasm. He tolerated his cousin as a 'dissenter'. He opposed interfering with the faith of Muslims, which he regarded as a perfectly satisfactory religion whilst condemning its addiction to empty ritual. He seems at times to be reaching for some sort of non-denominational faith:

> 'The great doctrine of the Koran is the Unity of God – to restore which point was the main point of Mahomed's mission, and to be candid, I think Mahomed has done a good deal of good in the world. I amuse and instruct myself for hours together with the Mahometans here, who to a man all believe in the Scriptures. They believe Jesus Christ a prophet and respect him as such. Mahomed's mission does not invalidate our Saviour's. One has secured happiness to the Eastern and one to the Western world, and both deserve our veneration.'

Raffles had encountered other religions as a functioning part of the social order and found a need to come to terms with them. He could not condemn them out of hand as he might in England, though – like present Indonesian officialdom – he always assumed that those who were not Hindu,

Buddhist, Christian or Muslim had 'no religion'. For Raffles's generation, the possession of religion was a mark of civilization; for the present generation of largely godless English, it is, of course, a mark of primitiveness. It may well be the non-denominational religiosity of Freemasonry that appealed to the tolerant and international mind of Raffles. For Freemasonry preaches a belief in God but does not clearly say *which* god. This too would link Sukarno and Raffles.

'There, between the two huge pillars where once the Governor-General stood to officially open the *Volksraad*, I unwrapped my five precious pearls: Nationalism, Internationalism, Democracy, Social Justice, and Belief in One God . . . "Let us build *merdeka* [freedom] in awe of the One Supreme God", but "Let every Indonesian believe in his own God. Let each worship as he chooses. Let us declare the fifth principle as the civilized way: Belief in one God with mutual respect for one another."' – C. Adams, *Soekarno: An Autobiography*

*

The guide saw me to the gate of the Great Garden like a well-mannered escort of the age of Raffles seeing his dancing partner home. A statue crouched coyly by the lily-pond. Surely that was a copy of the mermaid of Copenhagen? A gravel path led out into the trees of the botanical garden towards the looming bulge of Olivia's monument.

'I used to work here in the garden,' he said, peering round the gate. 'There are no more guests at the palace today. I'll take you round.'

The garden was full of birds and plump fruit-bats hung from the trees like Christmas decorations. On one side mouse-deer, *kijang*, were grazing. They had been there in Raffles's day, though *Kijang* now was a kind of locally made Toyota. A man sat by the side of the path sticking glass eyes on fruit stones so they could be adapted into novelty key-rings.

'All this was started by Raffles,' declared my palace – become my garden – guide.

'But all the books say it was Van der Capelan.'

He swatted the objection away like an importunate mosquito. 'That is when it was *officially* founded as a botanical garden. The man before Raffles sold off the land that went with the palace and stole the money.' That had been Daendels, 'the Dutch Napoleon'; grossly fat and corrupt, he had died of the piles in West Africa. Serve him right, too. 'Raffles bought the land back and planted trees. That is how the garden started.'

A phantom graffitist had been at work in the English tongue, doubtless some frustrated student. On one of the trees was chalked, 'Higher education is your ticket to instant unemployment.' It was necessary to walk round the whole tree to read it. Raffles would not have agreed with that sentiment. Further along was, 'Before you find your handsome prince, you will kiss a thousand toads.'

'Is there a *Rafflesia arnoldii* here?' – the huge parasitic plant discovered by Raffles in Bengkulu, the largest flower in the world. It can be more than a metre across and weigh twenty-five pounds.

'Yes. This way.' He led me down a dank path and pointed. There was what I can only describe as a small red flower on a stick.

'That's not a *Rafflesia*. A *Rafflesia*'s huge.'

'It's the same family.' He pouted. 'There used to be one, but someone stole it.'

'Why would anyone steal a flower weighing twenty-five pounds and stinking of rotten carrion?' He shrugged.

'In Bogor, people will steal anything.'

My guide was snorting great breaths of fresh air through

splayed nostrils, staring up smiling into the leaf canopy, feeling
the grass luxuriously through his thin shoes. He looked
absurdly revived, like a pit pony let up for air.

'On holidays, many boys and girls come here. Half the
people in Jakarta who end up getting married do their courting
here. Behind those roots there . . .' A lump came into his
throat, choking off speech. Suddenly he rushed off, leapt halfway up a tree and grabbed a handful of loose bark, like a dog
chasing a squirrel. 'This bark makes a man very strong. Eat
some of this and you can have ten women in one night.' He
cast it wildly away.

'Does it really work?'

He looked briefly crestfallen, then grinned manically. 'Whenever I wanted to test it, I could never find more than one
woman. Look!' He hurled a stone up into another tree bringing
fruit and branches crashing down. 'This tree produces fruit
like the members of little black boys – very popular with
schoolgirls. Look!' He rushed laughing into the greenery and
began swinging on a liana. 'Every holiday many Tarzans come
here looking for Janes.'

There was a clattering up in the top branches. 'Flying foxes,'
he whispered, black eyes shining. 'Good to eat but they make
a man . . .' He clenched his fist like the cannon in Jakarta and
groaned.

We came to poor Olivia Raffles's monument, rebuilt – as
the inscription informed us – after being 'destroyed by a great
wind'. A tiny schoolboy was doing his homework in its shade,
his face simultaneously puzzled and depressed. Above his head
the graffitist had struck again, proclaiming 'Raffles was here',
not the more idiomatic 'woz 'ere' of a home-grown scribbler.
On the first attempt he had written, 'has been here', crossed it
out and moved on to a tentative 'was being here'. Only after
mature reflection on the English preterite, or maybe the con-
sultation of his grammar, had he arrived at the final version.

7. *Noblesse Oblige*

'A great disregard for the *little people* is shewn throughout their [the Javanese] political history.' – T.S. Raffles, *The History of Java*

The native rulers of Indonesia saw the arrival of the British as a golden opportunity to regain their ancient liberties. The Dutch had been conveniently defeated for them by an unhoped-for outsider. After this windfall, they saw themselves as under no obligation to behave as spoils of war. The end of the Dutch administration negated all contracts. The British, somewhat legalistically, considered themselves as heirs to the Dutch and therefore heirs to all their agreements and treaties. Any attempt to break them would be an act of perfidy. So the two sides stared past each other in mutual misunderstanding.

Raffles was predisposed by long British habit to see native rulers as despots and to wish to reduce them to a 'constitutional' position. From the start he adopted a policy of stressing British supremacy, curtailing the independence of local monarchs and trying to make them salaried officials. It is curious that he has been regarded as an early exponent of the British art of indirect rule. The Dutch had left Java as commercial monopolists. They would return to find themselves unambiguously raised to the position of political masters.

Only a couple of months after the British conquest of Java, Raffles personally visited the royal courts of Solo and Yogyakarta (Yogya) to make friends and sign treaties with the two principal Javanese rulers. The Dutch had adopted the strategy of encouraging factions within the ruling houses, splitting them again and again. Raffles would ultimately adopt the same practice. Initially he had sent envoys. To Yogya, he had sent John Crawfurd. Raffles and Crawfurd did not get on. Between them was the rivalry of authors and researchers into the same topic, for Crawfurd prided himself on his Malay scholarship. He would write bad reviews of Raffles's *History of Java* yet produce only pale pastiches of it in his own works. Crawfurd appalled the Sultan of Yogya with his arrogance.

The Sultan himself played to all the worst of Raffles's fears. Having been deposed by the Dutch, he unilaterally resumed power and executed his own prime minister – the very model of 'an Asiatic despot'.

Raffles, aware of the need not to unite the native rulers against him, stopped at Solo first and found the Sultan conciliatory. A treaty was signed. But equally important to Raffles was his meeting there with Dr Thomas Horsefield, an American naturalist. He would prove to be Raffles's substitute for the dead Leyden as a formally trained scholar who could act as his academic partner. Henceforth, they would collaborate zestfully in the scientific investigation of 'the *other* India'. Compared to *that*, the treaty must have seemed of rather transitory importance.

*

There is a sadness about Solo, or Surakarta to give it its formal name, a greyness that belies its heat. It is the oldest royal city of Central Java, locked in eternal rivalry with its parvenu neighbour Yogya. But whereas Yogya enthusiastically embraced the Indonesian Revolution against the Dutch and was, for a time, capital of the infant republic, Solo thought it would all blow over and one day the Europeans would come back. Things were much the same in Raffles's day. The Sultan of Solo rapidly came to terms, whereas Yogya merely awaited its chance. So government money and preferment go to effervescent Yogya and Solo sinks in slow decline.

The bear-hug of Indonesian hospitality cannot be avoided. 'Solo?' they say. 'We have relatives or friends or friends of relatives there. You *must* stay with them. If you didn't everyone would be terribly offended.' And so I end up staying in a Muslim high school, where going through a wrong door can plunge you into the midst of schoolgirls at their devotions.

At five in the morning the boys practise the call to prayer, the untutored voices somehow much more moving to an infidel than the slicker cadences of the professionals. Their straining chords mingle with those of the caged birds on the veranda, lending themselves too easily to glib moralistic musings concerning freedom and constraint.

At seven the girls appear, swathed in cloth from head to foot, and immediately go into a routine of physical jerks to disco music in front of the boys. Then the boys struggle into tight shorts and demonstrate their prowess to the girls. But, the master emphasized to me repeatedly, they never dance *together*.

Outside the school is a *becak* or trishaw rank. They sit there for hours playing chess, which here has none of the Western connotations of pretentious intellectuality. *Becak*-drivers have sharp tongues. They call the whole business of dancing and praying 'Allah disco'.

A *becak* is perhaps the best way to see Indonesian towns. In many parts they take the children to school, the sick to hospital, the wives to their shopping. But they are gradually being banned from cities. They cause congestion, are unmodern – worse – colonial. I always seem to end up with very old *becak*-drivers pedalling me about. People stare, but are they thinking, 'See that good white man who has hired that hopeless old driver though a young one would have been stronger and quicker'? Or are they thinking, 'Look at that fat foreigner sitting there while that poor old man slaves away'? *Becaks*, for Westerners, are intimately associated with guilt.

Young drivers too can have their problems. In Solo, being caught in the first rainstorm of the year, I did what many others were doing and dived into a *becak*. I had just been to the royal palace, a run-down structure in the centre of town. A fire there a few years before had led people to recall legends that the destruction of the palace would lead inexorably to the destruction of all Java. In Java no one laughs at such legends, and suddenly government funding had become available for rebuilding. The principal curiosity of the palace was the collection of chastity belts. The guide, ever-eager to improve his English, wanted to know how he should designate the male version, a ticklish cylinder of gold covered with spikes, imposed by a jealous female ruler on her consort. Thinking of this, I hardly noticed the driver.

Becaks have a sort of plastic curtain at the front that can be let down as in a push-chair. The driver, of course, is outside in the storm and is reduced to a pair of glistening legs with muscles like giant pistons.

'Where do you want to go?' asked the legs.

'Ivory Street.' We haggled gently over the fare.

'Whereabouts in Ivory Street?' asked the legs.

'Do you know the Muslim high school?'

The legs laughed and a hand reached in and held out a plastic identity card. My driver's name was Joko. He was a pupil at the school.

'There are two shifts of pupils,' he explained. 'I get up at five and go to the school till noon. Then I take out my *becak* till seven. Then I do my homework and help my family till midnight. Then I go to sleep again.'

The *becak* cost forty pence a day to hire. Sometimes he did not earn that much and made a loss. He had seven brothers and sisters and his father had no work. He was seventeen years old.

When we got to Ivory Street, he stopped, put on a coolie hat, a pair of broken sunglasses and a mac that covered him from head to foot. This was curious as it had by now stopped raining. He looked like Greta Garbo on a shopping trip.

'It is the Chinese boys,' he explained, reluctantly. 'They go to the same school as me and their fathers own the shops along this street. If they recognize me they'll call out insults and jeer.'

This was too much guilt for one *becak* ride. One corner of the street had been curtained off and was being used as a milk-stall. 'Your custom,' said a sign sadly, 'is our only hope of advancement.' In the hills, I knew, there were grassy meadows, contented cows, Indonesian milkmaids with plaits and dirndl dresses.

'Ah,' I said, 'milk. You will know, of course, that all Europeans are mad about drinking milk. Let us go there and drink milk.' Once inside, I could invent some European obsession with walking, pay him off and spare him the embarrassment of the Chinese boys.

Behind the curtain was another young man. They seemed to know each other.

'Do you go to school too?' I asked warily.

'No,' said the young man, 'Joko is lucky compared to me. *I* am too poor to go to school but I love to learn English. At night, if there are no customers, I learn from the Australian radio. You can send off for a free book.' He waved a copy at me. 'Tell us about English schools.'

We sat and drank tepid milk. I told them of a place where education was free, where the government even gave students money to study. They found it hard to believe, mere travellers' tales. Such a thing could not really be possible. It was like stories of cities with pavements of gold.

'Would you,' asked the young man, 'have time to talk to us in English? They charge a pound an hour for English conversation at the colleges.'

The rain started up again and thundered wetly on the canvas roof. There was no escape. We spoke of irregular verbs. The more I tried to explain them, the more I realized I didn't understand them myself. But an hour of my time and a walk home in the pouring rain did not seem too much to atone for the guilt of even one *becak* ride.

*

Raffles's visit to Yogya was sheer 'Boys' Own' bravado. He arrived with a force of 900 light cavalry. He was treading a fine line, anxious to make it clear he was not here on a mission of conquest but not wanting to seem a mere mendicant. The policy was that he had come simply to confirm existing arrangements. There was a business with the carriages, Raffles taking the first and not the second, which had been intended for him. The Sultan tried to impose the reverse arrangement. Raffles knew that within the *kraton* (palace), precedence was the same as power. Minute regulations governed the smallest matters of dress and behaviour. To this day, the contents of the palace library have an obsessive concern with sumptuary rules – who has the right to wear combs and jewellery, to carry fans.

They entered the audience hall, Raffles and his small party being temporarily cut off from their escort by the press of excited, armed Javanese. Next there was a fussing about the precedence implied by the arrangement of the chairs – fighting with furniture. Swords were drawn on both sides. It looked as if there would be a massacre. At the last moment the Sultan backed down. The chairs were moved so that Raffles's buttocks had priority, or at least equality. They sat. An agreement was signed.

'The Sultan was accompanied by several thousands of armed followers, who expressed in their behaviour an infuriated spirit of insolence . . . Though at that time no act of treacherous hostility took place, the crafty and sanguinary Sultan drew from the circumstances he observed, a confidence in his own strength.' – Lady Raffles, *Memoir*

'. . . The Sultan had yet to learn with whom he had to deal. Raffles, it is true, lacked those few extra inches that can give a man the assistance of a commanding physical presence, but he lacked nothing in moral stature, and there was clearly something about him that compelled respect.' – C. Wurtzburg, *Raffles of the Eastern Isles*

*

Halfway between Solo and Yogya is the town of Klaten. It is sprawling and dusty, a junction on the railway line, a place devoid of charm apart from the emerald greenness of the surrounding ricefields. It is home to many small businesses. A hundred Javanese skills flourish here. There are carvers and brass-casters, iron is worked in a small way. Beds, cupboards, mirrors, lamps and brass knick-knacks flow to the market of Yogya. Raffles set up a fort here, but it is striking nowadays for being the source of antique English furniture.

The wood comes from the mahogany trees planted along the roads by the Dutch. Every traffic accident brings a windfall to woodworkers and police, for the principal victims are the ancient trees – otherwise protected by law. Even bicycle accidents seem to knock down trees. It is like that fine tradition of · the British Navy whereby every first shot received in warfare inevitably strikes the drink locker and disables further accounting.

The designs come from Chippendale pattern-books: chairs, tables, bureaux, tea-caddies. Inside an irrelevant modern factory, Javanese carvers sit crosslegged on the floor, carving freehand, as in their village – chatting amicably, eating, smoking. They produce perfect, alien furniture of stunning beauty with shrugging indifference. They would not give it house room. The finished pieces may be shipped to America via England to acquire a more acceptable provenance. Indonesians can make anything. The offcuts, too good to waste, are made into funerary urns for the ashes of American Christians, decorated with praying hands and round-eyed Western angels.

'We spent the night at Klatten. In the small hours, finding myself unable to sleep, I left my stuffy room and walked to the gate of the fort, where I met a sergeant of the 14th who had likewise sallied forth in search of a little fresh air . . . For a few minutes we stood in silence side by side, looking out over the still palm-tops to where, in the distance, Mount Merapi stood like a pyramid of jet against the silver moonshine, a flag of smoke from his lofty summit trailing right across the firmament.

"Rum country, this, ain't it, sir?" the sergeant suggested pleasantly.

"How so exactly?" I queried.

"Well, sir, take that mountain there for a start, smoking away like 'ell, if you'll excuse the expression. I suppose one o' these days it'll just spit out a few thousand tons of assorted muck and bury the 'ole countryside, and then go one smoking as calmly as if it 'adn't done a mortal thing, same as you or me might go on smoking a cheroot after stamping on a beetle."

"It's done that several times in the past," I told him.

"You know, sir," he continued after another short silence, "that crowd of 'eathens at Jocya reminded me a bit o' this 'ere mountain. There they was, as quiet as quiet, and yet you felt they was all on fire inside of 'em, and for two pins there'd be a blessed eruption . . . By God, sir, I give the salute to the Governor for the way 'e stood up to that little lot! I never seen a civilian before with that much guts, never in my mortal life."

"Oh, there's nothing soft about Mr Raffles," I agreed

heartily. "In spite of his shyness and gentle ways, he'll stand no nonsense."' – H. Banner, *The Clean Wind: An Historical Novel of Romance and Adventure*

*

I already knew where I would find Lukas, on the corner of the *alun-alun*, the big square that stands before the palace. As usual, he was drinking a potent drink of his own devising, beer mixed with strong, red wine. The square was shut off for the big festival of Mohammed's birthday, *sekaten*. Inside was a fair and a circus. I had to pay to get in.

'What's this?' I asked Lukas. 'Now you charge people to come and see you, like the Sultan?'

He let out a roar and grabbed me. Small as he was, it was no problem to lift me off my feet. He was in his late twenties, very dark and oddly simian. We ran through the familiar litany. All was well. He had another son. His wife had gone back to her village to show it to her mother. He still worked at the palace as a guard. It had been a good year for the seduction of easy tourist women. The rains would come soon. He could not complain.

We sat and drank his potent emetic. Friends dropped by, a schoolteacher, a *becak*-driver. Some started playing chess. He was concerned that I should know he had finished work for the day. He would never drink before going on duty. The palace and its works were taken very seriously.

'How is the batik, this year?' I asked. He grinned. When Lukas grinned, his face nearly fell in half. His family had a small shop near the water-palace where they sold batik paintings. In his descriptions to tourist ladies, he was always careful to call it 'an exhibition' and speak of the young artists who desperately needed encouragement through their patronage.

'This year was good! We have a new idea for paintings. Come, I show you.' He took me by the hand and we set off towards the *kraton*, picking his way through the stalls, pausing to shout greetings and jokes to friends in the crowd. A newspaper-seller hawked his wares. 'Good news! An accident. Many killed!'

We sidled through the palace gates and crunched across the outer court, strewn – I recalled – with sand from the sea-bed, home of the Sultan's mystical wife, Loro Kidul, goddess of the South Sea. The tinkle of *gamelans* announced that the palace dancers were practising their stealthy art in one of the inner courtyards behind the high stone walls. A palace guide, one of the intercultural pimps, was spieling to tourists.

'This cage you see is not for the animal. Is for the baby. A Javanese child must not touch the ground for eight months. We put in a little money, a pencil, flowers. If the child touches the money, it will be rich. Flowers make a girl a good mother, a boy handsome. Does it work? Look at me, ha! ha!'

Ramrod-straight guards nodded graciously to Lukas and obliged tourists to remove their hats with peremptory gestures. But, who knows, perhaps behind the motionless façade there was wiry Javanese anarchy barely kept in check by rigid etiquette.

We passed the museum, crammed with a huge accumulation of Western junk – hideous lamps, statues, humidors.

Another guide intoned, 'The late Sultan died *in Washington DC!*' – the place of his death more important than the fact.

The art gallery. The young Sultan in blank youthful beauty and the dignity of old age, accepting the surrender of the Dutch. He sits impassive. The Dutch bow and fawn. Curiously, I had seen the original photograph of the scene. This was no victor's adjustment of the facts. It really was like that.

'Why have you come back?' Lukas scanned my face. I told him about Raffles.

He dropped my hand like a hot potato.

'Raff-lesh?' he said, shocked, as if I had mentioned

something unseemly. 'Raff-lesh was here. He was a bad man, a very bad man. He attacked the palace, killed many Yogya people, looted the royal treasures. Ooh, he was such a bad man!'

*

Raffles did not expect the treaty with Yogya to hold. The small force he had was already mostly committed to dethroning the Sultan of Palembang, one of the major sultans of Sumatra, who had petulantly repudiated British claims to his loyalty and massacred the Dutch inhabitants of his town. He did not know he was being an archetypal Oriental despot. Gillespie was dispatched and rapidly 'reduced' the town. The wily Sultan kept the letters he had received from Raffles. Later, drawing on another demonology, he would be able to convince the Dutch it was that English devil that had put him up to it.

Raffles used the disagreement to annex the tin-rich island of Bangka. We see him, for the first time, greedy to seize an asset. He was desperate to find an export commodity for Java and to construct a defensive position in case Java were returned to the Dutch. When the tin proved unsaleable, with typically deft footwork he used it to issue a tin coinage. Bangka had been ceded to the *British* government. If Java were returned to the Dutch, Bangka would remain British. In a neat genuflection towards his patron, he renamed its largest town of Montok: it was now Minto.

*

We walked through the aromatic back lanes of the palace. Forty thousand people are said to live there in a tumble of whitewashed houses loud with bougainvillaea, reminiscent of the Mediterranean. We approached the water-palace, a proof the Disneyland had always had a place in Indonesia. It was an improbable structure, a ruined European mansion seeming to float on the water, with underground tunnels, a mosque. It was variously explained as the place where the Sultan received the goddess of the South Sea, where he dallied with concubines, where he asserted his Oriental mastery over water and ritual purity.

I knew it was a favourite prop in Lukas's hobby of seducing Western women. He pointed at it.

'Raffles destroyed the water-palace,' he declared unctuously.

'No he didn't. It was already in ruins when he arrived. There's even a drawing of it at the time.'

'All right, maybe it was the Dutch. They bombed it again in 1948.'

If they had, I rather suspected the planes had been British. But Lukas couldn't keep up post-colonial resentment for long. It was just a hat he popped on from time to time to see how it looked. He laughed.

'It's prettier as a ruin, anyway. Here's the house.'

The family lived in a small structure nearby. It was clear from its form that in Dutch times it had been a stable. The walls blazed with batik paintings in glaring chemical colours. Light ricocheted off the intense reds and blues. A little boy, with the angelic face of all sleeping children, was stretched out on the floor, a thin mattress under him. Lukas bent down and grinned a Lukas grin, giving the child an Oriental kiss, a gentle rubbing of his nose from cheek to ear while inhaling. He held the limp form up for me to see. The child frowned and batted in sleep with one hand.

'Wah! My son! You remember him?'

'Yes, but last time he was just a worm.'

He stared at the boy, entranced, incredulous at the magic of his own engendering, then folded him gently down.

'This is the new thing.' He pointed at the wall. Most of the paintings were typical tourist nonsense, dancing girls, peasants labouring in the ricefields, Borobodur temple at night, one curiously of pyramids. But there in the middle was, indeed, something new. It was Rambo, or rather a cross between Che Guevara and Rambo. The gun blazed. The moronic mouth snarled with perfect dentition. The hair raged in some imaginary wind. The eyes gleamed an insane *blue*.

'We sell dozens.' He took my hand again and led me to the next room, pausing to turn one light off and another on. In Indonesia, electricity is expensive. In front of us was another face. It was based on the famous official photograph that had hung in millions of Indonesian homes. In immaculate uniform, medals and *songkok* hat, it was Bung Karno.

We stared at it in silence.

'That's for the domestic tourists. Foreigners won't touch it. I grew up looking at that. Bung Karno too was here – in Yogya.' He slipped an arm kindly around my shoulders. 'Send me a photograph of your Raff-lesh and maybe I will do him in batik – if there's a demand. But I think the Dutch would not buy it and neither would Yogya people.'

*

The Sultan of Yogya had been misbehaving. He had strangled a number of the principal chiefs of the country and intrigued with the Sultan of Solo. Now he was building up his defences and refusing to keep the terms of the treaty. It all meant trouble.

Raffles decided he must act to prevent the whole island rising. Most of the army was still absent in Sumatra. Nevertheless, he set off, pausing only to throw a ball to celebrate the King's birthday. Luckily, Gillespie returned in time to rendezvous with Raffles, bringing a small force with him. They had less than 1,500 troops against an estimated 11,000 within the *kraton* and the whole army of the Sultan of Solo without. They were surrounded.

'"The City of Pilgrimage", as Jogja became known, numbered 170,000 inhabitants. In the next few weeks [of 1946], the entire government moved inland and the population swelled to 600,000 ... We operated more like a band of thieves than a government ... We also had no money ... The only way to get what we desperately needed was to smuggle. And everybody smuggled for the Republic. My current Ambassador to Japan ran sugar. My former Ambassador to America ran opium ... The one commodity we had was raw materials. Our Minister of Econmics arranged to export goods to Britain, and Britain guaranteed the shipments' safety from Dutch buccaneering on the high seas ... The Sultan of Jogja was a major liaison between the Dutch-held capital of Djakarta and the Republican-held capital of Jogjakarta ... At one point the total capital of the Republic of Indonesia was transferred into gold bricks, stuffed in shoe boxes and soap dishes and hidden in the back room of the Sultan's office ... In December 1948, the Dutch dropped a package of Christmas cheer down my chimney. At 5.30 in the morning of Sunday, the 19th, they bombed Jogjakarta ... One hour of heavy bombing interlaced with rocket-firing P-51's and the Dutch had captured the airport. Low-flying Spitfires strafed the streets lengthwise and crosswise. The heavens were black with airplanes. One thousand paratroopers took the post office and radio station, and set fire to the automobiles ... By noon Jogja was surrounded.' – C. Adams, *Soekarno: An Autobiography*

*

'We will go to the Social Ministry,' said Lukas, surveying the swimming pool. It was a very small pool, little better than a birdbath but, for once, it was not full of Chinese. This time it was crammed with raucous Australian children. 'White goats,' Lukas called them. But the Chinese were not to be spared.

'This guest-house is *owned* by Chinese,' he declared

irritably. He paused to run an eye over an Australian air-hostess type. 'I have,' he confessed, 'been drinking too much milk lately. It is bad for my health. It is time to drink a little chocolate.'

'What?'

He gave me a pitying look. 'Indonesian girls – chocolate.' He held out his arm and pinched the brown skin. 'Chocolate.' He pinched mine. 'Milk.'

'Oh, I see. But what has that got to do with the Social Ministry?'

A boy came out from the woodshop next door, sat down at our feet and began varnishing the headboard of a bed, humming to himself as he worked.

'There is a brothel there. You pay 500 rupiahs to get in, and if you see a girl you like you come to terms. It is very clean; they are inspected. I will take you on my motorbike. That, too, is very clean.'

'Mmm. I can't. I'm seeing a librarian from the palace. Anyway, this is work. I could only go to your brothel if Raff-lesh had been there.'

Lukas grinned. 'But of course he did. In those days there was no television. What else could he do? Of course your Raff-lesh went there.'

Raffles joyfully rogering away, a cheroot clenched casually in his teeth? Or Raffles smoothly efficient in his adultery, sex as an aperitif, a substitute for the sherry inadvertently left behind in Bogor? I couldn't see it. That was more Gillespie. Raffles had been so . . . unbendingly upright, despite the crooked back.

'I bet he didn't. I bet he worked every night, believing he was making life better for people just like you. But,' I recalled irrelevantly, 'when Bung Karno founded the PNI he recruited 670 whores from Bandung. He said they were the best spies and always had them greet Dutch officials by name when they were out walking with their wives – psychological warfare.'

We idly watched the boy sloshing on the varnish. Suddenly, I realized what he had on his fingers.

'Excuse me. On your fingers – aren't those . . . condoms?' He looked puzzled and stared at his hand openmouthed, as babies do.

'Yes, yes.' Lukas jumped up delightedly. 'Condoms. You're wearing condoms!'

The boy blushed. 'The boss gives them to us. He's Chinese and doesn't waste money. Rubber gloves cost money, but he gets these free from the government. What are they?'

Lukas jigged up and down on the spot, laughing. 'Condoms,' he roared. 'You put them on your dick so girls don't get pregnant. *I* only wear them with my wife. I don't want *her* getting pregnant.'

The boy pushed his hair back out of his eyes. 'Oh. Well, no wonder I don't know. I've never had sex.'

Lukas's laughter died on his lips. The air went out of him like a popped balloon. We had laughed at a man slipping on a banana skin only to find he was really hurt. Lukas looked aghast, a man whose whole philosophy had been called into question.

'How old are you? Eighteen, nineteen? Never? Why not? What's the problem?'

The boy sloshed on. 'Do you know what they pay me? Two thousand rupiahs a day [60p]. Girls won't look at you unless you've got money.'

Lukas was enraged. 'But that's crazy. You're a handsome boy. They'll do it for nothing. You can always have a tourist woman. Anyone can have them. They will pay *you*. But perhaps you do not speak English? This is dreadful.'

He turned to me, fired with moral fervour. 'We must take him to the Ministry.' It sounded very proper. He began to dig wildly through his pockets, throwing money on the ground – totting as he went.

'They will want two thousand from me because they know I like to play for an hour or more. But they have good hearts. A young boy like that. They will know he is excited. Two strokes and whoosh – all over! Perhaps they will do him for fifteen hundred. There is not enough money.' He looked at me pointedly.

'No,' I said. 'I'm not going and I'm certainly not paying for a total stranger to go to the Ministry. You must be crazy. Anyway,' I offered a little desperately, 'perhaps he isn't after sex but love.'

The boy looked up. His legs were trembling. 'No,' he said hoarsely, 'I want *sex*.'

Lukas was now very, very serious. He was whispering, angry almost. 'I have never asked you for anything.' It was true. 'You are a friend. But this is *keamalan*, an act of charity. He is a fellow human being. He suffers. We must help him. It is a moral duty.'

'But . . .'

He bit his lip. 'Yes, yes. You are right. It is wrong to seek money and give nothing in return.'

'But . . .'

There was no stopping him now. He was off with all the ethical momentum of a Jesuit sniffing out sin. 'So *you* must buy a Rambo from me. Then, I will get commission. I will use it to take him to the Ministry. There! All solved! Don't worry. I will make sure he wears one of those things – *not* on his finger. Everyone is happy!'

We looked at the boy. His hands were shaking so hard he had dropped the headboard. Varnish was dripping in unheeded symbolism off his quivering brush and running up his arm in a wiggly line. He was panting.

'No,' I said, truculently. 'He doesn't know what he's in for. Perhaps he doesn't even want to go. Absolutely not.'

*

It only took a few weeks for the Yogyans to build the forty-five-foot-high walls of the huge palace. The tiny fort the Dutch Company insisted on having took years. But the battle between them was all over in a few short hours. The British forces, running out of ammunition, turned once again to brute courage, escaladed the walls and turned the Javanese guns on their own defences. 'Gillespie was himself,' Raffles wrote. The Sultan of Yogya was swiftly taken and deposed, his son neatly installed in his place. The army of the Sultan of Solo played no part, but watched, saw wisdom and quietly crept away. It gave Raffles the opportunity for another outburst of estate-agent's hyperbole to Lord Minto:

> 'The European power is for the first time paramount in Java ... A population of not less than a million has been wrested from the tyranny and oppression of an independent, ignorant, and cruel prince, and a country yielding to none on earth in fertility and cultivation, affording a revenue of not less than a million of Spanish dollars in the year, placed at our disposal ... – By order of the Honourable, the Lieutenant-Governor

There was one shadow on all this. The troops had plundered the palace. The loot was assessed at $750,000. Raffles was furious. He had not come to Java to pillage it. He had come to free it from tyranny that it might rise to greater glory. It was an act worthy of the Dutch. This was the start of his bitter feud with Gillespie, the Commander of the Forces. Nevertheless, he took his share in manuscripts and diamonds. He was always a practical man.

*

Dutch paratroops stormed down the same road, past the same fort in 1948. Indonesians see the battle with the Dutch as simply a repeat performance of that with Raffles. They do not see the Dutch as enslaving them and the British as bringing them freedom from Oriental despots. On both occasions a small but well-organized foreign force seized the palace in an attempt to crush Indonesian nationhood. The similarity is clear to the little children visiting the Museum of the Revolutionary Struggle. But then they see no conflict with the message of their Rambo satchels, each showing the military moron zapping slit-eyed gooks.

Since the age of Raffles, the whole state has been harnessed to writing an alternative history of resistance and defiance – one more in keeping with present concerns. Local bandits have been dressed up as precocious nationalists, ineptness has become noble self-sacrifice, bloodthirstiness righteous wrath. Every area has to have its local hero for statuary purposes, dominating an important traffic roundabout in revolutionary fervour.

This time, for Bung Karno, there would be no battle to the death. Official history glosses lightly over what was a rather controversial phase in the development of the Republic. Bung Karno simply waited in the palace behind a white flag until the Dutch came to collect him. Finally, they hauled him off to internment in Montok on Raffles's tiny island of Bangka. It was no longer called Minto. Most of the army melted away into the hills to begin a bloody guerrilla war. Years later, when writing his memoirs, Sukarno would dwell on the indignity of being transported from the palace *in a jeep*. In Yoyga, people were still fighting with carriages.

One other thing stayed in his mind, the kindness of a Dutch soldier to one of the older freedom fighters who was ill:

'The soldier assigned to watch Hadji was no officer or intellectual. Just a human with a heart who could not seem to understand why all this fighting. "What is all this about?" he

kept asking. He had been told his army was *liberating* us.' –
C. Adams, *Soekarno: An Autobiography*

*

I awoke strangely tired and crapulous. There was no doubt
that this was Lukas's hangover, enjoyed by proxy. It was
difficult to open the door. A large batik painting was wedged
across it. I could not bear to look at it, wishing I had held out
for a Bung Karno, not a Rambo. On the ground outside the
door was a red plastic tub, the sort detergent comes in. I
picked it up. Someone had put in an inch of water and floated
frangipani blossoms on top. Their thick, whorish perfume
flooded the air, adding to the sense of hangover.

There was a loud whistle. I bleared over the edge of the
balcony to see the boy from the woodshop grinning and
waving, pointing to the frangipani tree over his head and
puffing out his chest. I raised the tub and smiled in a half-
hearted toast, then realized the awkwardness of drinking frangipani water, but it was too late, I was already committed.
What was it I was drinking to? To international friendship,
perhaps, or to the common core of humanity that underlies
difference. Or perhaps simply to the international conspiracy
of men.

8. White Elephants
and Other Beasts

The East India Company was a great white elephant. It had probably been technically insolvent for years. Its only profitable trade was that with China, while India had always lost money. In theory, it was a joint-stock company owned by all stockholders; in fact, it was run by twenty-four directors in a self-perpetuating oligarchy, and the government exerted authority through a Board of Control.

Curiously, for an enterprise of this sort, it owned very few vessels. Each ship was chartered for its separate voyages and divided up into sixteenths and thirty-seconds, owned by individuals. Often a particular individual would own a majority in a vessel and he became the 'husband' of the ship, with 'rights to bottom', deciding which charters it should accept. The freight rates were pitched artificially high in a system that extended from generation to generation, known as the 'system of hereditary bottoms'.

The Company employees were cross-cut with links of marriage and friendship, interests that led them to war on the aims and policies that they nominally supported. Most traded in their own right in the same goods as the Company, kept their own goods in the Company warehouse and shipped at discount on Company ships. A stroke of the pen could convert transactions that showed an unexpected loss into Company business, while those that made a profit became private speculation. The Company had unwittingly become an insurance policy for its employees.

White Elephants and Other Beasts

The great white elephant staggered from century to century, while the parasites that swarmed upon it grew fat. They never quite killed the beast, but slowly it grew more and more ponderous in its movements.

*

'A favourite and national spectacle is the combat between the buffalo and the tiger. A large cage of *bambu* or wood is erected, the ends of which are fixed into the ground, in which the buffalo is first, and the tiger afterwards, admitted, through openings reserved for the purpose. It seldom fails that the buffalo is triumphant, and one buffalo has been known to destroy several full-grown tigers, in succession. In these combats the buffalo is stimulated by the constant application of boiling water, which is poured over him from the upper part of the cage, and of nettles, which are fastened to the end of a stick and applied by persons seated in the same quarter. The tiger sometimes springs upon the buffalo at once: he very generally, however, avoids the combat until goaded by sticks and roused by the application of burning straw, when he moves round the cage, and being gored by the buffalo, seizes him by the neck, head or leg. The buffalo is often dreadfully torn, and seldom survives the combat many days. In these entertainments, the Javans are accustomed to compare the buffalo to the Javan and the tiger to the European, and it may be readily imagined, with what eagerness they look to the success of the former.' – T. S. Raffles, *History of Java*

Raffles was unusual in asking the meaning of these contests. Generations of Governors-General would sit through them – the symbolism occasionally upped a notch by the use of an albino tiger – and be baffled by the pleasure the Javanese took in a contest whose outcome was so predictable in advance.

*

'They no longer have the fights,' said Lukas. 'If they *did*, I'm sure the Sultan would have chosen me to apply stinging nettles to the private parts of the tigers. Nowadays, we have the circus. Let's go.'

It stood on the plain before the palace where the old combats took place, but many of the features of the European circus had been introduced and the dominant idiom was cheap tinsel rather than the warrior tradition. There was a Big Top. There was ice-cream – though skewers of spiced meat seemed to be in greater demand. There was that very Indonesian doubling-up of jobs. The clown, when excused from the ring, hawked sweets. The acrobat turned up again, extravagantly and im-plausibly toupeed, as a disastrously bad plate-twirler. He broke so many plates the act had to be abandoned halfway through. Lukas at first enjoyed it all without discrimination, taking alternate bites from meat in one hand and ice-cream in the other.

Then came a high-wire act with an extraordinarily fat tra-peze artist, who did nothing but hurl tiny children out into space from one swinging bar to another, where other members of the troupe approximately caught them by an arm or a leg. Lukas buried his face in his hands.

'Adu! The poor babies. I can't watch.' When he looked up his eyes were wet. 'They are stolen babies,' he sniffed. 'Or they are babies that have no fathers. Their mothers sell them.' In his world there was no possibility of a father doing such a wicked thing.

The dwarves he liked, screaming with laughter before they did anything. 'Small people are funny,' he explained without de-fensiveness.

Then the children came back, hideously rouged and lip-sticked, in Lurex suits with frilly cuffs, to tumble and somer-sault. A tubby boy of about four was the comic element through his inability to perform any of the tricks. This led to the other children constantly falling over him and sitting on his face. Lukas was unsure whether to laugh or not, muttering 'Poor babies' from time to time and crossing his arms over his chest in frustrated paternity. There was a delay of five minutes, then the chimpanzees appeared wearing the costumes the children had just taken off. It was immediately apparent they had been cut to fit the chimpanzees, not the children. Then dogs, clearly in terror of their trainer. When one misbehaved, he poked it very deliberately in the eye with his finger. Ponderous Sumatran elephants followed, extraordinarily hairy, like mammoths, and did very slow, inconclusive tricks, like jokes without a punch-line.

After a great deal of palaver a clanging, rickety cage was set up in the ring and tigers were introduced, together with a tall Chinaman in evening dress, but no buffaloes. Lukas took this very ill.

'Why couldn't they find an Indonesian?' he hissed. There seemed to be rather too many answers to that. The Chinaman stalked around with the feline grace of a narcissistic PT instructor, waving his whip so that the tigers roared and struck out with flailing paws.

'They are drugged,' declared Lukas huffily. 'I have seen. You can pay money to be photographed hugging the tigers round the back. They could not do that if they were not drugged. Also they have no claws. They pull out the claws and sell them to *dukuns*. Stinging nettles would be a good idea.'

The beasts leaped through fiery hoops, licked the Chinaman's face, jumped from stool to stool, running over his back. He did a final round with the whip and the flailing paws. Roars and applause. As he left the ring and passed near us, I saw him hastily pull down the cuff of his shirt to cover a trickle of blood.

We queued to get out.

'Shall we go and be photographed with the tigers?' I asked innocently.

'No,' said Lukas, hunched, hands in his pockets, suddenly small. 'We might see the poor babies. It would upset me.'

*

There are many loose ends to Raffles. Olivia, for example, is a shadowy figure. She has no voice of her own. History has reduced her to a fashion feature. She is known only for introducing itchy European clothes amongst the mixed-race ladies of Jakarta. Her successor, Sophia, Raffles's second wife, known as 'the Editor', would do her best to expunge her from the record and had the undoubted advantage of ready fertility. Later commentators have inferred that Raffles's first marriage was barren, though there are certain ambiguous references to 'family', in which term Raffles seems to include his entire circle of intimates. His most enthusiastic biographer, Boulger, speaks clearly of the children Olivia bore him. Were there children? Was Boulger merely confused or did he have access to information now lost? There is a possibility suggested by good Lord Minto:

'A rajah of Bali, an island adjoining the east end of Java, has sent me, amongst other presents, five boys and two girls all slaves, at my service. They have been some time kept at Mr Raffles's house, who has agreed to take one or two. They are all emancipated of course, but remain an orphan charge upon us. The boys are from about eight to thirteen years old, and are all, fine, spunky-looking boys. The girls are four or five years old. Now to give you a notion of the manners and scenes they are accustomed to: they were all dressed in their bettermost upon the occasion of their first being shown to me. They perceived that there was sort of solemnity, which seemed to give them some uneasiness. While they were paraded in this

114

manner, and they were all gazing around them, two Malay
spears unfortunately caught Taylor's eye, in the corner of the
room, and *of necessity* he began tossing and brandishing them
about, and at length the scabbards were pulled off the bright
blades at the ends of the weapons. The moment this happened,
the poor boys all huddled together, and the youngest left the
rest, and came with his little hands joined together, in the most
supplicating manner, and with the most imploring face,
walking from one of us to the other, and evidently begging for
his life, though he did not utter a word, nor even cried; but he
appeared terrified ... It was with some difficulty, even after
the spears were removed, that the children were reassured.
They certainly thought that they had been dressed out to be
sacrificed or put to death for some cause or other ... Next day
they were all very merry and happy. George [Minto's son] has
taken one of the boys to serve him on board of ship, and that
boy has fallen on his legs. Mr Raffles will take care of one or
two, and the rest have fallen to my lot. They will probably
grow into very good servants. The girls will puzzle me most. I
have some thought of baking them in a pie against the Queen's
birthday, unless I should strike out some other idea in the
meanwhile.'

Returned to India, he writes further:

'We have had a christening of seven souls at once ... Five of
them were presents from various Malay kings and potentates
... I have given the surnames of Man and Friend to the two
eldest ... I gave them the truly *Christian* names, of Homo
["man"] and Amicus ["friend"], that I may always be put in
mind to treat my humble property like men and friends instead
of cattle. Indeed, they deserve it; for better, gentler boys were
never born in Christendom. However, they were to have
Christian names in the usual sense of that word at their

115

baptism, and one of them is Francis Man and the other Edmund Friend . . .'

We hear no more of Raffles's 'one or two'. Given the crass sentimentality of Raffles about children in later life and his enthusiasm for Balinese, it seem unlikely that children as winsome as these should escape unadored and unadopted. Later, in Bengkulu, he will adopt another freed slave. So if there *were* children that died in Java, it is possible – not more than that – that they were the companions of Francis Man and Edmund Friend.

*

'Of course you must go to Borobudur,' said Lukas. 'You cannot come to Yogya and not go – even if you have been before. It is bad luck not to go. We Javanese have many beliefs of that sort but I am a good Muslim so I only believe 90 per cent of them.' he winked.

We were at his favourite tippling place. He had recovered from the post-circus depression and was cheerfully relaxed.

'You are my friend,' he said expansively. 'I will lend you my motorbike.'

A hush fell over the circle of drinkers. This was serious generosity indeed. Who knew how many years Lukas had worked to have enough to buy the sleek black machine that he wheeled, every night, into his bedroom.

'I have no driving licence.' He waved the objection aside.

'My friend here is a policeman. If there are difficulties, he can arrange them for you.' The man rolled over the collar of his leather jacket in a smooth, well-practised movement to flash some sort of a badge.

'What if I have an accident and wreck your machine?' Lukas laughed and pointed.

'My other friend here is a mechanic. He will mend it.' The

man reached in his back pocket, pulled out a spanner and waved it delightedly.

There was no escape.

'What,' I asked, 'if I just scratch it so it is not beautiful any more?'

At the last minute, Lukas decided to come with me.

*

Two years after his storming of the Yogya palace, Raffles would be credited with the 'discovery' of Borobodur, the great Buddhist temple outside the city. That is to say, the Dutch did not know it was there. It was unexpectedly revealed by the survey of landholdings necessary before the new land revenue system could be put in place. Unlike other scholars of the age, his first reaction was not to hack the temple apart to ornament the gardens of Buitenzorg but to have it promptly cleared of encroaching jungle and properly surveyed. Then, being Raffles, he had to visit it for himself. He has reaped a good press for this. It is regarded as a mark simultaneously of his disinterested, scientific curiosity and his boyish love of history. One is the mark of civilization, the other a human enthusiasm endearing in a public figure.

There is perhaps another facet of Raffles's passion for ancient architecture that invites attention. In Indonesia, as we have noted, he had become a Mason.

The myth of origin of Freemasonry deals with the murder of Hiram Abiff, the master architect of Solomon's temple. Becoming a master Mason, as Raffles did, involves identification with Hiram to the point of undergoing ritual death and resurrection through a Masonic handshake. The builders of ancient temples, whether Anglo-Saxons, ancient Egyptians or Jews, are all attracted into the sphere of honorary, Masonic ancestry. Within their structures is held to be embodied a secret, symbolic knowledge so that buildings may be 'read'.

They become a riddle to be solved, like the Sphinx. Perhaps this goes some way to explaining Raffles's unusual enthusiasm for Borobodur and his need for precise surveys. Its builders had, after all, been fellow Masons.

The discovery of ancient temples had a rather less than salutary effect on the Indian troops. This massive proof of former Hindu–Javanese alliance encouraged them to consider throwing their lot in with the local rulers and massacring their British officers. The plot was discovered. Raffles intervened personally, re-established good relations with the sultans and revived the trust of the troops. Critics carped sourly that not enough people got hanged.

*

Lukas drove with a good deal of panache. He would creep up behind buses, engine growling like a tiger, and suddenly flail out, swooping, screaming alongside long enough to ensure a large truck was coming the other way. At the last moment he would execute a manoeuvre, not with the handlebars but more by a deft whiplash of the buttocks so that we ended up precisely one inch in front of the bus.

'Prambanan?' he suggested – the ancient Hindu temple. 'I like the elephants.'

'Anywhere.'

We approached through a mass of stalls selling Borobodur T-shirts, carvings of Ganesha, Garuda birds, Coca-Cola. There were, as yet, no Rambos. Barbed-wire entanglements surrounded the temple itself, increasing the sense of ruin. It was still being patiently reassembled from a scattering of carved remains. In the shrines was a smell of fetid Western armpits, exposed in their hundreds, as cameras were raised to snap. Some workmen were scrubbing at masonry with toothbrushes as though being punished in the mindless fashion of the army. Touching fingers had left a high-tide mark on the legs of the figures, so that they seemed at first sight to be wearing welling-ton boots. The workmen were removing the wellington boots.

*

Raffles saw himself as a man of reason, a man of business – also a man of vision. He liked to think ahead. His enemies would call him a dreamer. He was always very careful to distinguish between the territories and rights acquired on behalf of the British authorities and those he held in lieu of the Dutch. One day, the Dutch might take Java away from him again. But they would only get back what they had given. The rest would stay British.

In the meantime, he was eager to unlock as many of the doors the Dutch had closed against him as possible. There was an idea niggling at the back of his head, as it turned out a very silly idea – Japan. He would gain access to the trade of Japan by sending the Emperor a white Siamese elephant, a Batavian almanac, 92 plants, 20 sheep, 10 birds, a carpet, a magnet, a table watch, cloths various, some Persian leather, 4 civet cats, a day-and-night spy-glass, 10 decanters and several pounds of ground Egyptian mummy – a trusted panacea.

Even before he gained control of Java, he had plotted to send Leyden on a mission to the Shogun. Japan at that time was totally closed to outside trade except through a small, closely watched Dutch factory near Nagasaki. The Japanese knew the dangers of foreign trade. They knew it led to foreign domination and colonization, and they were particularly hos-tile to the British. Raffles thought the Japanese might not know about the change of government in Java and that a daring imposture might deliver Japanese trade into British hands and so provide an outlet for Bangka tin and British woollens. He would recruit the Dutch at the Nagasaki factory to pretend nothing had altered. The captains of his ships would be nominally Dutch. English sailors would give themselves out as Americans. The Japanese would not even know they were trading with England. After many delays, two ships sailed with a cargo of tin, lead, sugar, pepper, cloves, nutmegs, woollens and cottons.

There was much prevarication in Japan. The Dutch in charge of the factory were uncertain whether to hand it over to Raffles's men. The Japanese were not sure whether they even wanted to know what was going on or not.

Eventually, a return cargo of copper and camphor was sent back to Batavia, but the bickering between Java, Bengal and the Dutch in Japan lasted for years, until Holland was able to resume the trade itself. The voyage was eminently suitable to fuel a dispute about Raffles's wisdom or folly, since it could be made to show a reasonable profit or a loss, depending on how the accounts were done. Accountancy was even then flexible. For years it had been important that the Company be able to dissimulate how much money it was losing, since it was technically bankrupt.

The saddest part was the elephant. It was returned to Java, where it disappears below the surface of history. Not that it was unappreciated. Japanese artists flocked to the harbour to view the exotic beast and portray it in their art. Its presence was regarded by the politically acute as a wonderful omen. But for once Raffles was short of exactly the sort of nuts-and-bolts information that he always prided himself on obtaining from local informants. He did not know that there was no dock in Japan and that cargo had to be unloaded into boats. There was no boat large enough to take an elephant. Elephants, he might have argued, can swim. But what they cannot do is *dive*.

It was not a total loss for Raffles. At heart he was, after all, a true scholar, with the scholar's ability to turn a dead end into a learned article. So he wrote up the Japanese in a paper and delivered it at the Batavian Society of Arts and Sciences.

*

The Buddhist temple at Borobodur is one of the few wonders of the world that does not disappoint on closer acquaintance. A whole, massive hill is encased in stone, arranged in tiers, carved and engraved. It has a quality of inevitability, of obsessiveness. Each part echoes the shape of the whole. It is impossible *not* to want to climb it.

At the summit sit the Buddha figures in poses of mantric significance. Many have a line around the neck like a choker. Thieves find it convenient to smash through the necks and sell the heads to the art-lovers of the West. The village stone-carvers are constantly in work making good the depredations of the headhunters.

Raffles may have felt reverential about the temple, but many visitors do not. At the bottom of the hill an American was arguing bitterly about having to pay 200 rupiahs (6p) to enter. At the top, a group of Jakartans were climbing the stonework like a rockface.

A little old Javanese lady accosted me, poking imperiously with her umbrella. It was a batik umbrella, carefully chosen to match her dress.

'You,' she said. 'Give us a hand here.' She indicated one of the Buddhas encased in a cage of stone latticework. 'I can't reach the hand of the Buddha through there to get his *sakti*, his divine force. You've got long arms. Reach in there for me and touch his palm while I hold your other hand. *Sakti* is like electricity. It will flow through you to me.'

'No,' amended an elderly man, probably her husband. '*Sakti* flows downhill. You must stand lower than him, even though you are older. He uses his right hand. You hold his left.'

We arranged ourselves in a line, like children crossing the road. Lukas joined, laughing, on the end, holding the husband's hand. I touched the palm but felt no confirmatory tingle, no flash of divine *sakti*.

121

'Thank you,' she said in ringing tones, then leaned forward to whisper. 'It's really for him, my husband. It's good for his asthma.'

*

'Parangtritis,' said Lukas. 'You will wish to go there. It is by the seaside, only 25 kilometres away. We shall be there in a few minutes.'

Raffles went there in 1813. But in 1813, the traffic was less terrifying. We stopped at a café on the foreshore. I staggered off to offer silent prayer for our safe arrival. Lukas disappeared to repair the ravages of the journey, comb out his hair and pay someone to guard his motorbike. The town seemed deserted.

'It is a place for the weekend,' said Lukas. 'When I was at school, I almost lived here with my friends. It is a place for lovers. You will see them on the beach.' He sighed nostalgically. 'Nowadays, I am too busy for such things.'

'Also,' I pointed out, 'you are married.'

'Yes. That too wastes a lot of time.'

We set off for the beach. It was largely empty apart from pony carts, offering rides to the non-existent lovers. A wind roared in our ears as on a British beach in high summer, kicking sand contemptuously in our faces. The whole beach was somehow messy and tired-looking, a building site waiting for the cement to arrive. The sea boiled and hissed over rocks, smashed against the cliffs. Two old ladies waded into the spume up to their hanks and began throwing flowers and emptying bottles into the waves while holding one hand each over their headscarves. One fell over in the undertow and laughed as she was dragged towards the deep on her buttocks.

'Loro Kidul,' grinned Lukas. 'They are offering to the goddess of the South Sea. This is her place. She has a palace out there, under the waves, all made of gold and gems. She changes with the moon. She is a young girl at the start of the month but at the end she is old, really old. She has a court of women – all women, no men. The court dances, the heirlooms of the palace, all come from her. When there was the fire at Solo, they brought lots of damaged heirlooms here to be given back to the sea. Every year, the Sultan of Yogya comes here to give her his nail-clippings and clothes. When the Sultan gives a formal audience, his wife sits behind him. There is always an empty chair beside him reserved for Loro Kidul.'

I thought of Raffles's wrangling over the chairs and wondered if he knew.

Lukas sighed wistfully. 'If young men round here wear green, her colour, she comes and takes them for her lovers. Parangtritis is a place of love.'

'It must be a problem for the army in their green uniforms. But isn't it her servant, Nyi Blorong, who does that?'

There is a busy Indonesian soft-porn industry drawing on the goddess of the South Sea. She embodies predatory, aggressive female sexuality, something Indonesian men find simultaneously titillating and terrifying. The films are unsubtle and usually consist of her coming ashore and tearing men's trousers off. Often, however, it is not the goddess herself who dips into male undergarments, but her earthier servant Nyi Blorong. The goddess, after all, is still a political figure in Java, being simultaneously wife, mistress and daughter to the various powerful ruling houses.

He shrugged. 'Nyi Blorong, Loro Kidul. It is the same thing. Every year young men are drowned swimming or fishing here. The young men she takes are never marked. The sharks and crabs do not eat them. Their bodies are returned perfect from the sea, washed and still. That is how you can tell.'

In the cliff was a cave for meditation. Lukas pulled me inside. It smelt strongly of paraffin. A man was asleep on a mat. He looked up, rubbed his eyes and grinned.

'He is only the guardian, not a meditator.' He looked around, eyes growing soft with nostalgia. 'When I was young, I came here one night to think of Loro Kidul but all I saw was a girl in my class. Wah! She was pretty. I forget her name.'

'Perhaps it was Tunjong Segara, "Lily of the Sea".' I don't know why the name popped into my head. Many years later, Raffles would have a daughter, born like himself at sea. A Javanese nobleman who accompanied him on his travels gave her the name Tunjong Segara.

'The name is wrong. It is Tanjung Segara, like Tanjung Priok. It is a place, near here.'

'A place? Can we go there?'

He shrugged. 'Of course.'

We walked back to the motorbike. Lukas tried unsuccessfully to start it. We checked the petrol. He played experimentally with the plugs. There was a garage across the road.

A cheerful mechanic came out, looked at it from afar and said, 'Your plug lead's broken.' We bent down, examined, yanked on it. It looked fine. He pushed us apart with his hands like man doing the breast stroke, whipped out a spanner and began to dismantle the entire machine. The lights came off, the saddle, the tank. He reached inside with an expert twist of the finger and tweaked out a broken copper lead. 'There!' I-told-you-so was in his eyes. He spliced it back in place, reassembled the motorbike. It started first time.

'How much?'

He batted the suggestion away. 'Nothing. That was easy.'

Lukas sucked on his lip. 'It must be the people where we left the bike. They expected us to eat there. We didn't, so they did this. So, nowadays you must pay people to break your bike. That is something new.'

We drove off into the warm air. After the buffeting of the seashore, if felt like a gentle bath. We turned off the main road and through a countryside that embodied tropic exuberance. No wonder the British could never quite get beyond the idea that agriculture here required no work. You knocked a fencepost into the ground and it grew leaves.

The roads became smaller and smaller, finally they were only dirt tracks. Lukas stopped to ask the way. He stopped several times and became more and more confused.

'It is *near* here. Only I cannot quite . . .' We emerged on to a beach of black volcanic sand like coal dust, parked and walked over to look at the sea. Parangtritis could be seen in the distance – the sea in between. It snarled and sloshed as if trying to get at us, a nasty, livid green, like chemical waste, lots of froth on top and swirling currents that told you how deep it was. It was horribly cold despite the sun. We both shuddered and looked at each other, surprised.

'This is a bad place,' I said.

'Yes.' We headed back for the bike. Lukas did a comic looking-through-pockets routine, playing with our anxiety to be gone. I smiled, not wanting to seem bad-tempered.

'I don't know why you're laughing,' he said, annoyed. 'The key's gone.'

He turned out all his pockets. I turned out mine – God knows why, perhaps to show participation in his loss. We walked back to the beach, staring at the ground. No key.

'This is not possible.' I knew what he was thinking. This was in some way tied up with Loro Kidul.

'Have you got any key on you?' I offered the guest-house key. He put it in the lock. It worked. We stared at each other in brief disbelief, then leapt on the machine and tore off.

*

Another *becak*-driver. This time in Yogya. He looked at the address I had written down. What was the problem? It could not be that he did not read. Illiteracy seems more common among the young in England than Indonesia.

125

'This is in the palace.'

'That's right. But *becaks* can go in there. I've seen them.'

'That is not the nature of the problem. *You* are a *bule*, a white man, so you can speak Indonesian. They will expect me to speak the Javanese of the palace out of respect, but I do not know how. I am from a village.'

'Are you from Tanjung Segara?' It was a wild stab in the dark, but the tide of serendipity seemed to be running so strong it was worth a try.

'Where is that? No. I am from near Jakarta.'

'Ah. Well. You take me there and I'll do the talking.'

He nodded and put the address carefully in his pocket. To throw it away would be disrespectful. It reminded me of the way Indonesians – even the most casual acquaintances – would always ask for your address on parting and treasure it up without the least intention of ever sending a letter. It was polite. It was – as they said – 'a memory'.

There was no need for any talk at all. We crunched on to the gravel by the south gate and saw the little house at once. The *becak*-driver got off and looked hopeful.

'Yes,' I said, 'please wait – but I may be some time.' He thought that was funny.

'I don't have anything else to do. This is my job.' He would tell his family that one, later tonight, and make them laugh too.

I knocked at the door and asked for Pak Suyono, an expert on the palace manuscripts. I was shown into a small room, immaculately clean but with an academic's scurf of papers on every flat surface. Through an open door I could see a very pretty girl in her teens reading a right-wing newspaper while sucking a lollipop.

Pak Suyono shuffled in, helped by his wife. She placed his cigarettes and lighter gently in his hand. It was clear he was blind. I looked questioningly at his wife.

'Please,' she said, 'it is good for him to talk, to use his knowledge.'

He told the story of his blindness, a silly accident, a blow from a window incautiously opened. He smiled as he spoke of the stupidity of an expert on manuscripts who could not read. He smiled and smiled in that Javanese way as he told of the pointlessness of a skill so slowly acquired in the absence of young people who wanted to learn it. The Americans call it the 'shit-eating grin'. You see a lot of it in Java.

I explained about Raffles. He nodded. 'To write a book,' he warned, 'is an arrogant thing. It is terrible to sum up the life of another man. But Raffles is hardly remembered here.' A hand groped over the tablecloth and fed a cigarette to sucking lips. I guided the lighter. 'Thank you. We remember Daendels, who was before him, because he killed so many of our people. You know Daendels, the Dutch Napoleon?' I knew him all right.

'The Javanese only remember the "bad guys". Raffles turns up in a couple of the manuscripts, but perhaps you should go to the other palace.'

'The *other* palace?'

'Yes, the Paku Alam, the title given by Raffles. The Paku Alam wanted to work with Raffles. The Sultan only wanted to fight him, so Raffles set up the Paku Alam as a royal house.'

Paku Alam, 'The nail of nature'. No, better, 'The pivot of the Universe'.

'The Paku Alam is now the Governor of Yogya, isn't he?'

'Yes. Impossible to see him, of course. Too busy. We were rewarded for our loyalty to the Revolution by being made a "Special Area", where the old families still have power. But you know, I used to play English games when I was a child here. They still had them in the palace, remembered from that time . . . You know your royal family was here the other year?'

127

'Yes, I read about it.'

'It was joke of course. The Sultan was supposed to meet them. "No," he said, "Paku Alam, you meet them. Your family always got on very well with the English." He still has the carriage.'

'The carriage?'

'Yes. It is bright yellow, very smart. *Kyai Manik Koemolo*, "the sacred jade bead", it is called. Raffles knew the way to his heart. He gave the Paku Alam the carriage. Carriages were important here.'

*

'Tunjong Segara,' said Lukas. 'I asked an old man in the palace. At first he said it as the name of an offering to Loro Kidul. Then he said the name was a man's name, an old-fashioned hero's name. It is from the Loro Kidul stories. It is Nyi Blorong's father-in-law. Why should they give Raffles's daughter a name like that?'

*

There is another town on the island of Java specially close to Loro Kidul, Pelabuhan Ratu, 'Queen's harbour'. At one end of the town, Bung Karno built a hotel. He had half the hillside blasted away to do it. It stands there now, a monument to the awfulness of the concrete architecture of the period, bland, grey, characterless, a Waffen-SS headquarters under the palm trees. On the beach they set an unfortunately worded sign, 'The sea here is very dangerous with many strong currents and many have been drowned – so always be careful to swim in the sea.'

On the ground floor was a marketing convention. 'A brighter future through more aggressive marketing' trumpeted a sign. I had seen another such in Jakarta; Indonesians with clipboards listening with serious politeness to strident Americans who poked them with suitably aggressive index fingers, called them impertinently, 'buddy' and 'sweetheart' and evangelized on behalf of acquired arrogance and rudeness. 'We are still a mentally colonized people,' one exquisitely polite lady had explained to me. 'Bung Karno always said we could only overcome it and become truly Indonesian through becoming like our colonial masters. That is the paradox of Indonesia.'

On the second floor is a room not available for letting, for it is already permanently let – to Loro Kidul, the goddess of the South Sea. You can drop the man on the desk a small sum to get the key. It's a perfectly ordinary room, but excessively feminine, covered in Barbara Cartland flounces and reeking of stale perfume. Blue watered silk and green frills recall the element in which the goddess moves. The bed is showered with rose petals, the floor with offerings of feminalia, mirrors, makeup, scent – the goddess is particularly fond of *Impulse*. Devotees come here to consult Loro Kidul. It is especially a resort of film stars. Before they dare shoot a single frame, the Indonesian soft-porn actresses, all good spiritual girls, have to ask polite pardon for their impersonations.

It is a curious experience for someone to go to the goddess's bedroom if they have ever lived in West Africa, as I had. Loro Kidul's portrait hangs over the bed, fair skin, flashing eyes, long storm-tossed hair. It is the face of Mammy Wata, the African goddess of love, wealth and fertility recorded in paintings and carvings from Mauretania to the Congo. Art historians will tell you that the Africans' idea of her has been fixed by a famous Indian print of a light-skinned Hindu goddess wrestling with snakes that was sold all over the continent in the early years of this century. European ships' figureheads also had a hand, or perhaps bosom, in her appearance. However you explain it, it is recognizably the same goddess.

The interesting thing is that the room was installed on the personal orders of Bung Karno. As ruler of Java, like the royal families he replaced, an aspect of his legitimacy had to be a relationship with the goddess. So they met in the modern way, a swift assignation on the second floor of a hotel where they take American Express, as Jakarta businessmen doubtless still meet their extra-marital friends nowadays.

Raffles, too, was a ruler of Java. What more natural, then, than that he should have been associated with Loro Kidul? He himself was born at sea. So was his daughter. Perhaps the name they gave her was a sign he was being slowly sucked into the currents of Javanese myth, a brighter future through more aggressive marketing.

*

I set off for the railway station. On a corner was a newspaper-seller. As he handed me a copy, he remarked sadly, 'Nyi Slamet is dead.' It was the big news. It had driven even the President's latest speech off the front page. She had died in the royal palace in Solo. Her many daughters had clustered round the body in inexpressible grief. There was to be a state funeral costing millions of rupiahs. Only after working my way through the whole article did I realize that Nyi Slamet was not a human being but a buffalo, a sacred white buffalo.

9. Hope and Glory

'"It's a good thing the British did come," Leonore said presently.
"How are Mr Raffles's reforms getting on, Dirk?"

"Why," I answered . . . "why you've only got to keep your
eyes open to find the answer to that question. Have you ever
seen the natives looking so contented and prosperous before?
That's because they're free now for the first time in memory.
No more compulsory coffee-cultivation, no more forced
labour, but every man at liberty to grow what he likes and do
what he likes with his own."

"And before long there's going to be an end to the
extortions of all the native officials, I hear," Bertram put in,
taking his cue from Leonore.

"Unless we have to give Java back to the Dutch, which
God forbid," I said.' – H. Banner, *The Clean Wind: An
Historical Novel of Romance and Adventure*

Raffles abolished the government licences for gambling and
cock-fighting, further cutting revenue. Gambling was an evil
because it led to debt and debt to people selling themselves
into slavery. He would fight tooth and nail to keep both out
of Singapore. Slavery, for Raffles, was simply bad in itself, but
could not be banned according to the Dutch law under which
he was forced to operate. Even British law was unclear on the
matter, possibly deliberately so. So Raffles revived the controls
on it that had fallen into disuse but were still on the statute

books. Gradually, he managed to ban the *importation* of slaves. In all this he showed himself carefully legalistic. It was revolution in complete accordance with the by-laws.

With opium, he was on more dangerous ground. It was a major source of profit for the Company, and could not be banned out of hand, so he controlled it and throttled back its consumption through customs regulations. Despite the protests from merchants, Minto backed him up. He had a firm friend in the Governor-General's palace. Always, justification of his actions had to be dissimulated into terms of financial sharp-dealing. It was not enough to argue that pushing opium was *wrong*. It had to be maintained that there was more profit to be had from a sober and industrious population. We should not necessarily believe such thoughts were uppermost in Raffles's mind. Elsewhere, he shows his true colours:

'It now becomes necessary that Government should consider the inhabitants without reference to bare mercantile profits and to connect the sources of the revenues with the general prosperity of the Colony.'

How different was the Dutch view, can be seen by the puzzlement expressed by Muntinghe, Raffles's loyal supporter and fellow Council member, to the proposed reform of the land revenue:

'The amelioration however of the natives of this island, though undoubtedly a consideration of the highest moment in the eyes of humanity, seems to me to become only a secondary object in a political point of view; and with the exception that every measure contrary to the principles of justice and equity it appears to me that the safest principle that can be adopted to judge of the propriety of any Colonial regulations, or of any changes or alterations to be introduced therein is that every

Colony does or ought to exist for the benefit of the mother country.'

Yet the new system was pushed through solely because of Raffles's own determination and conviction that this was the greatest contribution he could make to those neglected 'little people' of Java. Raffles was the first Westerner to notice that the 'little people' were there at all, except as beasts of burden or picturesque figures to pleasantly animate a landscape, and not until Bung Karno would most wealthy Indonesians become aware of them.

Raffles's new treaties with the sultans opened up wide areas of the country where the landlord was now the central government – which in fact meant Raffles. He was determined that as few middlemen as possible should stand between him and the peasants. Native officials would become salaried, not carried upon the backs of the farmers. Rent would be related to income. Economic freedom would be the guiding principle that would encourage enterprise and civilization.

Any man who invokes high principle will rightly be suspected of low hypocrisy. Some Dutch researchers have been keen to see in Raffles a Machiavellian humbug, as a way of comparatively reducing the viciousness of the Dutch system he replaced. His salary and expenses have been meticulously examined and held to show profiteering. The reforms he effected are dismissed as only paper reforms. The huge sums to be raised in revenue were never, it is said, collected. On his own estates, Raffles had slaves and he kept up forced coffee deliveries in his own area of Buitenzorg; indeed, he intensified the burdens on labour there. The survey on which the scheme was based was impossible at that time. The need to pay tax in money drove the peasants into the arms of Chinese money-lenders and debt slavery – and so on.

There is an element of truth in all this. Dreams, after all, can remain perfect only as long as no one tries to turn them into reality.

Complicated tasks of assessment and record-keeping were demanded of illiterate village headmen who were anyway firmly trapped in obligations of kinship to those they were to administer. But Raffles was desperately short of competent, honest staff and was in daily expectation of being replaced by a military governor. He held the levers of power, but was anything attached to the ends of those levers? The only way he could begin to know what was going on was to get out into the fields as often as he could. There, one suspects, he was told what people thought he wanted to hear.

Yet when the Dutch took back Java, they needed only to make small adjustments to Raffles's system to make the whole thing work. They had another hundred years. Raffles did not.

*

'The National Planning Council, founded in 1959, produced in 1960 a vast document containing an Eight-Year Plan of Indonesian Economic Development. The planners, however, seem to have been more concerned with the symbolic importance of the plan than with its implementation. The document contained 5,000 pages divided into 17 volumes, and eight books containing exactly 1,945 paragraphs. The implication, of course, was that the plan was based on the spirit of 17–8–1945 [the date of the Indonesian Declaration of Independence].' – C. Penders, *The Life and Times of Soekarno*

'Over there,' said Aneka, pointing with her knife, 'where the garage is now, is where we used to keep the rice. It was all ricefields where those houses are, but the farmers weren't allowed to sell us anything directly. The government bought it up and took it away. Then a truck would come once a month, with soldiers, and dump *different* rice in the garage. It was rice the government collected in tax. Because my father had been in a ministry and knew Bung Karno, we were in charge of doling out rice to the whole area. And it was *terrible* rice, but we had no choice, we had to eat it.'

We were in Jakarta at the end of the dry season, eating durian – the fruit like a football-sized conker, whose taste is halfway between caramel and swamp-water, with an after-whiff of rancid armpits. I remembered, irrelevantly, that the smell of it made Raffles sick. Aneka was in her thirties, very pretty, a doctor in one of the government clinics. She was obliged to work there for another fifteen years to repay her training. I was not quite sure that it was proper for us to be eating durian. After all, it lives in Indonesian mythology as a notorious aphrodisiac. She incised the fruit with unerotic, surgical pre-cision between good strong hands, as if lancing an abscess.

'My big brother used to steal the rice and give it to friends in school who had nothing to eat. Because we had government connections, he knew we could get more.' She pouted sulkily. No, she was not pouting, just ejecting an unchewable seed. She threw it away and waved her fingers. 'The boys were allowed to go out on demonstrations, but girls were not, and there were demonstrations almost every day against the im-perialists.' She grinned, plucked forth a slug of rich, yellow flesh and slid it into her mouth. 'One day they helped wreck the British ambassador's car. My brothers' contribution was to rip the door handles off. They brought them home.'

*

Raffles had fallen foul of the military. He was trying to send the troops back to Bengal to cut the costs of this, his 'other India'. Gillespie had not forgiven the business at Yogya, and other sources of friction had added personal rancour to pro-fessional disagreement. Gillespie had bought slave girls, refused to pay the peasants for labour on his estate. He and Raffles were temperamentally unsuited.

Gillespie was an upper-class lout of Irish extraction. His life was dotted with brawls and duels, debts, promiscuously sired bastards, acts of mindless heroism. He was the sort who is indispensable in war and unbearable in peace. Raffles was fifteen years younger, adamantly civilian, and would boast that he had never watched a horse race nor fired a gun in his life. Worse, he lacked breeding and had culture. He read books.

They bickered and snarled at each other over the Council table. For all his generosity of spirit, Raffles seems to have been unable to cope with opposition. It would be the same in Singapore with Governor Farquar. He wanted love. People either had to convert, almost religiously, to love – or go.

Finally he arranged for Minto to replace Gillespie, who had anyway asked to be recalled. But Minto himself was soon to be replaced by a soldier, Lord Moira, sent to India by his friend and fellow Freemason the Prince Regent to replenish his depleted coffers from the public purse. Minto tried, yet again, to protect Raffles. If all else failed, he assured him the posting to Bengkulu in Sumatra, but surely things could not come to that?

'Minto was not to depart until over two months after Moira's arrival, so there was the unusual situation of the old and the new Governors-General being in India at the same time. Minto, however, was not the sort to create any difficulties. As he amusingly put it: "I think the rising and the setting suns may drive their chariots very peacefully and amicably round the Calcutta Course."' – C. Wurtzburg, *Raffles of the Eastern Isles*

*

'Rice,' said Aneka. 'All my childhood, my dreams were full of rice. I used to dream about Bung Karno's rice coming every month.'

'You were hungry?' I pictured her, huge mouth and eyes, limbs like a stick insect.

'No, of course not. We always had enough food. It was all my father's fault. He scared us to death. It started with oranges.

'Oranges?'

'Yes. He told me that if I swallowed orange pips, orange trees would grow out of the top of my head and I'd have great branches coming through my skull. It's impossible to eat oranges without swallowing some of the little pips. Think of the agony! I used to run round holding my head and groaning for hours, thinking I could feel them starting to grow roots. In the end I stopped eating oranges.'

'What about the rice?'

'He told us if we didn't finish up our rice every day, the Rice Giant would come and get us – and we all believed it. People like you are always writing about the Rice goddess, how the people in the country worship her, though they are Muslims or Hindus. Well with us it was the Rice *Giant*. He said, when it was dark, the rice we left would turn into the giant and come and *get* us.'

She leaped to her feet, puffed out her cheeks and lumbered round the room, arms swinging in simian fashion. Out of her mouth came a great growling chant with thudding rhythms, a thud for each footfall:

> 'Where's that little girl Aneka?
> Left her rice. I've come to take her.'

She broke off, held her head and howled – laughing at the same time in recollection of childhood pain and innocence.

*

With the arrival of Lord Moira as Governor-General, the tone of letters from India changes abruptly. Gone are friendly support and fatherly advice. All is suspicion, rebuke and irritation. The father has become a headmaster. The Japanese trade is declared a disaster and forbidden. Waspish comments are made about the continuing failure of Java to make a profit despite the rosy prospects initially held out. Gillespie, arriving in India, files a long series of charges against Raffles, alleging arrogance, incompetence and corruption. They are taken very seriously.

The principal problem lay in the land sales to redeem the bad paper money issued by the Dutch. Raffles never made any secret of the fact that he was himself a buyer of land auctioned off by the government. It is the land bought in this transaction that will ultimately become the Botanic Garden at Bogor. It is clear that he used his participation to push up prices – to the great annoyance of his partners. There was an unwillingness to buy land from an administration whose title might not be recognized if Dutch government returned. By risking his own capital – actually borrowed – Raffles was able to increase confidence in the security of the transactions and so bring the sales to a conclusion of measured success. But it all looked very suspicious to a Company that assumed peculation in all levels of its officials, and it was hardly prudent behaviour.

Despite the firm support of the whole Council, Raffles would never quite clear himself of official suspicion. He would always be regarded as someone who got caught with his hand in the till. The Supreme Government in London was anyway increasingly inclined to write off the whole business of Java: Java had already cost it nearly five million Spanish dollars. With the defeat of Napoleon, it was the demands of a European peace that were uppermost in everyone's minds. Raffles and Java were suddenly irrelevant. Nobody cared. Raffles was slow to read the signs and foolishly submitted a plan for taking over the Philippines. He did not yet know that no one in London bothered to read his letters any more.

*

The house was an old Dutch building with thick walls and awkwardly high ceilings that made the proportions of the rooms seem all wrong. Aneka and her family lived there with haughty cats and purring servants. Fearing native pilferage and insurrection, the Dutch had built a strongroom at the rear of the house with a huge iron door, as in a bank vault. It had proved impossible to demolish, so it had been converted into a bathroom whose solidity was in keeping with a Muslim sense of eternally endangered physical virtue. In the evenings, when the television was on, showing American trash with subtitles, the cats would permit themselves to be stroked and the servants would creep in silently and crouch on the stairs to watch their favourite programmes.

Everyone had seen ghosts. Their existence was treated as a matter of established fact. There was a nocturnal revenant who took leisurely showers behind the thick, iron door and occasionally sang in Dutch. Another filled empty rooms with the smell of cheroots. At one time there had been many, many more – all Dutch, some unfriendly. In the end, a *dukun* had been sent for and, in a long ceremony, he had commanded them to decamp to the Town Hall, the proper place, it was felt, for dead Dutchmen.

*

The *Java Government Gazette* of 3 December 1814 appeared framed in funereal black. 'The numerous assemblage of persons of both sexes to assist at the mournful ceremony of paying the last duties and honours to the deceased, and the general and marked expression of grief which was there evinced, is the best proof of the respect and regard which her benevolence and manners had acquired amongst all classes . . .' Olivia Raffles was dead. She was buried beside Leyden in Jakarta and on her tomb Raffles set the first verse of a poem she had written to the dead poet:

'Oh thou whom ne'er my constant heart
One moment hath forgot
Tho' fate severe hath bid us part
Yet still forget me not.'

Raffles would soon learn of the death of Lord Minto. He was now terribly alone, exposed to his enemies. The news from Europe was good, which is to say bad for Java. Napoleon was defeated. Raffles now knew his beloved Java was about to be taken from him and restored to the Dutch. He collapsed and his friends feared for his life.

*

I was transported by taxi to Aneka's hospital, feeling very Indonesian, plugging into a circle of professional friends like this – also ill. Flu was sweeping the capital, a cold-season disease in humid heat. I could not breathe. 'My lungs,' I explained in resisting Indonesian, 'feel as though they are full of feathers.' *Bulu*, 'feathers', is also 'hair' and 'wool' and 'fur'. I could not imagine what it was this sentence made them picture. To have feathers in one's lungs was a precise sensation – but fur?

Aneka nodded and probed stethescopically. There was a flurry of excited voices outside the room and a woman was carried in, perfectly stiff, feet vertical, like a magician's assistant arrested halfway through an act of levitation. I made way before the urgency of the case and was waved outside to wait.

It was a thoroughly decent hospital, like those of my childhood, before four-hour queues and institutional arrogance were introduced. A clutch of schoolchildren, come for vaccinations, were radiating intense health like a fire radiates heat into an icy room. The man beside me had some unintelligible affliction that required an intravenous drip, but there were no stands for drips bags, so he was required to hold it for hours above his own head.

'The woman,' he flapped the raised hand sagaciously towards the door, 'she was hit by a truck.' As he spoke the door opened and she walked out, perfectly well – surely through some Lazarus-like resurrection – but sobbing, and I was beckoned back in.

'She was hit by a truck?' They stared at me, then laughed.

'No,' said Aneka, 'she was angry, that's all.'

'Angry?'

'Yes. It happens often. People put up with things and smile and smile, but inside they rage. Then, maybe after years, suddenly they cannot bear it any more and they scream and swear and fall over. The secret is to make them cry. They cry and at once they are better.'

The neat opposite, then, of the running amok so feared by colonial Europeans. She probed again, diagnosed congestion of the lungs, gave me a prescription a foot long that was condensed by a miracle of micro-technology into micro-pills in a micro-bottle. On it was written 'For hairy lungs'.

*

'"Look, look, Timmerhout!" my chief exclaimed, pointing to a streak of glittering silver on the north-western horizon. "There is the Batavia roadstead, with the ships as distinct as though they lay only a mile or two away ... And there see," he went on, wheeling to face the south, "is Wijnkoops Bay, clearer still ... Tell me, Timmerhout, are you susceptible to the spiritual exaltation of a great mountain such as this?"

"It certainly does make one's own personal troubles seem very remote and small, sir," I answered, not quite certain, however, whether I had rightly interpreted his meaning.

"Yes," he mused, "it does that indeed. But it does more,

Timmerhout. It fills a thinking man's heart with an overwhelming conviction of God's eternal presence; it leaves him strong in the belief that destiny is ultimately conquerable, that for the man who lays his life and fortune in the hand which shaped these noble summits out of chaos there can be no such word as defeat ... Whenever the darkness seems impenetrable, Timmerhout, climb a mountain." ' – H. Banner, *The Clean Wind: An Historical Novel of Romance and Adventure*

Raffles did more than climb a mountain. He went on a tour of the island, indeed, visited Bali. A fashionable belief of the nineteenth century was that a man was given a finite amount of 'vital force'. Once it was used up, you died. Therefore it made sense to be frugal in the expenditure of energy. Raffles, clearly, had nothing to do with this view. Energy, like money, had to be spent wisely but generously. Moreover it was not pantheism that revived Raffles. Rather, it was science and scholarship. The climbing of mountains was effected not with wild Romanticism, but with thermometers, so that the peaks' heights might be accurately calculated from the drop in temperature between bottom and top. He still wanted to really *know* Java.

Newly bereaved, he writes a long letter to Marsden, the eminent Malay scholar, on the comparative history and culture of the archipelago. A few months later, he is greatly revived by collecting information on the volcanic eruption on Sumbawa. But the greatest restorative is to retire with 'several of his staff, and a party of natives, whose good sense and intelligence had attracted his notice, and whom he had brought with him from the eastern part of the island.

'With these last he passed the greater part of every morning and evening in reading and translating, with the greatest rapidity and ease, the different legends with which they furnished him . . .'

'I have lately made a very considerable addition to my Malayan, as well as Javanese library . . . It has given a fashion for literary pursuits which cannot fail of being highly advantageous to all parties in the long run. A taste for letters is now the sure passport to preferment . . . The Dutch colonists accuse us of folly . . . Objects have a different appearance when received by the rising sun, to what they may present to one who is setting.' – T. S. Raffles

*

I had gone to an art show in Jakarta, paintings made in the field by an eminent Indonesian anthropologist whose un-suspected vice was art – a visual retrospective of a life of scholarship. There were all the standard ethnographic hits, Asmat, Toraja, Bali – the 'tribal' face of Indonesia. The gallery was full of the rich and famous, fluttering and cooing at each other. The Minister of Foreign Affairs, newspaper tycoons, their wives decked in gold and Dior – each worth twenty or thirty thousand pounds on the hoof.

In one corner stood a somewhat seedy man, paunched, batik shirt too tight, chain-smoking in defiance of signs to the contrary.

'I'm the manager of the gallery,' he explained, twitching.

'A difficult show?' I asked.

He looked at me and spoke with slow but deadly emphasis. 'When I get through here, I'm never going to have another show with a *living* artist, with opinions and views about how you hang his stuff. Only dead artists. And no widows. Widows are worse than artists. Widows "cherish the memory". And no loyal friends. Friends make you tired with their adoration. Ignore the whole bunch of them. They tell you lies. Dead artists, no widows, no friends. That's the only path to truth.'

*

It was a period of quiet content. Raffles was soothed by sheer busy scholarship. Then, out of the blue, came news from London. He was fired. He would not even be suffered to superintend the transfer of power back to Holland.

The English and Dutch accounts vary at this point. The Dutch tell of the rapturous joy amongst the settlers that greeted the realization that the Dutch were to return. The English dwell on their own dismay that the British hold over Java was to be so short. Typically, Raffles's concern was for the Javanese. He sought to make sure that the British treaties with the rulers would be honoured. One aged chieftain was asked how he felt about the impending change.

'Can't you fancy a young and beautiful widow, who has been joined to a harsh and withered old man, but has lost him and is wedded to a liberal and gallant young bridegroom – can't you fancy how she will rejoice when she finds the old man returned to life again and come to claim her?'

10. Arise, Sir Stamford

Raffles set sail on 25 March 1816 with two friends, Travers and Garnham, his physician, two Malay clerks and a Javanese nobleman, Raden Rana Dipura. Although the Company post at Bengkulu was assured to him, their destination was England, on medical grounds. Physically and emotionally, Raffles was exhausted. Raffles's thirty tons of baggage and 'native curiosities' would ultimately feed Britain's museums, but for the moment they simply drained his purse and proved his eccentricity. In London there would be much talk of a Papuan he brought with him and the excitement aroused by his physical similarity to the Africans. Raffles had acquired the boy, some ten years old, in Bali 'under very peculiar circumstances', and named him Dick. It is only by a chance footnote in the *History of Java* that we know he was alive at all and not a pickled specimen. Alive or not, he would remain a mere specimen to the West. A 'white Papuan' had been owned by the Batavian Society of Arts and Sciences for some time.

The other Orientals of the party were largely beneath official concern. They had only a ghostly existence, mere Javanese shadow puppets. Travers remarks on the presence of Lewis, a Malaccan servant who had been with Raffles for some years. The Malay clerks, we learn, were terribly seasick, and on the return journey only one will be mentioned. Once in London, Raffles clearly had fun astonishing Raden Rana with electricity and the opening of Parliament. On the return journey two boys will mysteriously appear, educated at Sir Stamford's expense, though one promptly does a bunk. One would like to know more of them, for it is not in the large flat planes that a man's life may be known, but in the interstices.

Recent events in Java had been of a kind to make Raffles reflective. He was still severely ill. 'The family' arranged for Travers to present him with a gift of plate and a loyal address on the third day out. His writings show us a man who is very nearly broken:

> 'This last and unexpected proof of your attachment and esteem is too much for me; it is more than, in the shattered state of my existence, I can bear without an emotion which renders it impossible for me to reconcile my feelings with the ordinary feelings of consideration . . .
>
> You have been with me in the days of happiness and joy – in the hours that were beguiled away under the enchanting spell of one, of whom the recollection awakens feelings which I cannot suppress. You have supported and comforted me under the affliction of her loss . . . You have seen and felt what the envious and disappointed have done to supplant me in the public opinion and to shake the credit of my public and the value of my private character; and now that I bend before the storm, which it is neither in my power to avert or control, you come forward to say that, as children of one family, you will hold to me through life. What must be my emotions I leave to the feelings which dictated your address to decide, for, in truth, I cannot express my own . . .'

In the recent past, Raffles was denigrated as paternalist. He himself would probably not have resisted the term. When planning to set up his free medical service for Java, he explicitly speaks of 'paternal care and consideration' for the local population. The term implied, for him, the responsibility and benevolence that go with power and – of course – love.

More recently, the term 'Orientalism' has been raised as a

stick with which to beat Raffles, incorporating him in an approach to the East that insistently imposes upon it an exotic, timeless and feminized quality. The age that has invented sexual politics inevitably sees it as much worse to treat someone as female than as a child.

Like all other interpreters, Raffles was always able to dismiss much of what he saw as adventitious, alien to the true character of South-East Asia. A wise interpreter – even then – usually found truth to lie some way *behind* the appearances, and Raffles was a committed optimist. The despotic nature of Javanese rulers was not seen as inherent to the political system as a whole. It could be neatly excised as an aberration. He honestly believed he could represent the interests of the people against their own rulers and be seen by them to do so. He did not realize that an outsider would always be seen as attacking the people by attacking their rulers.

The untidy state of Malay institutions, he was convinced, must hide some more historic unity or empire. He and Leyden invented the office of Bitara, the ancient ruler over such a unity. They strove to create its reality in a pan-Indonesian–Malay federation beneath the Governor-General, the good Bitara Minto, as Sukarno would later dream of a similar unity called Nusantara, with himself at its head.

Yet Raffles turned a page in the history of empire. He articulated in his words and actions the principle that the good of the ruled must lie above the commercial interests of the ruler. As a man of his age, he was blissfully unaware of the difficulty of defining what was 'good', but had he been less naïve, philosophical sophistication would surely have led to administrative impotence. That he was dismissed says much about the reception of his benevolent principles at home, but it should not lead us to doubt the intellectual honesty of Raffles himself.

'To us, a head of state is like a head of family. In Moslem

custom the father makes all decisions for his family. The elder or village chief shoulders all burdens for his village. This has been the Indonesian way through centuries.' – C. Adams, *Soekarno: An Autobiography*

*

On his way home, Raffles was to be presented with a chance to see himself in a distorting mirror. There was another man of energy and vision, an organizer, a revolutionary, a practical dreamer on his route. St Helena was a Company port. His initial disappointment on seeing Napoleon recalls that of Munchi Abdullah on seeing the Governor-General of all India, Lord Minto.

'Our first view of him was from the window across the lawn, where we beheld, not what we expected, an interesting, animated and martial figure but a heavy, clumsy-looking man, moving with a very awkward gait, and reminding us of a citizen lounging in the tea-gardens about London on a Sunday afternoon ... Now, then, behold me in the presence of certainly the greatest man of the age. I will not attempt to describe to you the feelings with which I approached him; let it suffice that they were in every way favourable to him ... His talents had always demanded my admiration, and in the brilliancy of this side of his character. In a word, I felt compassion for his present situation.'

The feeling was not to last. It is not fanciful to see Raffles as identifying himself in his own reduced circumstances with the broken Emperor. He must have been unusual in feeling compassion for Napoleon at a time when anti-French hysteria was still at fever-pitch. When he writes of Bengkulu, he will no longer term it 'this other India', but rather, 'this other Elba'. He had doubtless expected to see a noble vision of frustrated and wronged brilliance. Napoleon, however,

Penang Harbour.

A Dutch judge and dignitaries witnessing the execution of criminals.

Surveying Prambanang Temple.

View of Gunong Salak, near Buitenzorg.

The palace at Bogor.

The memorial to Olivia Raffles, Bogor.

SACRED
TO THE MEMORY OF
OLIVIA MARIAMNE
WIFE OF
THOMAS STAMFORD RAFFLES
LIEUTENANT GOVERNOR
OF JAVA, AND ITS DEPENDENCIES
WHO DIED
AT
BUITENZORG
ON THE 26 NOVEMBER 1814

OH THOU WHOM NE'ER MY CONSTANT HEART
ONE MOMENT HATH FORGOT
THO' FATE SEVERE HATH BID US PART
YET STILL - FORGET ME NOT

DESTROYED BY WIND, 4th JANUARY 1970
and
RECONSTRUCTED 17th AUGUST 1970

A Javan of the lower class.

A *gender*, a musical instrument from the Raffles collection.

Portrait of T. S. Raffles by G. E. Joseph, now hanging in the National Portrait Gallery.

Raffles House, Bengkulu.

Hamilton Monument, Bengkulu.

Raffles' country house, Bengkulu.

A flower of the species *Rafflesia arnoldii*.

The palace at Pagaruyung, Minangkabau.

The Raffles Statue, Singapore.

The Raffles Institution, Singapore.

offends. He is physically distasteful. He has no thoughts of courtesy or kindness. He fires off questions without even bothering to listen to the answers. He keeps his hat off, so that everyone else, out of politeness, needs must do likewise. He is bad tempered and arrogant. Raffles is shocked.

'. . . This man is a monster, who has none of those feelings of the heart which constitute the real man. I was favourably inclined to him; I compassioned his situation, but from the moment I came into his presence these feelings subsided, and they gave place to those of horror, disgust and alarm; I saw in him a man determined and vindictive, without one spark of soul, but possessing a capacity and talent calculated to enslave mankind. I saw in him that all this capacity, all this talent, was devoted to himself and his own supremacy. I saw that he looked down on all mankind as his inferiors, and that he possessed not the smallest particle of philosophy. I looked upon him as a wild animal caught, but not tamed. He is, in short, all head and no heart – a man who may by his ability command respect, but by his conduct can never ensure the affection of any one . . . The alarm I felt was lest he should escape.'

Raffles has been confronted with the face of naked power – devoid of love – and finds it unbearable. It was his own adherence to the creed of common humanity that would be the greatest obstacle to his memory in the East, a memory he thought was assured by his benevolence. For benevolence associated him with the common, with weakness. A true leader is admired for the display of power and ruthlessness. So it is Daendels, 'the Dutch Napoleon' as he was called, who is remembered in Indonesia, not Raffles. He simply didn't kill enough people.

*

To look at the Raffles Collection in the British Museum is to gain another picture of the man. There is the history, right enough, in the large and exquisite assemblage of Hindu metalwork that hearkens back to lost splendour and forgotten gods. It is housed in the Department of Oriental Antiquities.

Another Raffles emerges in the Ethnography Department. There is the *gamelan* orchestra, each type of instrument with its representative, building up the greater whole. Raden Rana Dipura, Raffles's Javanese protégé, gave solo concerts on the instrument called the *gambang kayu* for the delectation of European scholars. An eminent musicologist, Dr Crotch, attended and stoutly declared Javanese music closely to resemble the most ancient airs of the Scots.

There are the sets of Javanese puppets, of various kinds, the masks, some in miniature. Within each genre are the different characters, all painstakingly labelled in what may be Raffles's own hand. (Apart from the lacy 'R', it resembles that of the Raffles cigarette packet – a harmless joke from the Marketing Department perhaps.) There are the carvings depicting Javanese social types, the lady's maid, the farmer. In short, it is the work of a naturalist, a butterfly collector, obsessively classificatory with its types and sub-types, each one notionally pinned to a board that is the social whole. It is an extravagant exercise in learning a culture as one would learn an illustrated dictionary. It is a testimony to the belief in science and typology.

*

'It is a *gamelan* orchestra,' Agus said proudly. 'It is not only the people of Yogya and Solo who have *gamelan* orchestras. We Sundanese have them too.'

'*Are* you Sundanese?'

'My mother is Sundanese – well, sort of Sundanese.'

We were in Bandung, at a wedding. A woman from the

top of the hill was marrying a poor boy from the bottom. There was a lot of social disapproval in the air and much talk of how much land she had inherited. In Raffles's day this was the Preanger Regencies, an area of direct Dutch rule, the home of the coffee plantations with their compulsory deliveries at fixed prices. But the Dutch had been expelled long ago.

It was also the Day of Heroes, when Indonesians commemorate those who fell in the Revolution, especially those who fell in the Battle of Surabaya against the British or, rather, Indian army. It was that confused period at the end of the Second World War when the Japanese had surrendered and Indonesia had unilaterally declared its independence to an unheeding world. The British accepted the Japanese surrender but had no idea where to put it. Japanese troops under British officers policed an Indonesia that was nominally Dutch. The British should have learned from Raffles's experience that there was no future in this, that they would end up in the middle, execrated by both sides, but most of the British had heard nothing of Raffles in Java. He was merely the man who had invented 'Fortress Singapore'. British disgrace in the Far East was somehow Raffles's fault.

Mutual distrust had culminated in a fierce battle at Surabaya. The British had bombed the city flat, sustained heavy casualties from passionate Indonesian guerrillas and swiftly withdrawn with hearty cries of 'Over to you now, lads!' before a returning Dutch presence. But a group of Scottish gunners had found themselves more in sympathy with the agreeable guerrillas they were supposed to be fighting than their 'Haw-haw' English officers and gone over to the other side, becoming gunnery instructors in the Indonesian army and marrying locally. With great tact, my hosts had adapted my pedigree to link me with the Scots rather than Surabaya.

'English?' they said. 'Then you will know the men who

helped us in the Revolution. Yes, yes, they still live here, though very old. Perhaps you are related?'

It was very rough *gamelan*, the Javanese tinkles fine filigree, the Sundanese crashes and bangs basic metalwork. More, it has a definitely raunchy quality. The dancers were not the deft and wasp-waisted ladies of the royal palace, they were village girls, mostly children, with powerful thighs from the hauling of water. The men and boys did *their* dance, inevitably a martial dance, half tag-wrestling, half pointy-toed ballet. But this is the centre of the Indonesian rag trade, so they did it in jeans.

From the dance floor we could see where they worked in the suburb of Bethlehem and, when the sun shone, it glinted off the extraordinary architecture of the jean boutiques a mile or so away. Indonesian architecture is fairly conservative, but any frustration this must cause in the building community is worked off in the jean boutiques. There are ancient Egyptian pyramids; Dutch sailing ships; on the first floor of one a yellow cab is frozen as it crashes through the wall and plunges into the street; a shark leaps, multi-fanged, through the roof of another.

Inside the house, the young couple simper with modestly downcast eyes and greet their guests in whispers and the tenderest of handclasps. Outside, the dirty comedian is starting up, accompanied by the odd 'boom, boom' from the *gamelan* to press home the punch-line. Married ladies adjust their headscarves and thin their lips in disapproval. But there is nothing they can do; this is traditional. The comic, paunched, greasy, twirls his moustache with travelling-salesman macho and leers lubriciously at the microphone. No pop star could do it more suggestively. His delivery is astonishingly wet. He seems to have more saliva than is strictly necessary.

I don't speak Sundanese. It should be unintelligible to me.

But by some strange Pentecostal miracle I can follow all the jokes. They emerge unimpaired through the blur and blot of language and culture, as though I am listening to some pub comedian at home.

'There is one thing a wife will never forget about her wedding night!'

Cries of 'Tell us about it, then!' from the orchestra.

'She will never forget the tickling of her husband's moustache.' Pause. 'But *which* moustache? The upper *orrr* . . . the lower!!' Boom, boom. Clenched fist waved in phallic redundancy. There is a cannon like that in Jakarta.

Over it all, on the flagpole that normally demonstrates the family's devotion to the Indonesian state, flies a pair of elaborately soiled underpants, the sign – an anthropologist would think – of the licensed bawdiness of a rite of passage, the dissolving of all conventional norms as a new married status is about to be fixed. Not so, for these are the rainman's underpants. These seamy Y-fronts are stopping rain spoiling the ceremony.

'Is he good, the rainman?' I ask Agus.

'The best,' he whispers back. 'These people are landowners. They've got influence. They've borrowed him from the irrigation department. He's built into the five-year plan. There are times in the building of irrigation works when rain could ruin a whole year's labour. So they hire him to make sure there is no waste of money. He's the one they used when your Lady Di came. It stopped raining an hour before she landed and there wasn't a drop of rain till she left. The Pope refused to use one. The rain poured on his head day after day all the way from here to Flores. Still, I don't suppose it would have ruined *his* visit to get his hair wet.'

*

Raffles was to pass some sixteen months in England before

moving on to Bengkulu. He arrived, 'wretchedly sallow, with a jaundiced eye and shapeless leg'. The time was spent in typically energetic convalescence. His first act on touching English soil was to go down a Cornish mine. You never knew when such knowledge might be useful, and perhaps he still had hopes of hanging on to the tin of Bangka.

In the short time he would be home, Raffles wrote and published his monumental *History of Java*, kitted himself out with a new wife and a knighthood, extracted some sort of a grudging exoneration from the Company, did the Grand Tour of Europe, hectoring the King of Holland in the process, and met and charmed many of the most influential people in England. He arrived a sallow and emaciated failure and left as a knight, Fellow of the Royal Society, in high spirits and fine feather with a floating ark named *The Lady Raffles*.

*

There is a portrait of him done at the time by George Joseph, owned by the National Portrait Gallery. It shows Raffles, a still-young thirty-five, beefier-jawed than we shall see him again, hair still thick and brown. There is a suggestion of jowly truculence, almost squirish self-righteousness about the mouth that will soften, in later portraits, into disillusion. The pose is ramrod straight, the hunch has been dissimulated to signify probity. Behind him are generic Hindu antiquities and an inkwell. The presence of the latter is further explained by papers, arranged with deliberate casualness on tabletop and knee. It is the *History of Java*. He is an author in spate. Every picture must tell a story. He wrote a section of the book every morning, and it was sent off to the printers and ready in proof form by dark. When he returned from the social whirl late at night, he would correct the proofs. The whole thing was done and in the shops in seven months. It is an incredible hotch-potch, a ragbag of personal knowledge, a mere promissory note hastily issued on future scholarship. Yet it is the point from which all subsequent research had to start. Raffles always saw himself as merely clearing the decks for others who would follow after.

Portraits of the period often tell us more by what is in the background than by what the face of the sitter reveals. Lord Minto's portrait had him athletically snapping the instruments of torture before the port of Malacca. Over Raffles's shoulder is a classical pillar, part of the solidity of learning, and, beyond, a pall of flame and smoke – wait – no, not flame and smoke, not the spume of Javanese volcanoes, but fluffy English clouds.

Raffles dreamt of dukedoms, and later of standing for Parliament. He hangs now, on loan, in the Committee corridor of the House of Lords, amongst other illustrated highlights of the *Dictionary of National Biography*. He looks down on television monitors announcing the sober, serious work of worthy committees seeking to improve the lot of the natives. He must at last feel very much at home.

*

'"We have this area where all the prostitutes are. Periodically, we spot-check the district because it is our duty to keep them under constant surveillance. Yesterday, a team went in to inspect the conditions and do you know what they found? They found your photo, Pak. Right on the wall ... looking down on ... the whole thing. What shall we do? Shall we remove your photos from the walls?"

"Certainly not," I said. "Leave me there. Let my tired old eyes look!"' – C. Adams, *Soekarno: An Autobiography*

*

'If Marriage a Lottery is call'd
As all calculations it baffles;

155

Think of one who thus risks, unappalled,
All her future fortune in Raffles.'

A London newspaper of the time greeted Raffles's new marriage in verse. He himself announced his wedding to Sophia, the Editor, in one of the most ungallant letters ever penned:

'My Dear Cousin, –   You will, I doubt not, approve of the change I have made in my condition in again taking to myself a wife; and when I apprise you that neither rank, fortune, nor beauty, have had weight on the occasion, I think I may fairly anticipate your approval of my selection. The Lady, whose name is Sophia, is turned of thirty; she is devotedly attached to me, and possesses every qualification of the heart and mind calculated to render me happy . . .'

*

'One of his [Raffles's] first visits was to his aunt, for they were very fond of each other. He left his equipage, which was a splendid one – and private carriages with rich liveries were not so common then as they are now, and were indeed a great rarity in the quiet corner of London in which my father lived – and, walking the length of Princes Street, knocked at old No. 14, and on opening the door went at once into the sort of parlour–kitchen where my mother was, busied as usual about her household affairs. "I knew well," he said, "where at this time of the day I should find you," and taking his accustomed seat in an old armchair by the fire-side, where he had often sat, made her at once by his affectionate and playful manner, quite unconscious of the elevation to which he had attained since he had last sat there. "Aunt," he said, "you know I used to tell you, when a boy, that I should be a Duke before I die." "Ah," she replied, "and I used to say that it would be 'Duke of Puddle Dock'", which was a proverb in London of that day, referring to a wretched locality in Wapping, and with which aspiring lads, who had great notions of the greatness they should hereafter attain, were twitted . . .' – Dr T. Raffles

It is in rare asides like this that themes crystallize out of the mix of Raffles's life; for example, his great yearning for the reassurance of honours and recognition that he will then set lightly aside in the name of common humanity. Once he has been given viceregal powers, he loves to sit and eat with the natives. Given a palatial ballroom, he adores to receive junior officers. But he desperately needed to have that title and power, that palace and the liveried carriagemen of his eminence.

*

Raffles was to have a number of nicknames in the corridors of power. He was sometimes referred to sneeringly as the Tide Waiter (a minor customs official) or the Golden Sword (a title bestowed on him by the Sultan of Aceh). He had always coveted nobility from his Duke of Puddle Dock days. While still a nobody in Penang, he had urged his cousin to look into Sir Benjamin Raffles, an obscure baronet of the seventeenth century, to see if there was the basis of a claim to his arms and title. From now on, in the Calcutta ministries, he could be called 'Sir Knight'. In snide civil service fashion, it turned his elevation into denigration.

The dubbing occurred at the hands of the Prince Regent, to whom he had dedicated his *History of Java*. Rumour had it that 'Prinny' was jealous of Raffles's flourishing new friendship with his daughter. Otherwise, he would have been a duke, a proper one.

11. *This Other Elba*

'If, however, he [Raffles] is acquitted of those charges in which his moral character is implicated, still there is no reason why he should not be employed in a situation of minor responsibility and of more strictly defined duties, of which description the Residency of Bencoolen [Bengkulu] may be considered.' – Lord Moira

Bengkulu was a dotted line of British possessions on the barren west coast of Sumatra. Of all the botched British colonies, it was the worst. To end up here after Java was a dreadful comedown, a Siberian posting. It had been founded in 1685 in what was simply the wrong place, like Penang, in the false belief that it was on the direct route to China, and had ignored geography ever since. It had fierce malaria, a dolefully wet climate and a dangerous coast, to which Man had added slavery, Indian chain-gangs, forced delivery of pepper at fixed prices and savage repression. It lost £100,000 a year and the population was running away. The Company's agents were astonishingly slothful, corrupt, feared and detested. It had attained a terrible reputation in every single particular. The only appeal of Bengkulu to Raffles could be as a reserve of natural history. The Indonesian volcanoes that would rumble dyspeptically at the birth of Bung Karno belched and roared at the accession of the new Lieutenant-Governor.

'This is without exception the most wretched place I ever beheld. I cannot convey to you an adequate idea of the state of ruin and dilapidation which surrounds me. What with natural impediments, bad government, and the awful visitations of Providence that we have recently experienced in repeated earthquakes, we have scarcely a dwelling in which to lay our heads, or wherewithal to satisfy the cravings of nature. The roads are impassable; the highways in the town overrun with rank grass; the Government House a den of ravenous dogs and polecats. The natives say that Bencoolen is now a *tana mati* (dead land). In truth, I could never have conceived anything half so bad.' – T. S. Raffles

Even before Raffles's brutally frank reports, Bengkulu was a known hellhole. Governor Collet wrote of society there in 1712:

'And for the Ladies, I'll tell you in what Condition we are. There are but five White Things in Petticoats upon the Coast, one I am sending away with her husband, tho' she petitions to stay behind in the Quality of Nurse alias Bawd. Another is sent away by her husband with my consent because she is so free of Tongue, Tale and Hand that the poor man can't live in quiet with her. A third is non-compos and actually confin'd to a dark room and straw. A fourth is really a good Wife and a modest Woman but the malicious say that her person never provok'd anyone yet to ask her the question. The fifth is a young Widow suppos'd to have a little money, of the right St Helena breed, as well shap'd as a Madagascar Cow, – and so much for Women.'

Raffles, however, had brought the sturdy Editor and his first child with him. He refused to 'eat the bread of idleness' and set to work at once.

*

'It is difficult to get to Bengkulu. It is summer. All the planes are full.' It is a familiar story, but told by officials as if fresh and new. All the planes were booked solid. They are always booked solid. Should you manage to get on one, however, it will be half empty. 'Your name?'

'Barley.' I pronounced it 'Bali', as close as Indonesian will allow you to get to the original. The airline official looked at the flight list and shook his head. A group of young men in light-blue uniforms laughed kindly.

'Bali?' they said. 'Then you are one of us.' They whirled round revealing the same word stamped on their blousons. It was the Bali University football team. They were not the bunch of sullen, hunched louts an English football team would have been. 'We had to give him 20,000 rupiahs to get on the plane, though we are booked. It is a scandal. There is a football tournament. Wait.' They went into a whispering huddle with an older man who was clearly the manager. He looked at me, sighed and made an addition to the list of names. 'There,' they said. 'It's fixed. Give us your ticket. Now you're listed as our foreign trainer. It will scare the other teams to death. We will go to Bengkulu together.'

*

The population of Bengkulu was some 60,000 in Raffles's day, of whom about 10,000 lived in the town. Many were military, though the Company had come to rely on Buginese mercenaries, Topazes ('black Portuguese', like the Malaccans) and Malagasy troops. Behind many of the English names lurk Eurasians who had risen to positions of power within the colony. Raffles, as a nineteenth-century Westerner, seems to us Orientally aware of the duties of patronage. He fixed a commission for his friend Raden Rana in the militia. He would later assist in the founding of Singapore.

The trade was in the hands of some 500 Chinese, the rough

work done by convict gangs from Bengal or the 300 African slaves owned by the Company. The last shocked Raffles deeply. The female slaves lived promiscuously with the convicts, as the superintendent cheerfully informed the new Governor, 'to keep up the breed'. Sitting amid his cracked and collapsing fort and the wreckage of the town, his first thought was to free them all at once and set up a school for the children. The Editor adopted one, to set an example. At the end of his government she would be properly married off with a dowry supplied by Raffles.

The Company immediately disapproved, but Raffles had by now learned to ignore disapproval. His commerce with the great and the good in London had given him confidence. He abolished gambling and freed the pepper trade. Most of the local slavery came from the Company's policy of advancing money that would be paid off in pepper. Unable to ever deliver the goods, debtors and their children became slaves. Raffles wrote off the debts.

The convicts were encouraged to rehabilitate themselves, marry and become settlers. Instead of beating everyone with sticks, he tempted them with carrots. Raffles was up to his old tricks of treating natives like human beings.

*

With unexpected efficiency, a gleaming new bus met us at the airport to transport the team to an official reception and the first match of the series.

'You're on the manifest,' said the manager and shrugged. 'There's nothing else for it. You'll have to see it through.' And so I was embussed, given an identity tag and a blouson and disgorged at a crowded football stadium.

All over Indonesia are Balinese policemen. They gathered round, adored their team, hugged them in ecstatic solidarity, shook my hand in wet-eyed gratitude and homesickness.

'Thank you for helping our team. We are moved by your kindness. Lineker, Maradona.' Magic words, uttered like charms. More Balinese policemen escorted us through to the cinder track where the other squads in tracksuits looked us up and down in stony-faced semi-hostile appraisal, as at a sixth-form dance.

East Timur has been declared Indonesia's newest province, and its team was being propelled around the country to familiarize the idea. East Timur translates as 'Timor Timur', is abbreviated to Tim-Tim, and compounds with the loan-word 'team' to give *tim Tim-Tim*, 'the East Timur team'. The Balinese contemplated the ripplingly muscular tim Tim-Tim with horror. 'God, they're black!' someone breathed in awe. In the bright sunshine, their features disappeared into a matt blackness.

An American-style marching band, complete with drum-majorettes, formed up in satin uniforms and exhaled a patriotic air. The leader had a baton with a great dented knob that spoke of the need for further practice. The Balinese team went into an elaborate routine of synchronized bum-wiggling, thigh-stretching and shoulder-shrugging.

'This is quite irrelevant,' the captain confided, 'but it excites the girls.'

Someone blew a whistle. We set off, pounding round the track in a travesty of a military parade. Civilians marching are always unconvincing, like soldiers pushing prams.

It was already clear that some of the Balinese were very well off, the tribute of tourism flowing into their coffers, while others were very poor. The captain had revealed that, despite his youth, he owned a hotel and drove a BMW.

'Watch this,' he said. Drawing from his pocket a bundle of money, he casually tossed a couple of 5,000-rupiah notes over his shoulder. There was a thud and a furious scrimmaging behind as the *tim Tim-Tim* broke ranks and flung themselves on the notes in total shambles. It destroyed their impact splendidly. The Balinese captain smirked.

We formed lines in the hot sun. Heat rose from the track in a shimmering curtain and wavered across the pitch, bare of grass, earth impacted like concrete. There was a lot of military shouting from officials and painful stamping on the cinders in unsuitable plimsolls. In the heat, the Balinese began to wilt and slump against each other in comradely discomfort. Masters of beach technique, they flashed furious sexual semaphore at the drum-majorettes. The male members of the band flourished their trumpets in sexual rivalry.

'They are all too young,' announced the captain censoriously. There was a pause.

'God, but they're *pretty* young,' sighed an anguished voice from the rear. Everyone laughed.

'*Sporting spirit and the five principles of the nation are the eternal watchwords of Indonesian youth. . .*'

An official had stood up, shrugged on the glasses that were the sign of his learning and come to rigid attention with a huge wad of foolscap from which he intoned.

'My fiancée is white,' the man behind whispered. 'I'm off to Australia when I finish university. I really miss her. She's not a tart like most of the tourists, a nice girl, keeps her blouse on on the beach. She works in a cheese factory. Will you help me write a letter to her?'

'Of course,' I said. Hadn't Alfonso, the Malaccan Portuguese, said he was going to work in a cheese factory? Perhaps Indonesians saw all of Australia as one vast cheese factory.

'Tell me,' whispered another voice, 'what are groupies? I have heard the word but the idea seems strange.'

I explained. They heartily approved of the notion.

'*. . . as a step towards the completion of the purposeful harmonization of the common people beneath the banner of unity within diversity . . .*'

The teams wilted further.

Another voice. 'It's funny. I can't *stand* the smell of cheese. Yuk! It's like the way you *bule* people talk about durian.'

'. . . *moving forward in the spirit of solidarity towards the expression of the cultural value of the vaunted ethic . . .* '

'Which team are you playing?'

The captain yawned and absently ogled a chubby girl untangling her pom-poms like a chimpanzee grooming its young. 'We're not playing today, just watching. You'll know when it's our turn because we can't shave that day. It's our religion.'

'. . . *in accordance with the presidential instruction making official the upgrading of the programme for sustained youth development and conscious implementation of . . .* '

He talked so long, it began to get dark. By the time the match started no one could see the ball, let alone the *tim Tim-Tim*.

*

One reason that Bengkulu looked so depressing to Raffles was the absence of verdure. Later he would come to see it as a place of natural rather than human history. But for the moment, every shrub and tree had been cut down, the English fearful lest hostile natives skulk behind them. They had good reason to be fearful. In 1801, Parr, the British Resident, had been beheaded.

His memorial is still there, at the crossroads by the fort, standing empty, like, indeed, a body without a head. In local memory, Raffles is credited with building it, but then local memory has Raffles doing everything, including constructing the fort – an ungainly beetle-browed thing of battlements – which was certainly there before him. Parr's memorial is remarkably similar to Olivia's memorial, and to her tomb in the original form, with its circular shape and roof like an inverted saucer. But this is simply to argue that it is a Company monument, class A, higher ranks for the use of.

Bengkulu impresses for other monuments. It was a hotbed of Freemasonry. We know little of Raffles's connections with the sect but his secretary, Travers, was ardent in his attendance. The lodge in Bengkulu was named 'The Rising Sun'. The name is significant, suggesting the lodge takes its origin myth from the cult of Osiris in ancient Egypt, fashionable at that time from Napoleon's recent campaign. Belzoni the Great, mountebank and explorer, would shortly claim to have discovered an ancient Masonic temple in Thebes, and the conflation of the builder of the Temple of Solomon and the god Osiris would be complete. Freemasonry would have ingested Egypt wholesale. The mark of the cult was the obelisk, inevitably interpreted as the god's erect penis, and Freemasons of the time laboured to bring obelisks into the hearts of many major Western cities.

In Bengkulu, obelisks are everywhere. The cemetery of the English church is full of the obelisk tombs of Company men. The church itself was rebuilt by the Dutch and is now colonized by Christian Bataks, the tribe whose dedication to cannibalism would later provoke Raffles to anthropological fieldwork. The mournful cemetery is nowadays bathed in the music of Mozart, played on a Japanese organ by Christianized Batak fingers. On some tombs locals have chalked 'Watch out – the Devil', writing perhaps truer than they know. A marble angel, wings snapped by local children, is associated in popular memory with a child of Raffles. But it is obelisks, buckled and heaving following the attentions of goldhunters, that dominate the place.

By the sea stands another, the Hamilton monument, scrupulously whitewashed. But the biggest erection by far rears up, sharp-edged and mathematical, in the main square by the new Governor's palace. Made of great blocks of stone it commemorates the Indonesian Revolution and has harnessed modern technology to the making of obelisks. I was stopped from photographing it by an officious policeman.

'The design,' he huffed, 'is Bengkulu copyright.'

*

'I treat them [local rulers] as a wise man should his wife, am very complaisant in trifles, but immoveable in matters of importance.' – Governor Collet

Parr brought his death upon himself. He had arrived with orders from the Company to cut costs. It was no longer willing to tolerate the onerous losses of Bengkulu. Many were thrown out of work and the Company employees were prevented from trading in their private capacity. Bengkulu was a place of mafias within mafias – the Company, the Freemasons, a shadowy association called 'the Concern'. Instead of mitigating the situation with regard to pepper, he tried to introduce the forced cultivation of coffee. He insulted and humiliated the chiefs. Worse, he tried to abolish the Buginese corps which was the muscle behind the government and so met the fate of every despot who forgets to pay the army.

The Malays had a meeting and it was decided, in accordance with customary practice, to take Parr's head. The other Europeans were warned to stay at home on the intended day, lest they be inadvertently injured.

'Just before midnight the first blow was struck; someone shrieked, "The Malays have come!" and the fighting was on ... They cut down the guard and entered the house in short order, three of them finding their way to Parr's room and dragging him out of bed. Parr had been ill and was no match for even one healthy man, let alone three, so that the execution would have been swift if Mrs Parr had not fought valiantly for her husband's life. Patiently, the Malays asked her to let them proceed, explaining that they were afraid that they might accidentally injure her, but the unreasonable woman persisted in interfering, throwing herself upon Parr's body and generally trying to get herself killed. At last, when she managed to be slightly wounded in the hands, the men were reluctantly compelled to use force on her. They shoved her under the bed and went about their business. They cut off Parr's head and then, as quietly as possible, without any ill-bred fuss, they went away with it. As far as they were concerned, the revolt was over and everything was quite satisfactory.

The Malays were astonished and aggrieved when the English seemed to resent the affair. At first it all went according to a design they recognized; a reward was offered for the heads of the assassins, and that, the chiefs thought, was intended to be the customary compensation paid for murder. They only wondered why the eccentric English didn't ask them to pay compensation in turn for Parr's murder. They were perfectly willing to stump up, shake hands all round, and thereupon forget the whole business.' – E. Hahn, *Raffles of Singapore*.

The British were unwilling to let matters rest there. What the Malays viewed as a regular judicial procedure was seen in London as an example of the dreaded 'running amok' of the natives. Afraid to tackle the chiefs directly, they seized lesser protagonists, tied them to the mouths of their cannon and blew them to pieces. Then they systematically destroyed the peaceful villages within a certain radius of the town, shot the buffalo, razed the buildings, grubbed up the fruit trees and dispersed the inhabitants. This hardly helped the colony to thrive.

Raffles recognized the need for a fresh start. He invited the chiefs to ponder with him how they could all make things better for everyone. He abolished the harsh regime of body-guards and asked the chiefs to dinner. As a final sign that he understood the Malay point of view in the matter, he repealed the law forbidding men to carry the daggers that were the sign of freeborn dignity. Thus, when Sukarno married and was unable to attend the ceremony in Bengkulu, he sent his dagger. In accordance with tradition, the bride married that.

*

Bung Karno was exiled to Bengkulu by the Dutch in 1938. He had been in Flores for five years and hated it. He was half dead from malaria and it was said the Dutch moved him to Bengkulu for his health. It is hard to believe this was not a cynical joke. Bengkulu is notorious for its malaria. It was true in Raffles's day and it's true now.

Bung Karno did not enjoy the town, describing it as 'outstanding in absolutely no regard'. Fort Marlborough, Raffles's fort, was in the hands of the Dutch police and for a while he was sequestered there, looking out perhaps through a Georgian window at Ambonese troops under Dutch officers and trying to make sense of the world.

On the other hand, he disliked the orthodox Islam of the locals. Being half Balinese, half Javanese, florid religious syncretism was in his blood. The mosque he built is still there, a plain, unfussy structure with a multi-levelled Balinese-ish roof, just down the road from the Bengkulu obelisks. The locals ungenerously complained because it did not segregate male from female worshippers.

Nearby is his house. There are several 'Bung Karno' houses in Indonesia. The one in Flores has a well, dug with his own hands, to whose waters are attributed healing powers. Once someone tried to heal my swollen feet with it. The house contains relics with their various – often unsought – symbolisms; the marital bed, the walking stick, the violin rotted and collapsed through termites' mining, its strings a pubic tangle.

The Bengkulu house also has its cult objects, the imponderabilia of everyday life, exactly the sort of thing we miss for Raffles. Its simplicity and homeliness seem incapable of bearing its burden of history. There are the photographs, Bung Karno somehow always staring into the camera, aloof, solitary, looking as if his face has been glued in afterwards. There are the clothes of his wife, sequined and outdated, the books – Dutch, French, Indonesian, politics, music, a study of manuscript traditions concerning the adoration of the Virgin Mary, another on the use of parachutists in war. A big red book on malaria has a slavering, golden mosquito on the cover.

In front of the house there is the bicycle, a moral object, like George Washington's axe or Nelson's telescope. Generations of Indonesian children have been invited to consider the ethical implications of this machine with its vicious iron spikes projecting through its exploded saddle.

'Because he truly loved that bicycle, he [Sukarno] cleaned it morning and evening until it shone. As it happened, there was only the one bicycle in the house. But Tjokro also had sons who wanted to try to ride Soekarno's bicycle. But they hesitated to borrow it because it was still regarded as new.

But one evening Harsono could no longer contain his urge to ride Soekarno's bicycle. Quietly, he wheeled the bicycle out of the house and he even rode all round the town of Surabaya. But, unluckily, on one street he rode into a tree to avoid a horse-drawn cab. The front of the bike was damaged. Harsono tried to get it mended in a garage. But it could not be put back like it was before.

In this affair, Harsono's mistake was not to be honest with Soekarno. It would have been only right that Soekarno was angry with him to the point of booting him up the backside. After this, Soekarno was sorry. In secret, he saved up again cent by cent until he had eight guilders like before. Once more, he went off to buy a Fongers bicycle but not to replace the old one. Instead, he wanted to give it to Harsono. Of course, Harsono was amazed to receive such a gift. But what could he do? Refuse it? Of course not!

Looking at this affair, one sees that Soekarno's spirit was often unpredictable. Shortly before, wasn't he so jealous of something a friend of his owned – that was better than his own – that he grabbed it and flung it away? (Remember the story of the spinning top.) However, now that his bicycle had been bent by Harsono, did he not save up his money in secret so he could give it away?' – R. Rahim, *Bung Karno Masa Muda*

*

Raffles had no intention of vegetating in Bengkulu. He immediately began to fret at the constraints placed upon him. Raffles was one of the first people to realize the importance of public opinion, and Dutch historians have seen him as someone who cynically constructed for himself a totally spurious reputation with blocks hewn from the moral credit of their own nation. He certainly understood how to arouse British chauvinism, but the constant references to British national honour and credit should not be too swiftly seen as hypocritical – as they would be if our own politicians had made them. Honour still meant something in the age of Raffles. His officers still fought duels.

The first thing to do was to redraw the frontiers of his domain. He began a war of provocation with the Dutch, arguing about the interpretation of the Anglo–Dutch treaty, refusing to hand back the Dutch city of Padang, issuing protests. They were as nervous as cats at having him in the archipelago, convinced he was their dedicated enemy. They were right; he was. And the basis of that enmity was quite simply that it was in the best interests of the natives to be under benevolent British rule rather than groaning beneath local tyrants or Dutch oppression. Nothing steels a man's purpose like moral indignation.

He started a toytown war, short on actual gunfire but full of military posturing, seeking to extend his southern frontier to Semangka Bay and so give the British a toehold in the channel between Sumatra and Java. The little forces marched up and down in brave uniform, threw up stockades and blew bugles at each other like dogs barking in the night. He signed treaties of friendship with local sultans, regardless of Dutch claims to exclusivity. In all things he opposed Dutch monopoly.

*

There were two men sleeping under the Parr monument, or rather resting, for they were both staring up at the inside of the roof where paint and plaster eased themselves free to flutter down like snow. The coastal wind was here mitigated to a fresh breeze that swirled the motes of plaster as they descended. Occasionally the men would reach out and swat an importunate mosquito. We shared the inevitable cigarette.

'Are you from Bengkulu?'

They laughed. 'No one is from Bengkulu. Everyone here is from somewhere else. From Padang, from the Batak country, from Java. We are from Java – you know – transmigration.'

Transmigration is the scheme that shifts the excess population of Java to the outer islands where, in theory, they receive land, a hoe and a new future. Raffles had always fretted about his lack of population and even ended up dreaming of white settlers. The Company had soon put a stop to *that*. His own figures showed that marriage was dying out in the colony. When you married, you had to produce more pepper for the Company. So people simply stopped marrying. The mosquitoes, immune to marriage, bred on with unconcern. My arms were already dotted with bites.

We sat and we talked. Slowly the story emerged. They had come from Java three years before, received their land, but it had not been good land. They had cleared the trees themselves, raised a couple of crops. But the settler towns were boring. One had gambled and mortgaged his land to a Chinese. The other had married off his son and had to pay a huge bride-price. The land had gone.

'If things go on like this,' he said, 'in a few years no one will be able to get married.' It could have been Raffles talking. 'So now we come to town to look for work. But today there is no work.'

'What work do you do?'

'We are coolies. When there is a ship, we unload it.' That had been the job of Raffles's African slaves. They had all gone, merged into the general populace somewhere. They had left little trace, though I seemed to recall a festival introduced by Gurkha soldiers. Had there been Gurkhas here? It seemed unlikely. Surely the chronology was wrong.

'We have not,' they said pointedly, 'eaten today. A thousand rupiahs is enough for a man to eat in Bengkulu.' I took the hint. It would be easy to slip them a couple of thousand rupiahs, but then I remembered Raffles and the chiefs.

'No,' I said, 'no money. But over there, by the English fort, is an eating place. Let's go and eat together.'

*

Raffles determined to visit as much as possible of his domain in person. He had a belief in the reality of human contact, in human contact as the only reality. There was also that craving for distinction that had marked him from a boy. It was always terribly important in his perambulations that no European should have been there *before*. His botanical expeditions masked an urge to deflower the whole country. He set off on great hikes, the Editor gamely in tow though usually pregnant. On receipt of the order to arrange bearers, Residents were wont to toss the piece of paper to one side with a laugh: it would never happen. The next thing was that Raffles would arrive, furious, on their doorstep, demanding to know why nothing had been done.

There comes a stage in middle age where every fine prospect is not simply a moving experience for the eye; it becomes the site for a house you plan to build some day. Thus it was with Raffles and the Bukit Kabut, 'Hill of Mists', a few kilometres outside Bengkulu. Here, he ordered land to be cleared:

'... A comfortable cottage is erected ... The only inconvenience will arise from the tigers and elephants, which abound in the vicinity ... In many parts the people would seem to have resigned the empire to these animals, taking but few precautions against them, and regarding them as sacred; they believe in transmigration and call them their *nene* or grandfather. When a tiger enters a village, the foolish people frequently prepare rice and fruits, and placing them at the entrance as an offering to the animal, conceive that, by giving him this hospitable reception, he will be pleased with their attention, and pass on without doing them harm. They do the same on the approach of the smallpox. I am doing all I can to resume the empire of man and having made open war against the whole race of wild and ferocious animals, I hope we shall be able to reside on the Hill of Mists without danger from their attacks.'

He was also making war on smallpox with an inoculation campaign.

*

All was not well at the hotel. A wave of malaria had swept over us until it more closely resembled a hospital than a hostelry. Five of the staff were ill in bed. In a strange reversal, the guests looked after them, for this was no snooty Western establishment. The Balinese footballers took over the kitchen, Muslim culinary fears being soothed by the revelation that two of the reserves were Muslims not Hindus. I had assumed these two to be from the army, as they had ferociously scalped skulls.

'No,' they explained, 'we nearly had to leave university this year, so we gave God our hair. And the girls used to *love* our hair.'

I sat in my hut, called – a sign informed me – 'Rafflesia', doling out aspirins and anti-malarials. An ineffectual doctor made tentative visits to the sick.

'Take this medicine,' he would say. 'You will find it no help whatsoever,' or 'We must test your blood for parasites. Whatever the case, the results are always negative.'

The Balinese dispensed bitter papaya leaves, a folk remedy, and played football. They held long, earnest conversations on equipment. A particular concern were shin-pads, called *skin-skin* in Indonesian, in a manner that neatly healed the ancient fission between West and North Germanic dialects. After a few days, I fell ill too.

'I expect,' smiled the doctor, 'you are feeling terrible. Never mind. Tomorrow you will feel even worse.'

He was, of course, right. The usual symptoms followed, fever, chills, vomiting, the spike being hammered into the top of your head. I heard him chortling to one of the footballers.

'We expect about four in ten to die with this. This looks to me like it's turning into cerebral malaria. He should die in the next couple of days. I'll get in touch with the Christian pastor.'

So that was it. I would end my days in the graveyard that had nearly claimed Raffles and *had* taken his children. I snivelled as I worked out that I was much the same age as he was when he finally left Bengkulu. Our birth- and, it seemed, death-days were almost identical. Like Parr I had brought this death upon myself. There had been a too strong identification with Raffles. It was as if I was to die in his place. There would be no commemorative obelisk.

The hut was infested with bees. They flew in through a hole

on one side, circled agonizingly round my head, and plunged into holes they had drilled in the roofbeams. My fevered brain kept making links between Raffles and Sukarno, Raffles and myself. Their droning drove me crazy. What was worse was the knowledge that in English they were called 'mason bees'.

*

The great triumph of Raffles during this arduous cross-country campaign was the discovery of the 'Devil's betel box', the *Rafflesia arnoldii*, a vast parasitic flower, a metre across, big enough to hold a gallon and a half of fluid. His pride is that of a true botanist. No one else could be as proud of being identified with such a hideous growth that stinks of rotten carrion.

'There is nothing more striking in the Malayan forests than the grandeur of the vegetation: the magnitude of the flowers, creepers and trees, contrasts strikingly with the stunted and, I had almost said, pigmy vegetation of England. Compared with our forest trees, your largest oak is a mere dwarf. Here we have creepers and vines entwining larger trees, and hanging suspended for more than a hundred feet, in girth not less than a man's body, and many much thicker . . .

We got on, however, very well; and though we were all occasionally much fatigued, we did not complain. Lady Raffles was a perfect heroine. The only misfortune at this stage was a heavy fall of rain during the night, which penetrated our leafy dwelling in every direction, and soaked every one of the party to the skin. We were now two days' march beyond the reach of supplies; many of our Coolies had dropped off; some were fairly exhausted and we began to wish our journey at an end. We, however, contrived to make a good dinner on the remaining fowl, and, having plenty of rice and claret, did not complain of our fare.

... The utmost good-humour and affection seemed to exist among the people of the village; they were as one family, the men walking about holding each other by the hand, and playing tricks on each other like children; they were as fine a race as ever I beheld; in general about six feet high, and proportionably stout, clear and clean skins, and an open ingenuous countenance. They seemed to have abundance of every thing; rice, the staple food of the country, being five times as cheap as at Bencoolen, and every other article of produce in proportion.

... Hitherto we had been fortunate in our weather; but before we reached this place, a heavy rain came on, and soaked us completely. The baggage only came up in part, and we were content to sleep in our wet clothes, under the best shade we could find. No wood would burn; there was no moon; it was already dark, and we had no shelter erected. By perseverance, however, I made a tolerable place for Lady Raffles, and, after selecting the smoothest stone I could find in the bed of a river for a pillow, we managed to pass a tolerably comfortable night.'

Bung Karno and his family undertook a similar journey from Bengkulu to Padang in 1942, their departure lit by the burning supply dump at Fort Marlborough – the Japanese army was only a few miles away and advancing. They were seized by Dutch troops and marched off.

Despite his identification with the peasantry, Sukarno was a city boy, unattracted by the jungle. His resentments against the Dutch were city resentments. As a child he had had to watch films dubbed with Dutch subtitles, but – greater in-dignity yet – not from the front of the screen but from behind, with the poor people, so that the Dutch text was backwards.

He makes much of their sufferings in sleeping in a plain native hut, trudging 300 kilometres on narrow paths, living in terror of wild animals. It is an epic tale of heroism. On the fourth day, however, they emerged from the trees and caught a bus.

*

It was like a scene from a Verdi opera but instead of monks there were footballers, dressed in that oddly textured, iridescent satin, dark-blue in colour but mostly black against the light. And shorts. Monks would not have worn shorts. There was the strong, not unpleasant, odour of Oriental sweat. Not the sour-milk smell of Europeans, nor the rank fat of Africans and West Indians. It had fundamentals of light musk and high tones of jasmine tea. There was something else. Yes, it was the rheumatism-balsam reek of the moustache tonic they rubbed into their upper lips.

The players were praying with heads lowered, a deliberately non-denominational prayer – in accordance with Bung Karno's five principles – invoking a carefully non-specific High God. The Muslims and Hindus, unshaven like mafia mourners, were together asking mercy on someone who, nominally at least, was a Christian. They were gathered in a semi-circle around the foot of the bed, led in devotion by their captain as if in some public school ideal of life. They finished, touched their hands briefly together over my racked body and uttered a single piercing shout that made me groan. Then they formed the only orderly queue I have ever seen in Indonesia and each stroked me lightly on the shoulder, murmuring softly, 'May you make a swift recovery', turned and clattered out on studded boots.

The captain and I were left together. He sat on the end of the bed and looked down on me, hefting a four-foot high trophy from one hand to the other. No celebratory symbol had been spared. It incorporated the goddess of victory, laurel branches, a chalice, a Garuda bird and a small golden footballer.

'You won, then,' I croaked.

'No,' he said, affronted. 'We lost.'

Of course. In Indonesia *everyone* gets a trophy. The sideboard has made a glorious entry into the modern Indonesian home, groaning beneath the weight of honours accumulated in even the most undistinguished of lives. The winners' trophy would have been six feet high.

He shifted in obvious discomfort and peered down at his gashed left knee oozing blood.

'It was not football so much as karate. Every time we got near them, they turned so as to be on the referee's blind side and thumped us or kicked us. In ordinary football that's well enough, but we are university men. It is not fitting.'

He felt my brow. 'You are still hot. I need to talk to you. You must offer something to God. You will not recover until you promise him something.'

I thought of the boys who had given their hair.

'I don't think God would want my hair. Anyway,' I quipped, 'he seems to be taking it all on his own.' I thought it was a pretty good joke for a man who felt as bad as I did, but the captain was not in a joking mood. He looked saddened by my lack of solemnity. That was not fitting either. I suddenly recognized this scene. It was a man-to-man chat, a talk to the troops. He would have ticked off his team members in just the same way.

'Pay attention. You are a rich tourist, so you must give God some of your wealth. You must promise a good deed and if you get better, you must perform it. That is the way. If you ask, he will hear. But you must give, too.'

I thought about it. It was not hard to find a good deed. One of the team, Nyoman, had confided that he had had to drop out of his course for a year to work. He was at his wits' end to find the money to carry on. If I recovered, I would pay his fees.

He looked at me hard, perhaps detecting a spiritual change. 'Have you promised to God?'

'Yes, I have promised.'

He sighed. 'Now you will see. You will get better. It is a simple matter.' He rose, carrying his trophy before him like a cross and patted me kindly.

'Excuse me, I must go and make sure the men are cleaning their boots. If they do not, after defeat, they will get depressed. And if their boots rot it is not certain they will all be able to find new boots for next season. You are a good man. I hope you recover.'

It was the moment for an Indonesian proverb. I pulled my mousy, greying hair. 'Hearts vary,' I pronounced enigmatically, 'but *everyone* has black hair.'

He looked at me, unsure whether I was being solemn or not, sighed and went through the door.

*

'The pleasure of this journey was great to Sir Stamford, as it opened to him a field of future usefulness. He saw that it was not only the barren coast which he had to improve, but a country rich in all the bounties of nature, and a people ready and willing to profit by his influence and advice. One old chief, on taking leave, actually fell on his neck and wept; and soon after walked the whole way from Tanjungalum, the most distant place visited, to see him again at Bencoolen. Such simple uncivilized people are soon won by kindness; they are like children, easy to lead, hard to drive. It was Sir Stamford's extreme simplicity of mind and manners that rendered him so peculiarly attractive to them, as they are always ready to be kind and attentive, provided they meet with encouragement and sympathy, thus affording a proof that the heart is the best teacher of true politeness. The Editor on reaching Merambung laid down under the shade of a tree, being much fatigued with

179

walking: the rest of the party dispersed in various directions to make the necessary arrangements, and seek for shelter; when a Malay girl approached with great grace of manners, and on being asked if she wanted anything, replied, "No, but seeing you were quite alone, I thought you might like to have a little *bichara* [talk] and so I am come to offer you some *siri* [betel] and sit beside you." And no courtier could have discussed trifling general subjects in a better manner, or have better refrained from asking questions which were interesting to herself only; her object was to entertain a stranger, which she did with the greatest degree of refinement and politeness.' – Lady Raffles, *Memoir*

*

After five days, I could move again. The Balinese had disappeared back to their own island, but heaped their addresses upon me after the Indonesian fashion. The doctor returned occasionally for purely social reasons, celebrating me as proof of the power of his healing skills. It was time to take the overnight bus to Padang, but first I would test my legs and see the myriad activities of the beach.

The fishermen were busily defecating under their stilted houses and heaving boats about in feats of community solidarity.

'We are not from Bengkulu,' they shouted before I even asked. 'We are Padang people.'

Out there was Rat Island, where the British had landed their goods and built a malaria hospital. The permanent wind grounded the mosquitoes. Line after line of fierce waves rushed in from the Pacific and smashed on the coral. Little figures slipped and slithered out to the very brink of the deep. Two men waved a greeting and beckoned me out to share their danger. They were the men from the Parr monument. One was scraping fuzzy weed from the rock into a basket. Fried, it would be a relish. The other was plunged up to his neck in the water, occasionally diving under to hack at the coral with a crowbar and emerge blue with cold and spluttering.

'Fishing?'

'No. I am smashing up the coral. It is for the lavatories of rich people. They are crazy. They polish it up and stick it on their walls. Rich people are not prepared to come to the beach to crap. The beach must come to them. Look, there goes the Korean.'

It was the manager of the Korean noodle factory. Every morning he practised golf on the sand while his top employees were forced to carry a tree trunk up and down the beach in an athletic display, giving gung-ho cries. It was not the Indonesian way and they were bitterly ashamed.

'I *am* from Bengkulu,' said a man striding resolutely into the gale. 'We have lots of words from English in our dialect, *kubod*, *pokit*, *stokin*, *trai*, all from English. And when we sit on the *selokan* at night, we call it *vranda*.'

'What do you do for a living?'

'*Me?* I drive a bus to Padang.'

Further along the beach the army, clad in shorts and drenched T-shirts, were standing up to their knees in the water and practising shivering kung-fu. I declined the offer to join them. An immaculate recruit, cropped hair, pressed trousers, sat on the beach watching them.

'You are not from Bengkulu?'

'No,' he said. 'I'm from Java. But I'm not in the army either. I'm a fake. I've got lots of friends in uniform so I'm going round Indonesia. As long as I have this haircut and wear these trousers no one minds. I can sleep and eat in the barracks. After a couple of months I'll be off to Padang.'

12. Empires of the Imagination

'It was near Simawang that we first found feltspar, granite, quartz and other minerals of a primitive formation. They were here mixed with a variety of volcanic productions in the greatest confusion, strongly indicating that this part of the country had at some distant point been subjected to violent convulsions. Dr Horsfield got specimens of these, which he gave in charge to some coolies who attended him; after the day's journey he wished to examine the collection; the men produced their baskets full of stones, but on the Doctor's exclaiming that they were not what he had given them, and expressing some anger on the occasion, they simply observed, they thought he only wanted stones, and they preferred carrying their baskets empty, so they threw away what he gave them, and filled them up at the end of the day's journey, and they were sure they gave him more than he collected.' – T. S. Raffles

The bus had been advertised as air-conditioned and possessed of a toilet. It had neither of these features; instead it had large cockroaches that ran over your feet and sneered at you from the windows. It had the standard cast of characters – crying babies, embittered army men with bundles wrapped in newspaper, fat Chinese ladies who stood for long periods in the aisles and made ingress and egress impossible with their rumps. To all this, they had added something new, karaoke.

The fat Chinese ladies were addicted to it. They simpered and whined Chinese pop numbers that sounded like Norwegian entries for the Eurovision song contest. Their menfolk clapped rapturously and puffed ecstatically on cheroots. My neighbours, not having spent years learning to be disturbed by noise as have Westerners, wrapped themselves round each other with an elaborate matching of convexities and concavities and fell immediately asleep. It was hours before I could nod off fitfully.

> 'They ees a huss in Noo Orleen
> They core the rising sun . . .'

It was pitch dark and the singer was at first invisible. As my eyes accustomed to the gloom, I saw that he was a bony little man in a civil service shirt, with the dramatic gestures you see in the films of Bung Karno's speeches. He should really have been Japanese.

It was bitterly cold, with thick mist swirling in and out of the lights. We were up in the mountains and creeping down towards the coast, brakes groaning arthritically. No matter how alien and exotic the daylight scene, darkness, in that it draws on the inner world of the imagination, returns it to the familiar. It was impossible not to see the lights in the houses as shining from the mullioned windows of Sussex cottages. The trees, thrown up for a second in the headlights, were manifestly the oaks and pines of English hedgerows. Then the first fingers of dawn began poking about in the forests, picking out the huge, carved ancestral houses of the Minang people. The dam was breached. Indonesia flooded back in.

The man next to me was asleep with his head in my lap. He stirred, opened his eyes astonished, grinned and sat up, giving my thigh a 'thank you' squeeze. He looked out of the window and yawned.

'Nearly home.'

'You are not from Bengkulu then?'

'No. I'm Minang. I was in Java, in Semarang. A Dutch woman wanted to pay my university fees. I didn't tell her I left school years ago. My business was going bust, so I took her money and ran.' It was said in an offhand way, without shame or boasting, a thing among men, a matter of fact.

He dug in his bag, pulled out two oranges, gave me one. We sucked on our oranges as the Chinese women, bleary-eyed, staggered down the aisle, already reaching for the karaoke microphone to sing a duet about the beauties of Surabaya. They had brought their own backing tape with them.

'We here [Minangkabau] found the wreck of a great empire hardly known to us by name and the evident source whence all the Malayan Colonies now scattered along the coast of the Archipelago first sprung, a population of between one and two millions, a cultivation highly advanced and manners, customs and productions in a great degree new and undescribed. I can hardly describe to you the delight with which I entered the rich and populous country of Minangkabau and discovered after four days' journey through the mountains and forests this great source of interest and wealth.

'To me it was quite classical ground and had I found nothing more than the ruins of an ancient city I should have felt repaid for the journey . . .' – T. S. Raffles

*

'I am looking for Yet and May.' All over the East, people have aromatic, polysyllabic names shortened to the form of splat, thud and ouch. In their full glory they were classical, circumambulatory, Sanskrit appellations, though their owners were Minangs, therefore Muslims. We were at the university, or more precisely, at a drink-stall near the university where I had been told these two friends of a friend might be found.

184

A wall of dark eyes considered me. I felt like a mouse surrounded by cats. Everyone looked shifty.

'We do not know where they are. If we see them we will say you were looking for them. What is your name? Why are you looking for them?' I explained, invoked known names, produced photographs of group outings promised but never sent, showed books requested but unable to pass the Indonesian postal service.

Two young men looked up from their Scrabble board. They were playing in English.

'We are Yet and May.' They spoke quietly. 'Come and play Scrabble.'

We played. Yet read English. May was an anthropologist. I was able to pull a few sharp moves with words of doubtful – possibly only anthropological – existence, technical terms of the trade. May backed me up. Yet finally drove me from the board with 'expostulate' on a triple-score square. It was clear they played a lot. They were apologetic.

'We have to play in English. For Indonesian, all the letters are wrong and there is no "x" and "v"s are impossible and there are nothing like enough "k"s . . .'

I could see a paperback copy of *Pride and Prejudice* projecting from Yet's back pocket.

He gave me a cigarette and settled to formal introductions. 'You have arrived from where?'

'Bengkulu.' I explained about Raffles.

'We, too, have only recently returned. We were in jail.' Yet studied my face for response and was gratified at my surprise. 'It was a minor matter, fighting with knives at a guest lecturer's talk.' He held out an arm decorated with a great X of sticking plaster, as in a children's comic. Either scholarship was taken more seriously here than in England or other forces had been in play. I could not remember the last time one of my lectures had ended in a knife fight.

'It was outsiders,' he explained. 'Come to make trouble.

We don't like it when outsiders make trouble.' I tried hard to look like the sort of outsider who would never make any trouble.

'How long were you in jail?'

'Five days.'

'And your – opponents?'

'We had to share a cell with them. It was *very* awkward. I never want to go back in jail.' He shuddered. 'They make you eat out of the pail you use for slops.'

'How did you get out?'

'Our rector came and signed a piece of paper and we were released into his care.' Their faces were blank, but studying my own. There was a different conversational idiom here. People were more circumspect. They gave less away till they knew what *you* were thinking.

'You must have been glad to see him.' May had been waiting for that and leapt in.

'Not really.' There it was again, he grinned the shit-eating grin and savoured his moment of contradiction. 'He couldn't be bothered to come before. He said he had to go to a wedding and that was more important. All the other students had to stage a demonstration with banners and everything before he would get off his arse . . .' He was shaking with anger. 'It was . . .' He groped for a word and found only an English term from Jane Austen. 'It was most unbecoming.'

*

'The houses are for the most part extensive and well built; in length seldom less than sixty feet; the interior, one long hall with several small chambers in the rear opening into it. In the front of each house, are two *lombongs*, or granaries on the same principle as those in Java, but much longer and more substantial: they were not less than thirty feet high and capable of holding an immense quantity; many of them very highly ornamented, various figures and flowers being carved on the uprights and cross-beams; some of them coloured. The taste for ornament is not confined to the *lombongs*; the wood-work of most of the houses is carved, and coloured with red, white and black. The ridge-poles of the *lombongs*, houses etc. have a peculiar appearance, in being extremely concave, the ends or points of the crescent being very sharp. In the larger houses, they give the appearance of two roofs, one crescent being, as it were, within another. The whole of the buildings are constructed in the most substantial manner, but entirely of wood and matting . . .

In approaching Pageruyong, we had an excellent view of this once famous city . . . The entrance to the city, which is now only marked by a few venerable trees, and the traces of what was once a highway, is nearly three-quarters of a mile before we came to the Bali [meeting-hall] and site of the former palace. Here little is left save the noble waringin trees, and these appear in several instances to have suffered from the action of fire . . . Three times had it been committed to the flames by a remorseless fanatic; twice it had risen to something like splendour: from the last shock it had not yet recovered.' – T. S. Raffles

It has now. Like everyone else, when the Minangs do not have enough history, they build some more. A gleaming new ancient ancestral house stands on the spot. Yet and May took me there.

It is a couple of hours by bus into the mountains, a place of waterfalls and rich cultivation. It is easy to see why Raffles was impressed after the wilderness he found at Bengkulu. Everything here speaks of order, tradition, man's shaping hand, regular hours put in, regular harvests confidently expected. Minangs never stop pointing out how clean even the towns are compared to Java. Minangs are very proud of themselves and Raffles would have liked that.

There, by the side of the road, were the ancient stones Raffles inspected to find evidence of civilization. In the West, buildings are one of the infallible marks of civilization, though wood is less conclusive a claim than stone. Extraordinary wood buildings were all around him, but Raffles wanted the Minangs to rise to the level of having stone constructions, so he looked for them till he found them.

The streets were full of erect, self-assured Minang ladies on their way down to the market. Yet and May greeted them all in tones and postures of deepest respect. Minangs have a proverb, 'Men are like dust'. It is women who are the fixed points of the world here, not men. It is women who own the houses and the land. The whole of male life is an exile from the paradise of the house. Boys are born into their mother's house, but from the age of six or seven are required to leave it every morning with the men and spend their time at the mosque – nowadays at school. For a man to be in the house during the day is either to be ill or a public scandal. He spends much of his time in the public arena of the coffee house, often talking about the problems of being Minang. I had never met a people so self-obsessed.

At puberty, boys go off to make money by trading, so that Minang merchants are found all over Indonesia. You find them in the most desolate harbours, slumped in cheap lodging-houses, frequently afflicted by homesickness. The social problems of unruly youth are thus neatly exported and, in return, Minang culture provides a ready stock of wet-eyed songs about the glories of home to be sung in exile.

On marriage, the exile is mitigated but eternalized. A man goes to live in his wife's house, where he is always a guest and every evening he must ask permission to re-enter it afresh. It is not quite the matriarchy that it is often described as. After all, the women have brothers who are important in the affairs of the house and a child's mother's brother is rather more important in his life than his father. A father gets love but an uncle respect; you can go hunting, all-men-together, with your father but never with your mother's brother.

Minang women, on the other hand, are held to be bold and domineering compared to most Indonesians. It is the teenage girls who whistle after the boys these days, not vice versa. If a man and woman are walking in the rain, it is the woman who carries the umbrella that shelters them. After all, an umbrella is a *sort* of house. Men seem strangely shy and tongue-tied, rather prone to seek comfort in the male-stressing austerities of Islam so that periodic bouts of fundamentalism shake Minang society like a domestic affray. The destruction Raffles witnessed was at the hands of one of these movements. Within Indonesia, a soothing, academic sub-industry devotes itself to the study of the conflict between patrilineal Islam and mat-rilineal Minang tradition and is structured in advance to prove, comfortingly, that there is no difficulty whatever in reconciling the two.

*

Yet stood in the palace at Pageruyung and churned out the standard 'introduction to Minang culture' lecture. I looked out of the window and saw two buses come down from the Christian Batak country – in Raffles's day a land of cannibals. The first was named 'Adam', the pursuer 'Delilah', a very Minang ordering. May sat, leaning against a beam, and listened, saying nothing. But the native will seldom accept the anthropologist's account of the world that he, himself, lives and feels in. He looked up at the ceiling dripping with its intricate layer-on-layer of carved leaves, flowers and tendrils, the shutters with their interwoven lianas of red-and-gold blos-soms, the lush hangings in the alcoves where each daughter of the house received her visiting husband. And said nothing.

Every house is to some degree a map of the culture that

built it. In our solitary Western bedrooms is encoded that whole practice of expelling sexually mature children from the house that baffles most of the rest of the world.

'No one lives here,' May finally commented into thin air, 'except perhaps a couple of old grannies, but if you come back and try to stay they always say, "No room. It's full, it's full." That room's for this daughter and this one's for so-and-so's sister. But it's only full of ghosts. People don't come and live here.'

We wandered round the garden, full of shyly trysting lovers.

'It's a different matter once they're married,' said Yet eyeing them with an old man's cynical wisdom. 'Then the women don't want to know you. Look, you must come to the house and meet my sister. She's married, so everyone gossips if she leaves the house alone while her husband's away. But you are a guest and the duty to look after a guest has priority. That means she can get out to visit you as long as I'm there.'

It did not *sound* as if Minang women were the terribly liberated creatures of Yet's lecture. We set off down the hill back to the bus station.

'Bullshit!' cried May suddenly, kicking at a long skein of buffalo turd. 'Bull*shit!*' He stamped in another lying by the roadside. 'More bullshit!' He pointed at Yet. 'It's just not like that any more. All this Minang tradition crap has got nothing to do with *my* life. I lived in the house till I was fourteen and went away to school. No one cared.'

Yet looked hurt. 'What you're leaving out,' he remarked coolly, 'is that you were brought up in Java.'

'When I marry my girlfriend, we'll live in town in *my* house. My children will grow up with me, not their uncle. Look,' he said, pointing, 'look there. Round the traditional houses, you see those bungalows. They're the houses built by the sons-in-law so they don't have to go through all that Minang crap.'

'Your girlfriend's Chinese.'

'She's *not* Chinese. She's a Muslim. Her mother was a Minang anyway.' In sociology, discussions of fact always turn out to be discussions of terminology. It was only a matter of time before they got to the old chestnut of 'What does it really mean to be Minang?'

A crowd of tiny schoolboys, coming up the hill, stopped to watch these madmen who stamped in turds and shouted at each other.

'Are you going to the palace?' called Yet. They nodded. 'Then you must all be little princes.' They squealed with laughter. Yes, yes. Of course. That's what they were. They were all little princes. The little princes started poking each other.

'Princes are bullshit!' shouted May, but his rage was undermined by giggling too and he and Yet staggered off down the hill, arm in arm like comradely drunkards, May pausing now and then to wipe his shoe with great deliberation.

*

'Politically the greatest results may accrue. At no very distant date the sovereignty of Minangkabau was acknowledged over the whole of Sumatra, and its influence extended to many of the neighbouring Islands; the respect still paid to its princes by all ranks amounts almost to veneration. By upholding their authority, a central government may easily be established; and the numerous petty states, now disunited and barbarous, may be again connected under one general system of government. The rivers which fall into the Eastern Archipelago may again become the high roads to and from the central capital; and Sumatra, under British influence, again rise into great political importance.' – T. S. Raffles

Once again Raffles was trying to pick up the dropped

stitches of history, re-tying broken threads, re-establishing a past which was a mere illusion, a creation of his own wishful thinking. He quickly 'discovered' that the treaties between the Dutch and the Minang were purely commercial, having no political implications! The stage was set for a great British takeover in Sumatra, a new province centred on Padang, reviving the fortunes of a vanished empire and the glories of a classical world. In his treaty with the 'Emperor' of Minangkabau he was careful to have himself named as the emperor's representative to all the Malay states. The Company was not impressed and sent him what would in later times be termed 'a rocket'. They told him to stop messing about and give Padang back to the Dutch.

*

May leaned back and sighed contentedly. The demons of doubt that usually nagged at him seemed, for once, at peace.

'Indonesians,' he said dreamily, 'are the happiest people in the world.'

'How do you mean?'

'Some time ago, two of our friends had an accident. Their motorbike hit a bus. One was killed outright. "Better to die like that," we said, "than to live a cripple." The other was horribly maimed and what did we all say? "Well, he was lucky really. He could have been killed!"'

Yet was in no mood for anecdotes. The anthropological urge was upon him. He was soon in full flight, trying to grasp and encapsulate the Minang with the desperation of a home-grown ethnographer who constantly stubs his toe on the contradictions and inconsistencies raised by his own broad generalizations. It is impossible to paint with a broad brush when standing so close to the canvas.

'There is one legend that tells you everything about the Minang social system. The house holds on to its women, its fields and the children. But what if the men get lost? What if they forget their own house? Have you heard of Malin Kundang?

'Once upon a time, there was a poor widow who lived with her only son, Malin Kundang, by the sea. She had only a tiny, tiny field, so however hard she and her son worked they never had enough to eat. Her son also worked very hard for the neighbours and he fished. He did everything a man can do to earn money and by the time he was fifteen he had saved a little, enough to go away on a trading trip.

'He got on a ship and set off. His mother cried. He cried. Week followed week. Year followed year. She had no news of him. Five years, ten years. Still no news.

'One day a big ship came to the village. The neighbours called to her, "Hey, mother. It is Malin Kundang who has come back with great wealth."

'She set off, trembling, tears in her eyes. There on the bridge of the ship she saw him, dressed all in gold, with rings and jewels on his fingers and necklaces of diamonds. He had become a man. He had grown tall and handsome, with dark eyes and flashing teeth.

'She called out to him from the crowd and he looked to find her. She was skinny, poor, dressed in rags. At first he did not recognize her, then he was ashamed. His beautiful wife was beside him, horrified at the hideous old woman claiming to be her husband's mother.

'"Is it true?" she asked.

'"No," said Malin Kundang, his heart full of pride. "That is not my mother."

'Then his mother called out on God and cursed him and God heard her. He turned the ship and her son into stone. You can still see it at the village of Air Manis. I will take you tomorrow but it is not nice any more. They have repaired it in cement. It is like Disneyland.'

We were sitting on a big rock, not Malin Kundang's, in the middle of a hotel. They were drinking beer. When Indonesian students drink, they drink to get drunk. They told with glee the story of a foreigner who had come and asked where he could get beer *because he was thirsty*.

It was a strange hotel. The décor was extraordinary, a cross between a rock-garden and a gigantic, seedy Indian restaurant with rooms replacing the tables. But it was football again that overshadowed the whole establishment. The owner was a football fanatic, and his passion had driven him to form his own team from the staff. They were posed athletically in portraits all over the walls, dangerously close to those of the President and Vice-President. The man who did the cooking had been hired for the outstanding strength of his left foot. The man who worked out the bills had recommended himself by his ability to leap six feet in the air and catch a football in one hand. The indispensable players knew they could not be fired under any circumstances and had abandoned all further dissimulation to sit all day in the hall frankly gossiping and eating copious meals of their own devising.

Yet's audience listened to the tale and nodded. 'Malin Kundang was a bad son. What does it matter what a man does as long as he loves his mother?'

I was tempted to tell the Jewish joke about Oedipus – 'Oedipus Schmoedipus, so long as he loves his mother' – but knew it could not possibly survive translation.

*

Out of the blue came one of those turning points that make Raffles's life more the stuff of fiction than of fact. An incautiously worded sentence from inimical Lord Moira lent itself to misreading as an invitation to visit. Raffles and the Editor did not even wait for a proper ship. They were off like a flash to Calcutta in a tiny vessel at great risk to life and limb. Then something inexplicable happened. Lord Moira underwent an almost religious conversion. The change is coincidentally marked by Moira's change of name to Lord Hastings. He was transformed overnight from nonplussed, reluctant host into a supporter – more – a 'fan' of Raffles. The man must have had charm.

13. Flotsam and Jetsam

I had not meant to go to Bali. It was all a matter of planes and the high tide of the tourist season. I had been before and found it, in May's word, 'unbecoming'. Tourism is not ennobling either for the givers or the receivers, reducing humanity to its lowest common denominator. Australians were everywhere, organizing pub-crawls around the beachside drinking halls, fornicating, fighting and vomiting. A leaflet pressed into my hand at the airport was a rich ethnographic document. It dwelt on the tedium of Balinese cuisine, which had neither chips nor Vegemite; no wonder it gave everyone diarrhoea. The punch-line urged, 'Avoid hangovers. Stay drunk!' There were many people in the streets avoiding hangovers.

Raffles had not meant to come here either. It was contrary winds that had blown him to Bali just after the death of Olivia. This suggested to me a common destiny that should not be fought, a divinely ordained chance to visit the places Raffles had seen. Moreover, from Bengkulu I had an unpaid debt, a promise made to the God of the Five Principles that must be kept – Nyoman's university dues.

The threatening hand of the God of the Five Principles hovered over me at the airport, mysteriously withholding my luggage. The idea of a kind customs official seems strange to English ears, yet in Bali I found one, who took me on a tour of vast, hissing sheds piled high with homeless suitcases. I was told to wait, and sat upon the suitcases of others as a child is given a dummy to suck.

One by one the security men filed in and lined up for parade before a thin, etched man covered with gold braid.

'I have loved you,' he cried in tones of strangulated anguish. 'You are professionals. Trained. You are famous.' The word called for amplification. 'Famous even as far as Italy.' He wrung his hands. 'We were brothers: I was your big brother, you were my little brothers. And now this. This terrible thing. A broom has disappeared – stolen – from this very shed!'

Securely invisible behind a screen, two security men giggled silently and wagged reproving fingers at me in silent mockery of their superior.

'The natives of *Bali*, although of the same original stock with the Javans, exhibit several striking differences, not only in their manners and the degrees of civilization they have attained, but in their features and bodily appearance. They are above the middle size of Asiatics, and exceed both in stature and muscular power, either the Javan or the *Malayu*. Though professing a religion which in western India moulds the character of the Hindu into the most tame and implicit subserviency to rule and authority, and though living under the rod of despotism which they have put into the hands of their chiefs, they still possess much of the original boldness and self-willed hardihood of the savage state.' – T. S. Raffles, *History of Java*

The hotels were all full. I trudged from one to the next, humping newly restored luggage. It was unbelievable. There were so many hotel rooms some of them must be empty. I sat down at a stall and moodily sipped a cold drink.

There were a lot of men sitting about in sarongs, smoking. They waggled their eyebrows at me, we began to talk. They were building workers, Muslims, from the neighbouring island of Lombok, fleeing drought to seek work jacking up tourist hotels in Bali. One man had brought his three sons, aged fourteen to eighteen. He had not seen his wife for a year.

'This is the last job,' he sighed wearily. 'I have to go home.'

'Yes,' chorused his friends, 'his hand is nearly dropping off.'

I explained my own plight.

'How much,' they whispered, 'do they charge for a room?' I told them. They fell about laughing. It was twenty times what one of them could earn in a day.

'That's crazy. Have nothing to do with it. Come and live with us,' they offered. 'We're building the hotel next door. It opens next month. There are lots of rooms. Pay us what you like.'

It was an establishment of extraordinary but gap-toothed luxury. It had a marble bathroom but no water. Most of its contents were mysterious to the men who had installed them and as a thing of beauty and no utility, to enter it was for them almost a religious experience. For Muslims, with their ritual ablutions, cleanliness is indeed next to godliness. A bucketful of water was left outside my door every morning like an offering.

'Would you like a window?' they had asked.

'A window would be nice.'

'Wardi – a window!' One had appeared in an hour.

There were no ordinary light-bulbs, but chandeliers had arrived, so one was mounted temporarily in my room. You had to walk round it to get to the marble bathroom.

They worked from dawn to dusk but in the evenings engaged in a parody of domestication, washing, cooking and dreaming of home. I was scandalously caught one evening sewing a button on a shirt I was already wearing. This, they warned me, was a terrible evil. To do such a thing was to risk being lost for ever in the forest.

Their great private preoccupation was the construction of a

roulette wheel. It was a complicated device made of wood and coat-hangers, built by a syndicate of hopefuls.

'There is a Chinese who comes every Saturday and wins the men's wages. It would be much better if I won the men's wages,' the foreman explained with irrefutable logic. 'However, there is one problem. We cannot remember the sequence of numbers around the wheel and on the board. There is a place where white people go to gamble, where we would be shy. Could you dress up and go there and make notes and . . .?'

'Of course.'

*

'In the arts, they [the Balinese] are considerably behind the Javans, though they seem capable of advancing rapidly. They are happily not subjected to a frame of government so calculated to repress their energies or waste their resources. They are now a rising people. Neither degraded by despotism nor enervated by habits of indolence or luxury, they perhaps promise fairer for a progress in civilization and good government than any of their neighbours.

They are strangers to the vices of drunkenness, libertinism and conjugal infidelity: their predominant passions are gaming and cock-fighting. In these amusements, when at peace with the neighbouring states, all the vehemence and energy of their character and spirit is called forth and exhausted.' – T. S. Raffles, *History of Java*

*

It was not easy to find the house of Nyoman, my footballing friend from Bengkulu. Not intending to stop here, I had not brought his full name, just the appellation that revealed his place in the sequence of children born to his parents. To look for someone named Nyoman in Bali is like trying to find Paddy in Dublin. I found the area with some trouble, then the street with more, then the alley after quite a lot more, but all attempts to get to the house failed. Then, in the distance, drying on a washing line, I saw a familiar blue blouson with the single word 'Bali' engrossed upon it.

I entered the gate and there he was, lined up with mother, grandfather, sisters and nephews, all adorned for the temple in cloths of gold and with flowers and gold leaves in their hair. Father was wafting incense in their faces, spraying a paternal blessing upon them with scented coconut water. They made me sit down and began to shower me with food and news. Behind the house, a pig was turning on a spit, slick with oil like a sunbathing tourist.

'It is wonderful that you have come. It is an extraordinary day. We have just received the best possible news.'

'What news?'

Nyoman took a deep breath and grinned. 'There is money coming. Money from God.'

My mouth must have hung open. 'From God? How do you know?'

The family settled as for a group photo and he began to relate the story, they nodding emphatically. Only later would I discover they did not speak Indonesian so could not possibly have understood a word.

'It was this way. Like all Balinese, my father has his village temple. Always he pays more for its upkeep than his brothers. It has led to fights in the family. Well, one day an old man came to the house and tried to sell my father a coconut for 50,000 rupiahs so the money could go to the temple. My father was angry. "What?" he shouted. "How much does a coconut cost? 50 rupiahs? 100 rupiahs?" He chased the man away. But that night my mother had a dream. In it she saw we should buy the coconut, so we went round the family and friends and got together the money and bought it. And when we opened it, what do you think? There were four gold rings inside. They're over there on the altar.'

I went over and looked. There were four cheap gold rings

like they sell to tourists on the beach. I nodded.

'It is the best possible sign. Money from above. We are taking the rings back to the temple. They will be used to cure disease.'

They looked at me. I seemed to be cast in the role of scientific observer sent to witness the truth of the event and set my seal of authenticity upon it.

'Is there any sign of this money?' I asked cunningly.

Nyoman shrugged. 'Not yet. In fact my father has just lost his job. But it's certain it's coming.'

I felt vaguely annoyed, irksomely trapped, reduced to a minor motif in someone else's greater design. 'Look,' I said. 'I have a story to tell too.' I told them about the promise made in Bengkulu, my unexpected visit to their island. I felt like the party bore longwindedly dissecting a joke everyone had already instantly grasped. They nodded and shrugged. Right, well, there it was then. The whole thing was explained. There was no need for me to be so surprised about it. They accepted the money in a matter-of-fact way. After all, it was not from me, it was from God.

'And now,' they said, 'you had better borrow some proper clothes from us and come to the temple so it can all be sorted out by the priest.'

We drove for hours. I had forgotten to stand with legs apart while they tied the sarong, so I could hardly sit down in it. Fruit was passed around. In other cars, on other motorbikes, sat people of all ages going to temples. They were all laughing. It was most unlike church.

By the time we arrived it was dark and there was a great fussing with parking, officials with torches adding greatly to the difficulty of the whole operation. The younger members had to be enticed past the men selling fish satay and into the temple itself, where there boiled a sort of spontaneous riot. A priest was found and the story told again. He seemed delighted and drenched us in scented water, bustling off with the rings. I received rudimentary instruction in the right gestures and motions of worship, the sequence of colours of the flowers and was entrusted with my own incense stick. But there seemed to be some disparity between our relative colour systems.

'Now a white flower,' Nyoman would hiss, passing me a blue one. 'Now red.' And gave me orange.

We progressed from court to court, the women hefting the piles of offerings about with brisk efficiency. At the highest point was a priest in white, arms raised in lengthy supplication. It turned out that he was only trying to mend the lights. At the crucial point of the ceremony, the electricity failed entirely and the congregation set up a great wail, being now unable to see the colours of the flowers in their hands.

'They have no money to mend the lights,' said Nyoman, 'but who knows. Maybe now there will be more money from on high.' It did not feel like a hint.

Torches began to circulate, passed from hand to hand after the surreptitious fashion of comic-reading choirboys during lengthy sermons. A boy took advantage of the dark, leaning forward to tremblingly inhale the long, black hair of the beautiful girl in front, then slumped back on his heels, sated and stunned, with a post-orgasmic expression of exhausted ecstasy and wonder.

As we left, they pushed flowers into my hair. The smell was evocative, thick, curdling, whorish. It was frangipani, 'dead Chinaman flower', again.

*

Tampaksiring was Bung Karno's retreat on Bali. It was no problem to get in. The French waiter's *pourboire* 'drink money' is the Indonesian soldier's *wang rokok* 'cigarette money'. This probably says a lot about both cultures.

The palace was an uninspired building, blandly Germanic, like the villa of a particularly dull Bonn executive and painted in shades of matt-pink and grey. Its glory was the setting, perched over the temple whose waters gushed everywhere.

Water has always been significant in Hindu culture, and the influence lives on in the nominally Muslim culture of Java. The king's association with water and rainfall is a manifestation of both his power and his purity. The Balinese still remember that the worst drought in living memory broke the day Bung Karno flew in for a visit. Not just the sea but the rain, too, was harnessed to declaring his legitimacy.

I commented on the cripplingly small bird-cages everywhere, mostly empty.

'Bung Karno loved animals,' I was told. 'But he sent the elephants back to the jungle. Anyway, they are not practical animals.'

Raffles would certainly have agreed with that. After his removal the Dutch had learnt nothing from his white elephant. In the 1840s they were driven to distraction by a Balinese ruler's repeated and vociferous demands for a rhinoceros. It took months of work and cost a fortune to get it to him. In return, all they got back was a black horse.

*

'On Java we find Hinduism only amid the ruins of temples, images, and inscriptions; on *Bali*, in the laws, ideas, and worship of the people. On Java this singular and interesting system of religion is classed among the antiquities of the island. Here it is a living source of action, and a universal rule of conduct. The present state of *Bali* may be considered, therefore, as a kind of commentary on the ancient condition of the natives of Java.' – T. S. Raffles, *History of Java*

*

'Buleleng,' I said. 'I must go to Buleleng. Raffles was there.'
'You are not going to hire a car, I hope.' Nyoman was shocked.

'No, I thought I'd go by bus.'

'But you cannot. You would get lost. It would take for ever. Give me a moment. I have a cousin, Ketut, who has a car. He will take you. You must not pay. That would be shameful.'

The cousin turned up, stocky, shaven-headed, cheerful and slow-revving. I wondered whether he had given his hair to God. He was revealed to be a mechanic. With stage whispers, he was taken into a corner and talked to most emphatically by the family with energetic gestures.

We set off.

'You got business in Bali, shop, hotel maybe?' he inquired.

'No. Just a tourist.' It saved time explaining but I was to regret that rash statement. Of course – I was not wearing shorts or an Australian romper suit, so he thought I was one of the many illegal businessmen.

'Elephant cave,' he said.

'No. No elephant cave. I only want to go to Buleleng.'

'Elephant cave beautiful. You can't come to Bali and not see elephant cave. It would be an insult. The family would be angry.' We went to the elephant cave.

'Now bat cave. Very impressive. You like.'

'No bat cave. Buleleng.'

He looked desperately hurt. 'Please. *I* want to go to bat cave. It's only nearby. Not take much time.'

We went to the bat cave and the monkey forest and every temple along the way, with holy water and magic meteorites, a list of the weird and wonderful, all groaning with tourist appeal. It began to get dark.

'We have to stay for night. Where we stay? Candi Dasa?'

There was no escape. We stayed at Candi Dasa.

The next day, we got up early.

'Buleleng,' I suggested.

'You sure you want to go to Buleleng? Is nothing there. No shops. No discos. Why you want to go there?'

I explained at length about Raffles. Ketut became upset. I seemed to be suggesting that the British had conquered Bali. No one had ever conquered Bali. Not even the Dutch – properly.

'No, no,' I soothed. 'Raffles never conquered Bali. He was merely an early tourist, an ally of the Sultan of Karang Assam.'

As I said it, I wondered whether the blatant untruth hid a deeper wisdom. Was it mere coincidence that where Raffles had been tourists followed? He had imposed the Grand Tour, the search for the phoney classicism of ancient Greece and Rome, on the Indonesian archipelago. He had set up Bali as Java's museum annexe, living history.

But no. Raffles's interest at least went beyond mere superficial sensation-seeking. After all, he had been to Buleleng, not Kuta Beach. But all anthropologists and writers bring a deadly infection, for to make a place known is to contribute to the destruction of what makes it interesting.

Ketut jammed on the brakes and looked at me annoyed. This morning, I was being a very bad tourist indeed.

'Karang Assam? Now you want to go to Karang Assam, not Buleleng? Which?'

'I'm not sure. Raffles definitely visited Buleleng, but I thought it was because he wanted to see the Sultan of Karang Assam. They wrote to each other.'

He sighed. 'Buleleng and Karang Assam are cousins, brothers, anyway one family. They were always attacking each other, then making friends. No one remembers what was what any more.' A motor mechanic summarizes history, but he was at least a *Balinese* motor mechanic. 'If it is letters you want we should go to Karang Assam. In the palace at Amlapura is an ancient library, many *lontar* leaves. You want history, you go there. The different courts of the palace have crazy names, London, Amsterdam, Tokyo – maybe that was your Raffles. It is better you go with me. If you go alone, you are a tourist. If you go with me, I can speak Balinese.'

In the face of such apparent certainty, there was nothing else to do. We went to Amlapura.

*

The palace was a place of still ponds, lilies, old gnarled tree roots clamped into the soil in long shady alleys, a place of peace and contemplation. In the centre stood a carved wood pavilion used for the filing of human teeth, a ceremony by which the young formally join the human race at puberty by losing animal dentition and acquiring Hollywood smiles.

On the gate, selling tickets, was a young girl of stunning beauty, wrapped in a crisp sarong. What was clearly her brother emerged similarly clad. They displayed those Hollywood smiles. They were children as advertised on television, physically perfect, sweet-natured, helpful. Surely this was crass Orientalism. I looked harder. There was a small spot, just coming to a head of pus, by the side of the girl's nose. The boy had dandruff. The world was safe from Orientalism after all.

Ketut began his spiel. I was annoyed to note he spoke Indonesian. Like many young Balinese he could not speak the language of the court. He began a long unfocused ramble about our journey. I interrupted ungraciously and asked if there was a librarian. We were pointed to the library.

We passed through a stone gateway and down some steps. The courtyard was dusted with gravel, full of flowers in pots, singing birds. A stout man emerged, drying his hands from some domestic activity. Could he help?

I was, I explained, interested in Raffles. He had certainly written to the Sultan. Perhaps he had even been here. I wondered if there were any traces of him. The man sucked his lip.

'When exactly was he here?'

'Ah . . . Well.' I did some rough calculations.

'What month was he here?'

What *month*? I was impressed. The archives here were marvellously organized if they could pin down documentation to the month. It had been after the death of Olivia, on the way back from the East, so it was probably in June or July. The man nodded.

'He was a tall man, fair?' This was astonishing. There must be a palace tradition about him, living on through the ages, Oriental hyperbole amplifying the reality of the small, mousy man.

'He had two children?' Wait, there was something wrong here. At that time, he was childless . . . unless . . . unless he had adopted local children. This was very exciting.

'You were asking whether he left anything behind. Wait.' He bustled off. What would it be? Letters? A silver medal bearing the image of George III? He returned with a Balinese parody of a Hawaiian shirt, covered in pink-and-green lizards. He held it out.

'He left this. It has been washed and ironed.'

The palace, it turned out, had adapted itself to the modern age. It now took paying guests, some of whom forgot their laundry. One of them had been an Australian with a name like Raffles.

*

'The inhabitants of these islands are strikingly alive to a sense of shame; a feeling which is heightened by the influence of a tradition amongst the Melayus, that, on the first establishment of the Melayu nation, the islanders stipulated, that neither they nor their descendants should ever be put to shame . . . "None of the Malayan rajas ever expose their Malayan subjects to disgrace or shame: they never bind them, nor hang them, nor give them opprobrious language; and whenever a raja exposes his subjects to disgrace, it is the certain token of the destruction of his country. Hence also it is, that none of the Malayan race ever engage in rebellion, or turn their faces from their own rajas, even though their own conduct be bad, and their proceedings tyrannical."' – T. S. Raffles, *History of Java*

*

'Buleleng,' I said.

Ketut shook his head. 'No Buleleng. The clutch is going. To get to Buleleng we must go through the mountains. The clutch will not take it. Believe me. I am mechanic, I know these things. We must return to Denpasar. Pass me the map.'

'Where is the map?'

'*There.*'

'Where?' I could not see it.

'*There.* At the eastern end of the car.'

'Which is the *eastern* end for God's sake?' Balinese are like homing pigeons, constantly orienting themselves with regard to Gunung Agung, the central volcano, the 'navel' of Bali.

So the God of Pancasila did not want me to go to Buleleng. We drove back to the town, Ketut humming to himself. He dropped me at the hotel. The Lombok men were supposed to be mixing cement but instead had adapted the hose to pleasure purposes, spraying each other in damp horseplay. There was the delicate problem of finance.

'Let me pay for the petrol,' I offered Ketut.

'Wait. I must take the car back to my father. I come and see you again.'

In an hour, he was back.

'I am ashamed.' He hung his head like a silent screen actor to show that shame. 'My father was angry. He said I could borrow his car for a few hours and, see, I have been all over the island with you, wearing out his tyres and his clutch for days. Also I have not fed the pigs so my father had to do it. You must give me money so my father will not be angry with me any more. The money is not for me. It is for my father so he is not angry with me. I think it is up to you to make us friends, since you are the one who has made us enemies.'

I sighed. We looked at each other, both knowing more than we wanted to. A little more Orientalism withered within me. As I gave him some money, he whispered,

'You must promise not to tell Nyoman. You would make *him* ashamed.'

In the odd economy of honour and shame I realized that was probably true.

14. Founding Father

'We are now on our way to the eastward, in the hope of doing something, but I much fear the Dutch have hardly left us an inch of ground to stand upon. My attention is principally turned to Johore, and you must not be surprised if my next letter to you is dated from the site of the ancient city of Singapura.' – T. S. Raffles

Raffles was about to secure his greatest triumph and create what will always be regarded as his memorial – the city of Singapore. The Company in London was still fuming over his anti-Dutch manoeuvrings in Sumatra, and with slowly malevolent penmanship confecting a damning dispatch that would put him finally in his place, scotching, once and for all, his distressing tendency to extend Britishness to other parts of the world as an act of human compassion. But the Company could not keep up with him. Once again, he did the impossible. While the Company scribes were still sharpening their adjectives, he convinced Moira, now Lord Hastings, of the intention of the Dutch to exclude Britain from the whole archipelago and of the urgent need to establish a British station to the east, near the mouth of the Straits of Malacca, to stop that mouth snapping shut.

He also intended to found a station at Aceh. Two commissioners were appointed to look into the succession to the throne. Raffles supported one candidate for the Sultanship, the other commissioner, in thrall to Penang, supported another. The Company's two commissioners sat for seven weeks in Aceh harbour, while Raffles bombarded his fellow official with a thousand pages of memoranda until the poor man submitted.

A free agent, Raffles was at his best, liberated from Bengkulu to wander the archipelago, Aceh, Carimon, Riau, Penang, Malacca, looking for a site for his new outpost and engaging in swift, energetic moves of personal initiative, unshackled by bureaucracy and the cramping dictates of accountancy. No wonder he exulted in the Dutch description of him as an 'unquiet spirit'. Yet, with Raffles, there was always the practical touch. Bricks, he hinted to a naval commander before they set off, would serve very well as ballast for his ship. They would also came in handy for building his new city.

Historians have understandably homed in on this period, as crucial to the interpretation of British policy. It would later be thrown into prominence by endless bickerings over whose original idea it was to form a settlement at Singapore, precisely who had rights in the matter, what was the legality of the treaties, what dark and hidden economic forces really moved their human hearts.

It would be unwise to overlook one essential fact. The Raffles of this time was at least as concerned with natural history as with politics. He was visiting the botanical gardens in Calcutta, hiring botanists to work with him in Bengkulu, corresponding with British specialists in many branches of the sciences. He had a long, involved relationship with the Sumatran tapir, having tracked it down from early reports in Penang and Malacca until finally he was able to present one to the Governor-General's park in Barrackpore in redemption of his studies. For Raffles, this was no mere distraction or consolation, the creation of knowledge was what he considered the ultimate justification of the European presence.

His first deed after taking possession of the harbour of Singapore was to set draughtsmen to work on the natural history of the island. By the time they got back to Penang, even the Editor, heavily pregnant, was loyally plugging away at botany while her busy womb was gestating his son, Leopold.

*

Singapore was formally founded on 6 February 1819. A number of accounts of the proceeding are preserved.

'... Mr Raffles himself came and shook hands with Tengku Long [the Sultan recognized as having authority], and a great many cannons were fired from the ships and from the cutters. Mr Raffles showed Tengku Long every honour and respect ... At that time, Mr Raffles was speaking with smiles and a pleasant face, and kept bowing his head, and was as sweet as a sea of honey. Not merely the human heart but even a stone would be broken by hearing such words as his, with a gentle voice like the sweetest music, in order to remove any sadness, and that the doubt which might be concealed in the treasury of the human heart might also disappear, and so all the waves of uncertainty which were beating upon the reef of doubt were stilled, and the cloud which threatened a squall of wind with darkness such as that of a great storm about to break was all dissipated, so that the weather became fine and there blew the gentle breeze which comes from the garden of love, and then suddenly there arose the full moon of the fourteenth day with its bright light so that the sincerity of Mr Raffles became evident to Tengku Long. In a moment his sadness changed to gladness and his face lighted up. As Mr Raffles looked out of the corner of his eye, his face changed colour, and he rose from his chair, and taking the hand of Tengku Long he led him into his cabin, and closed the door. In that cabin, these two men conversed, and no one knows the secret of what they said. If I knew the secret of their conversation, I would certainly write it in this story, but God alone knows it. After a considerable time they both came out smiling and holding one another's hands, and then they went down into the boat.' – Munchi Abdullah, *Hikayat Abdullah*

'During the whole of the ceremony the vulgarity of the Sultan's expression, the want of expression and the perspiration running down his face, combined with the wicked and dastardly proposal he made a few days ago for the murder of the Dutch at Rhio, raised in the feelings of the English spectators a horrible and disgusting loathing of his person, and several in pretty audible whispers, expressing these thoughts on the occasion sufficiently loud for Sir Stamford to hear, and in which sensation I suspect he inwardly accorded. The Tomagan [local chief] had a countenance more of dark cunning with some sparks of duplicity than otherwise, if I might be allowed to form an account of his heart from the index of his face; his certainly hard expression marked him to be fit for treasons, stratagems, war.' – Captain J. Crawford

'I shall say nothing of the importance which I attach to the permanence of the position I have taken up at Singapore; it is a child of my own. But for my Malay studies I should hardly have known that such a place existed ... Our object is not territory, but trade; a great commercial emporium, and a *fulcrum*, whence we may extend our influence politically as circumstances may hereafter require. By taking immediate possession, we put a *negative* to the Dutch claim of exclusion ... I shall leave this for Bencoolen in a few days, where I hope to remain quietly until we hear decidedly from Europe ...' – T. S. Raffles

Raffles must have known full well what wrath he had called

down upon his head. The livid Penang government character-ized his calm return to Bengkulu as 'like a man who sets a house on fire and then runs away'. But despite the crackle of a paper war with the Dutch and London, heavy with the thud of mortal memoranda, Raffles would not hear definitively from Europe for years. In the meantime, it might be expected that he would keep his head down. Not so. He was ready for another adventure.

15. Leaps and Bounds

'My attention has been drawn to the Island of Nias, which is opposite the settlement of Tapanooly and Natal, and on which the Resident has always maintained a small establishment.' – T. S. Raffles

You arrive nowadays by air in one of those small aircraft that preserve the sense of flying as logically unsustainable. Nias is 100 kilometres out into the Indian Ocean, and flying off into the open sea is still an act of faith. This is as far west as Indonesia goes. Beyond is ocean all the way to Africa.

Constructors of fanciful genealogy have chosen to see Nias as the primal home of the Malagasy before their sea migration to the coast of Africa. Their act of faith would have been considerably greater than my own. Although Raffles had Malagasy troops at Bengkulu, this was one historical reconstruction that was to elude even him.

There is an airport at Gunungsitoli with a few dispirited tourist knick-knacks under dusty glass, for nowadays Nias is become a place of tourists. Some 3,000 a year make it to the island. The Australians are immediately recognizable by their twelve-foot-long surfboards, sheathed in florid surfboard cosies, possibly sewn by loving mothers. The Japanese cluster in groups. They come in search of surf and sun and stone-age culture – a sort of Bali with rocks. Raffles was attracted for much the same reasons.

The chiefs had petitioned the Company for protection against slavers in 1811 and been refused. Since Nias was the source of most of the imported slaves in Bengkulu, Raffles, with his abolitionist principles, was more sympathetic. Also, Nias was a source of rice and Bengkulu was incapable of feeding itself. But it was the culture of Nias that drew him.

'I have a long account . . . of my discoveries in Pulo Nias. I believe I formerly told you that I was engaged in some arrangements for bringing that Island under British authority. I am now happy to say that I have succeeded; the people have unreservedly become the subjects of Great Britain. As this is an Island almost unknown, and I may at least claim the merit of first visiting and exploring its interior, some particulars may be not uninteresting . . .

The Island is in sight of Sumatra, and seen by most ships passing. I find the population to exceed 230,000 souls, on a surface of about 1,500 square miles, which gives a population of about 153 to the square mile; the country most highly cultivated, the soil rich, and the people the finest people, without exception, that I have met with in the East. They are fair, and a strong, athletic, active race; industrious, ingenious, and intelligent, and forming a striking contrast to their neighbours on the opposite coast of Sumatra. What has most astonished me is, the high degree (comparatively) of civilization to which they have attained, without communication from without. We have no trace, no idea whence or how the island became peopled; the people themselves say, a man and woman were first sent from heaven, from whom they are all descended. Their language, their habits, their character, and institutions, are strikingly different from all others with which we are acquainted.' – T. S. Raffles

*

'We are not interesting,' they tell you matter-of-factly at

Gunungsitoli. 'If you run you can just catch the bus to the south, to Lagundi. All tourists go to Lagundi.'

They are right. Gunungsitoli is the least attractive of towns. Wood and thatch are immediately picturesque, concrete and corrugated iron – such as here – are eyesores. Being insufficiently different from the West, they fail in their duty to be exotic, remote in time. They are slums because they are of the present.

The people know just what it is they are selling in Nias, a view of a savage yet noble past. To travel to Nias, the pamphlets urge us, is to travel in time. This can only be because we still arrange the world in an evolutionary sequence, just as Raffles did, from savagery to civilization. This is an absurd view – as if knowledge of the world is like a bucket that is simply filled or emptied up to a certain point. Such a perspective is riven with internal inconsistencies and it was these inconsistencies that generated the puzzles that, in turn, attracted Raffles. The natives were headhunters and slavers –clear marks of savagery – yet they had stone streets, baths and architecture – 'Roman' features, therefore clear signs of civilization. How could they be both civilized and savage?

The same question had hung over the Sumatran tribe, the Bataks. In the midst of the furore over the founding of Singapore, Raffles had diverted his ship to meet and question Bataks about their alleged cannibalism. What fascinated him here was that cannibalism appeared to be not some product of a wild fit of communal madness but a civic duty, required by regular legal process. The Bataks, moreover, bore the ultimate mark of civilization: they had books and their own writing system. Raffles was deeply baffled by this and invested time and energy in trying to overcome the enigma. He determined to visit them in person – with the Editor.

The only answer to his bafflement would have involved letting go of the notion of civilization itself and that he would never be prepared to do. For Raffles saw the British as bearers of civilization. This was their justification and their mission. Without this unexamined notion, he could not have gone on. So Nias challenged him and he was dimly aware that this was so, but he never truly rose to meet that challenge.

*

Telukdalam was the chief port in Raffles's day. It was with the chiefs here that he signed a treaty. Later, Krakatoa (west not east of Java, as the film moguls would have it) would erupt and wipe it from the map with a huge tidal wave, as the memory of British presence has been eradicated by the overlay of Dutch occupation.

Again they will not allow you from the bus.

'No,' they say with gentle firmness. 'We have told you. We are not interesting. You must go to Lagundi.'

It is striking how quickly an official route is established. Not to submit to it means you have not 'done' a place. You have not really been there; your passport is unstamped. To digress from it is to be awkward or eccentric. And so tourism builds up mutual caricatures. It narrows the mind wonderfully.

They finally push you off at a crossroads in the middle of nowhere.

'No, no. You cannot stay. You must get off. Lagundi.'

Gentle brown hands hustle you off and deposit luggage at your feet. They smile. They wave. You are left wrapped in the terror of strange places.

There is a cough. You turn and there are gentlemen of a certain age, grave and reserved, pointing to their motorbikes.

'Taxi?'

*

'The Nias slaves are highly valued throughout the East, for their industry, ingenuity and fidelity; and observation has

shown that these are no less the characteristics of the people in their native country. The intercourse with them has given us a most favourable impression of their native character, and of their capabilities of improvement. Notwithstanding the disadvantages of a secluded situation, the absence of all instruction and example, and the insecurity arising from a state of internal division, they have drawn forth, by their industry, the resources of their fertile country to a greater degree than has yet been effected by any of their neighbours on the coast of Sumatra.'
– Dr Jack and Mr Prince, *Account of the Island of Nias*

*

The bay at Lagundi is a broad sweep of sand. Out to sea, huge waves are crashing against the rocks and coral. Within the reef, the sea is a warm bath. A line of huts made of thatched palm leaf stretches away on stilts, around their feet a rabble of bars and eating-houses, offering spaghetti and toasted sandwiches. The accents are heavily Australian, sheep-jawed men and big-boned women chewing on broken vowels. Everywhere are surfboards and those absurd cosies again.

A woman passer-by stops to consider me with distaste.

'Aw, Jeez, not another bloody surfer!'

Considering my physique, this is hardly likely. I look at the terrifying waves, big as houses, cruising by the other side of the coral.

'No proper waves for a week,' she says, 'only this piddling stuff and there's not enough to go round.'

'Actually,' I say, 'I don't surf.' Relief and contempt sweep over her face.

'A Pom! They've brought you to the wrong part. Here's for Aussies. The European Quarter's over there.' She hooks a thumb at the other end of the beach and I set off with my luggage only to be overtaken by my motorbike chauffeur.

'I am sorry. I thought you were Australian. I will take you where you belong.'

He explains the difference. In the European Quarter rooms are Rp. 5,000 (£1.50) a night and you can swim, as there is no surf. In the Australian section are the waves. They know an Australian may drink five or even ten bottles of beer a night, so they may give the room entirely free and make their money from the beer.

The European Quarter is basic, small bamboo huts that the wind blows straight through, water from the well. Everything is still owned and run by village people. Fishermen wander by and sell you fish and squid that locals will cook for you on the beach of white sand. The loudest noise is the rustle of palm-fronds. It is recognizably the Gauguin fantasy made flesh.

The tourists are a mixed bunch, young travellers, middle-aged schoolteachers, a wicked woman who sleeps with the locals two at a time, a gnarled, tortoise-necked spinster called Maud who wears sandals and a leather hat. They have in common a distaste for package holidays and seem unaware that the locals are packaging *them*.

Everywhere are children, small, brown, consciously endearing. In the morning, they come and sell you hot bread rolls filled with sweet 'cocknut' and pay you back with dynamite smiles. Children are among the first to acclimatize to tourism, and these have all developed hard-luck stories for the consumption of foreigners, speaking easily of calamitous death and hideous disease. One does an outstanding performance as a deaf-mute, producing strangulated squeaks and agonized gestures with an extended hand of supplication.

'An Australian man wanted to adopt me,' he confides. 'But I think he wanted to sell me in Sydney so I let him know I could talk and he ran away.'

It is easy to blame tourism for all that is unattractive, praise traditional culture for all that is picturesque. Tourism's carica-ture extends even to the economic relations between West and East.

'You are rich,' the locals tell you. 'White people never work.

We know, we have seen. You just lie around all day, get drunk, fight with each other. *We* work all day, every day.'

But the pornographic sandcastles built by the children on the beach probably owe more to the shapes naturally suggested by the coconuts they use as moulds than to any outside influence. On Nias, after all, there is almost no topless bathing but the traditional sculpture glories in the erect male member.

'On the subject of religion, the people of Pulo Nias have but few ideas; they acknowledge a supreme being, whom they call Sumban Quit or the Lord of Heaven, but they had no distinct notions concerning him. Wooden images are to be found in all their houses which are regarded as a kind of lares or protecting household gods, but no worship is addressed to them. They are rather considered as representatives or memorials of their ancestors, for whom they have a great reverence. A belief in charms is common and every man carries a bundle of these attached to his kris . . .' – Dr Jack and Mr Prince, *Account of the Island of Nias*

The Raffles Collection of the British Museum includes three such carvings. Two are standing figures, identical to those peddled on the beaches to modern tourists. They look quite new, phalluses unbevelled by time, as if plucked from a modern ethno-tat stall, and must have been produced specially for Raffles's delegate – probably Dr Jack. The other is an old seated figure with a more convincing patination. Nowadays, such carvings tend towards gigantism, their ability to impress tourists relying on sheer size.

One other item is included, a necklace of fine-grained coconut shell and brass, as worn by the ancestral carvings.

*

One morning two Japanese surfers are delivered to the European Quarter in error. The Nias apartheid has broken

221

down yet again. In Indonesia, as in South Africa, it is the children of the Rising Sun who resist categorization. The Indonesian beach urchins rush up to them, climbing on their knees, stroking them the way people do here when being friendly. The Japanese are almost in tears. They are not used to being *touched*.

'We have surfed around the world,' Ito tells me proudly. 'See.'

He shows his photo album. All the pictures have been taken by pointing the camera straight out to sea at the encephalograph of the waves. There is no land or human figure to give scale. The only difference between the pictures is in the density of the little, grey squiggles – a surfer's view of the universe.

'You speak Indonesian?' Ito asks. 'Would you help me? I want to buy a souvenir, a necklace. There is a man who sells them. Would you come with me?'

We set off for the house of the dealer, a man of oleaginous sleekness who flaunts himself and his goods before the sun-bathing tourists. His is an economy of seduction. We sit on his veranda, handle his wares absently, offer prices offhandedly. He produces a coconut-shell necklace.

'Antique,' he declares. 'The Japanese stole most of the good stuff in the war, but this was hidden.'

There seems no need to translate that to Ito. I hold the necklace. It is warm. The day before, I had visited one of the villages. The royal treasurer had been kind enough to show me the royal heirlooms, including such a necklace.

'Always look at the fastening,' he had warned. 'The metal should be worn on one side but sharp on the other. Sometimes they file them down to look old. But one thing the forgers cannot fake. Touch it!'

The necklace was icy cold, though the day was hot. The treasurer looked at my face and nodded.

'Cold like the grave.'

This necklace, on the other hand, is warm, therefore new. Ito and I demur, disdain the necklace, condescend to look at it again, sigh, look bored, haggle and finally buy it and some other odds and ends for a modest price.

As we descend the ladder of the house, I turn to see the dealer pressing a banknote into Ito's hand. My first thought is that I have botched the negotiations, that the price we paid was so absurdly high that even the dealer's conscience is troubling him to the point of offering a rebate. Then I hear him mutter, 'That's enough. I can't afford any more for you,' and the penny drops. If a South-East Asian turns up with a European, he must be the latter's employee or guide, whatever pretence is made to the contrary. He is giving Ito his commission.

*

'They dwell in excellent and commodious houses, the interior of which are laid out with neatness, not devoid of elegance; streets are regularly formed and paved, with avenues of trees, and stone stairs to the pinnacles of different hills, on which their villages are mostly situated, enbosomed in the richest foliage imaginable. The slopes of the hills and the valleys are covered with one continued sheet of the richest cultivation, and there is not a forest tree standing in the Island: all have disappeared before the force of industry. To each village are attached stone baths, appropriated to the different sexes, which remind us of Roman luxuries. They wear a profusion of gold and other ornaments, than which nothing can be conceived more original. I have a large collection now before me, and only wish I could at once transfer them to Park Lane.' – T. S. Raffles

*

The villages admired by Raffles are still there. But in Nias, tourism is the last in a long line of withering outside influences that have destroyed the culture Raffles revered. Foreign governments suppressed the system of alliances and feuds. Missionaries smothered the religion in a blanket of Christianity. What is left is a ceremonial that is rightly termed 'brain-dead', for tourism often preserves the empty outer forms that have lost their meaning. The ancient houses with their rich ornamentation are as impressive and irrelevant to everyday life as English cathedrals. The stone streets, the carved rock seats and slabs are testaments to a stone-working technique that is gone for ever. But Nias are still excellent carvers of wood. So when you get to those villages 'hidden in the hills' the locals are already struggling from their houses with the new antique carvings before the buses and jeeps have disgorged their camera-clicking hordes through the gate.

An important local ritual involved young men performing gymnastic feats over stone vaulting horses topped with spears. Nowadays, as the tourists arrive, a schoolboy is already slipping into his red shorts ('They look better on camera') and offering two leaps for Rp. 12,000 – sorry, no spears. The children who practise surfing on tree trunks in the morning will be plucked off to learn the war-dance in the afternoons. They are needed to fill in the crowd scenes in the shows put on for visitors.

Yet culture is not the same as ceremonial. When you talk to Nias people, they speak matter-of-factly of their battles with witches and sea-spirits. There *is* an intriguingly different view of the world there, but not one that tourists can photograph.

*

In Java, Raffles had argued for free medical care for the inhabitants as part of the responsibility of 'paternal care' assumed by the British. This would include the training of native personnel and campaigns to introduce vaccination against smallpox and eradicate syphilis. It was one of Raffles's paper projects that never came to anything. Historians have noted that the plan fell flat owing to mortality amongst the medical staff. They have not gone on to the doubtless proper conclusion that this demonstrated that such medical help as was available at that time was largely useless. In Bengkulu, the project would resurface.

On his trips in the province, Raffles was willing to offer vaccination. An early effort had resulted in many deaths, but the effect of this was largely overcome by Raffles's own, much-adored children being vaccinated in the market-place. The urge to supply medical care . . .

'Sorry to bother you, Mister . . .'

I looked up from the page I was writing. It was the little boy who sold the coconut rolls that I ate for breakfast. He held up a leg and looked as pitiful as a lame puppy. . . . 'Have you got anything for my leg?'

It was an ingrowing sore, eating into his ankle. Scars all around it spoke of previous infections, now overcome. I sat him down and cleaned it, spread it with antibiotic cream, overlaid all with a bright-pink waterproof plaster, patted into place. He winced but made no complaint.

'Have you got any pills for it?' he asked, looking very small.

I gave him a vitamin pill from the bottle I had brought but not bothered to take after the third day.

He looked up with melting brown eyes. 'Haven't you got an injection you could give me?'

'No injections.' I felt guilty at having no injections. Why did I have no injections?

He gave me a hug, then thanked me more formally and shook hands with great ceremony. His friends admired the big plaster as he went down the ladder, limping judiciously. They clustered round and began to exhibit wounds as claims to attention. Gently but firmly, they were repelled.

The plaster would stick until the first time he went in the sea, which would be in about ten minutes. I had really done nothing for him, but *he* had offered *me* certain proof of my own benevolence and selflessness. Thus it was with Raffles.

'Sir Stamford was anxious to do the utmost possible good for such an Island and such a people ... The Court of Directors "had no hesitation in declaring that his proceedings in regard to Pulo Nias were deserving of their decided reprehension. And they were inclined to visit him with some severe mark of their displeasure for the steps he had taken," and threatened to remove him from his government.' – Lady Raffles, *Memoir*

16. Dust to Dust

'God willing, we hope to depart from this for England, if not in 1823, certainly in 1824 ... Neither my health nor that of Lady Raffles is very good; I never was strong and during my first residence in India, the climate made a considerable inroad on my constitution ... I have seen enough of power and wealth to know that, however agreeable to the propensities of our nature, there is more real happiness in domestic quiet and repose, when blessed with a competence, than in all the fancied enjoyments of the great and rich.' – T. S. Raffles

After the founding of Singapore, there was a new stress upon the pleasures of the domestic sphere. Raffles had his country plantation, Permatang Balam, 'the abode of peace', his four children, his wife. He shunned international politics and reverted to his favourite model of a colony as an extended gentleman's estate, founded an agricultural society, planted coffee himself. We have glimpses of him striding the fields building a sugar refinery from drawings in the encyclopedia tucked under his arm or proselytizing his neighbours on the virtues of a new homemade fertilizer. He founded another journal, largely devoted to practical matters. British colonial administration after Raffles would always have an earnest air of applied domestic science about it, government by Women's Institute.

'Perhaps this was one of the most happy periods in Sir

Stamford's life; politically he had obtained the object that he felt so necessary for the good of his country. He was beloved by all those under his immediate control, who united in showing him every mark of respect and attachment, and many were bound to him by ties of gratitude for offices of kindness, or private acts of benevolence and assistance which he delighted to exercise towards them.

The settlement, like many other small societies, was divided into almost as many parties as there were families on his first arrival; but these differences were soon healed and quieted and a general interchange of good offices had succeeded. The natives and chiefs appreciated the interests which he took in their improvement and placed implicit reliance upon his opinion and counsel. The consciousness of being loved is a delightfully happy feeling and Sir Stamford acknowledged with thankfulness at this time that every wish of his heart was gratified.

Uninterrupted health had prevailed in his family, his children were his pride and delight and they had already imbibed from him those tastes it was his pleasure to cultivate; this will not be wondered at, even at their early age, when it is added that two young tigers and a bear were for some time in the children's appartments, under the charge of their attendant without being confined in cages, and it was rather a curious scene to see the children, the bear, the tigers, a blue mountain bird and a favourite cat all playing together, the parrot's beak being the only object of awe to all the party.

Perhaps so few people in a public station led so simple a life; his mode of passing his time in the country has already been described. When he was in Bencoolen he rose early and delighted in driving into the villages, inspecting the plantations and encouraging the industry of the people; at nine a party assembled at breakfast but separated immediately afterwards; and he wrote, read, studied natural history, chemistry and geology, superintended the draughtsmen, of whom he had constantly five or six employed in a verandah, and always had his children with him as he went from one pursuit to another visiting his beautiful and extensive aviary as well as the extraordinary collection of animals that were always domesticating in the house.

At four he dined and seldom alone, as he considered the settlement but as a family of which he was the head. Immediately after dinner all the party drove out and the evening was spent in reading and music and conversation. He never had any game of amusement in his house. After the party had dispersed, he was fond of walking out with the Editor and enjoying the delicious coolness of the night land wind and a moon whose beauty those only who have been in tropical climates can judge of; so clear and penetrating are its rays that many fear them as much as the glare of the sun.

Amidst these numerous sources of enjoyment, however, Sir Stamford never forgot that the scene was too bright to continue unclouded and often gently warned the Editor not to expect to retain all the blessings God in his bounty had heaped upon them at this time but to feel that such happiness once enjoyed ought to shed a bright ray over the future however dark and trying it might become.' – Lady Raffles, *Memoir*

*

Madu ditunda, read the caption, 'honey postponed'. The picture showed a pouty, sluttish-looking Western woman in her bra, sitting up in bed and looking annoyed. A man, his shirt open to reveal a hairy chest, sat on the other side of the bed and hung his head in shame. The flaps of his shirt hung in sympathy. The all-male crowd gaped at it in horror.

The pedlar held the picture aloft like a priest the eucharist and turned slowly round so the people behind him could see it too.

'This,' he announced, twirling the microphone professionally like a Las Vegas crooner, 'is what comes of sex before marriage. All you young men are threatened by male weakness. Scientific research has proved that the male should have intercourse three times a week to be healthy, but never before the age of twenty-five and never after the age of sixty. The result of excess is deformed children and impotence. You, clear off!'

He pointed at a lad of about twelve squatting in the front row of the audience, wide-eyed, taking it all in. The boy scowled and slouched reluctantly away. Two schoolboys, a year or two older, clung to each other willowishly and basked in the implicit confirmation of their maturity.

There followed a lengthy presentation on sexual disease, impotence, homosexuality and sterility, lavishly illustrated with photographs of hideously deformed or ulcerated white genitalia. It was accompanied with rap music fed through the loudspeakers, the whine of bony-ankled ghetto macho, over which the man shouted as if heroically defying heckling.

'Europeans fornicate with their own children,' the man declared roundly, glared at me and held up an article on child abuse, 'which is why they have AIDS.'

One of the schoolboys whispered in his friend's ear, bumped his backside against the other's groin, looked at me and giggled. His friend looked at me and giggled too.

'Their women are like dogs on heat. Their men cannot control them so they become impotent . . .'

The crowd looked at me questioningly, in good-natured puzzlement. Why, they wondered, did I not keep my wife in order? Why had I allowed myself to be made impotent? I began to feel this was excessively personal.

'. . . Which is why whites have drink and drugs. But *we* have none of these problems. *We* have Islam and these pills.'

He held out a handful of matt-black capsules, vaguely evocative of rubber, leather and bondage, or maybe the understated power of military hardware – though perhaps such associations were only a manifestation of my own non-Islamic perversity.

'These pills are compounded from over a hundred essential ingredients from the densest forests of Sumatra and the rocky coasts of Nusa Tenggara, rare sandalwood oil, seeds from the Devil's sirihbox . . .' Raffles's grotesque parasitic flower, harnessed, then, to modern marital insecurities.

'. . . The normal price is 2,000 rupiahs each, but today, not 1,000, not 500, only 200 rupiahs apiece! But you must promise me this . . .' He looked warily round the circle of onlookers. '. . . No one must take these pills till he is safely at home with his wife. The urge will be so strong, the effect so POWERFUL, you won't know what hit you! It will be like this.' He pulled out a plastic model of a monk. When you pressed the top of his bald head, the robe flew up to reveal an erection. 'Wah! There you go!' Press, erect. Press, erect. He threw back his head and guffawed, showing broken teeth, then suddenly serious. 'These must be used in a godly way, not for the encouragement of vice. So I won't sell them to unmarried boys or men whose wives are dead or foreigners or transvestites.'

A sizeable number of men seemed not to fall in any of these categories and pressed forward waving money. They emerged from the scrum triumphant, secreted the pills in their trousers and sidled off in search of honey to be now more promptly delivered.

*

It was all too good to last. Quite suddenly, Leopold, the adored eldest son, was dead. In the space of six months Raffles lost his three eldest children. He and the Editor were gravely ill. They were frantic to preserve the life of their youngest child. Raffles declared himself almost mad with grief, heartbroken. As the doctors slowly poisoned him with mercury treatments, only two concerns could even momentarily hold his attention: Singapore and the collection of plants and animals to be shipped to England. He packed off his infant daughter to England post-haste, together with a shipment of Bengkulu spices, both fragile tokens of hope for the future. But the decision was taken. He must return to England or die. Only then did he realize that he was a sort of prisoner. To resign he needed the approval of at least thirteen of the Court of Directors of Calcutta.

*

Raffles's house is still there, down the hill from the fort at Bengkulu. At least they tell you it was his house. It is not an obviously English structure, but perhaps a century of earth-quakes and Dutch rebuilding can change a house considerably. An added complexity is the existence of two Government Houses in the town. But still they tell you this was Raffles's house and a sense of history, like a lost puppy, will attach itself to any minimally acceptable object.

The walls are massive stone, mocked by the intrusive roots of creeper that tunnel and split their solidities. Natural History is reclaiming it. Outside the door where carriages once wheeled to a halt sit Bengkulu labourers, faces wrapped in cloths like steamed puddings. The coach-houses to either side have become salt warehouses, *gudang garam* – the name – not Raffles brand – of the clove cigarettes I offer them. The irony is not lost. It must be, to them, an old joke but they are polite enough to laugh at it. *Gudang Garam*, yes, yes. A sign declares the property to belong to the Indonesian Department of Justice.

'You cannot come in,' says an officious foreman with a clipboard. 'Government property.'

'Leave him alone,' says one of the labourers with a flexing of authoritative shoulder muscles. 'Come and sit by me.' He digs me in the ribs. 'The house is full of priceless antique furniture. He does not want you to see it.' We laugh. A glance at the interior shows collapsing roofbeams, no stairs, rusting ironwork, cartoons of human figures engaged in fumbling sexual acts, a smell of urine. Someone has planted orderly rows of maize inside what must have been the dining-room, now open to the sky. Raffles was always for encouraging agriculture. Was this the place that was the haunt of tiger and parrot and Mr Silvio, the pet monkey who sported trousers?

'Do you want to buy the house?'

'You would have to do it up a little first.'

He looks at the house with a long appraising glance and puffs on his cigarette. 'No,' he says, shaking his head and looking along the line of blind, gaping windows, 'it's not a house to live in any more.' He shivers. 'Too many ghosts. Even this time of day you feel it.'

*

'Whilst the Editor was almost overwhelmed with grief for the loss of this favourite child, unable to bear the sight of her other children – unable to bear even the light of day – humbled upon her couch with a feeling of misery, – she was addressed by a poor, ignorant, uninstructed native woman of the lowest class (who had been employed about the nursery), in terms of reproach not to be forgotten. "I am come because you have been here many days shut up in a dark room, and no one dares to come near you. Are you not ashamed to grieve in this manner, when you ought to be thanking God for giving you the most beautiful child that ever was seen? Were you not the envy of every body? Did any one ever see him, or speak of him, without admiring him; and instead of letting this child continue in this world till he should be worn out with trouble and sorrow, has not God taken him to heaven in all his beauty?

What would you have more? for shame, leave off weeping and
let me open a window."' – Lady Raffles, *Memoir*

That window was, more and more, to be Singapore, a city
named after the Singha or lion, initially without lions but
cursed with a plague of rats. They killed the rats and there
was a plague of poisonous centipedes. No one worried about
biblical precedent.

Bengkulu was now a sub-plot. The real story lay elsewhere.
Bengkulu was Raffles's penance, but he would not leave it as
he had found it. He had set up schools for the local children.
There had been a reform of the administration. While in Java,
Raffles had chiefly reduced power, here he determined to
bolster it.

'In order to render an uncivilized people capable of enjoying
full liberty they must feel the weight of authority and must
become acquainted with the mutual relations of society . . .
Power we do and have possessed; we have employed it in the
most arbitrary of all modes, in the exaction of forced services
and in the monopoly of the produce of the country . . . We
have destroyed the power of the native Chiefs; both reason
and humanity would urge us to take the management into our
own hands and to repair the mischief of a hundred years by
affording them a regular and organized government . . .
Tyrants seldom want an excuse and in becoming a despot I am
desirous to give you mine . . .'

The out-stations of the province, Tapanuli, Indrapura, etc.,
were no longer to be leased out to the highest bidder or
administered by the Company directly but to be run by Buginese regents as the Buginese Corps was to be disbanded. Revenue was to come from land revenue, as in his reform in
Java, but in fact, there was no one to collect or oversee the

new system. It was a cosmetic reform, on paper only. Native chiefs were not paid their salaries nor were the producers reliably paid for their pepper by the new Buginese overlords Raffles had imposed on them. It is hard to know how far Raffles deceived himself in this as in his reforms in Java. There is an increasing cynicism in his reports. By now, he knows no one bothers to read them. His thoughts are already of home.

Raffles's promotion of spice, sugar, potatoes and coffee was another disaster. Despite the use of convict labour, i.e. *de facto* slavery, it was never economic. The soil was unsuitable and a huge investment in resources and labour was required to coax fruit from it, fertilizer, a little shelter for each tree. Moreover, the Company had crammed its warehouses with cheap spices while it had the run of the Moluccas during the Napoleonic Wars. As a result, Raffles was paying 4s. 7½d. a pound for nutmeg in Bengkulu while it was selling in London for 3s. a pound. The Company were appalled to discover that Raffles by 1824 had half a million coffee trees in Bengkulu, every single one of which was costing them money. It is not to be wondered at that they were unconvinced by his claims that the new settlement of Singapore would make money. It would be a reversal of their 150 years' experience of the area and the whole tendency of Raffles's working life.

17. Almost My Only Child

Singapore gleams in the national neatness of . . . the Malays?
the Chinese? the Tamils? No . . . the Singaporeans. The phantom graffitist of Bogor would here be quite without occupation. Here all graffiti are government approved.

New Year in Singapore. Outside, no snow deep and crisp
and even but air still and damp and stifling. The normal
evening breeze has failed to appear. Lightning flickers over
towards the east like a defective neon tube. From the tenth-
floor balcony you can see the lights of the gloriously ramshackle Indonesian blocks of flats across the water. A hundred
televisions are radiating Malay Islamic virtue from Malaysia
as well as local Chinese pizazz and the gurgle of Tamil down
into the stairwell. Raffles kept the different races apart under
their own leaders; modern policy jumbles them up.

The Indian family down the hall are cooking a sauce that
exudes musky heat. Its insidious aroma penetrates locked
doors and windows and provides an, as it were, smelltrack for
a public-service advertisement urging Chinese parents not to
beat and scream at their children every time they see them.
My Malay hosts nod in approval. Yes, yes, Chinese indeed are
like that – that woman on the next floor, for example – not
like philoprogenitive Malays. Content brown children are
hefted on to laps in proof, clutching storybooks nowadays
written in English. One looks at me.

'Uncle,' he says, 'will you help me with my Mandarin homework?' I demur. Modern youth, I feel, have got beyond me in their wisdom.

'Then perhaps you will help me with my English essay. I have to write a story about my favourite toy.'

I think of the story of Bung Karno and the spinning top, or maybe Harsono and Bung Karno's crashed bicycle. It will pass easily into Malay cultural terms. Tomorrow. But now it is time for the big programme to start.

*

The founding of Singapore mobilized all the factions within the Company's orbit in totally predictable ways. The Dutch rattled sabres and shrieked of perfidy and the danger to the general peace in Europe. Raffles bombarded all and sundry with letters expressing wide-eyed surprise that any doubts should be entertained about either the legality or desirability of what he had done. The government and Company were engulfed in an initial wave of blind rage and foot-stamping that gradually weakened and gave way to dithering as they began to smell a profit. Lord Hastings maintained a blandly shifty façade, a series of non-committal 'Oh reallys?' like a man woken from a deep sleep with shocking news. It looked as if his promissory notes of protection for Raffles would go unredeemed. Also slow to rouse was British national chauvinism in the Eastern seas, having been preoccupied throughout living memory with drubbing the French. Now, in newspaper reports, it began to make itself heard like the irritable trumpetings of some monster stirring offstage. Raffles knew that the first few months were vital. If he could only hang on to the colony and show some black figures in his accounts, it would survive.

Curiously, it was the Penang government who forced Hastings into active support of Raffles. They were delighted that the Golden Sword had really gone too far this time and settled back comfily to watch his downfall with undisguised glee. Bannerman, the Governor, wrote letters of shocked sympathy to the Dutch, sneeringly refused troops and money to the Singapore garrison and addressed Hastings in the smug terms of the school sneak, confiding that he had limited assistance to advising them how best to evacuate the settlement.

Hastings rapped him furiously over the knuckles, threatening to hold him responsible for any harm that might befall the infant colony, and Bannerman collapsed. 'I have received a lesson which shall teach me how I again presume to offer opinions as long as I live.' His words were prophetic. He dispatched money and troops to support Singapore and – shortly after – died.

*

The achievements of Singapore were not to be detailed, merely celebrated. The New Year programme was utterly slick, West Coast American hype – the theme a funky song 'Stand Up for Singapore!' presented by Chinese bump-and-grind dancers rotating their groins in strobe lights and pink smoke. The history of the nation was presented in a pageant, but history began about 1960 with the rampant disorder of the late colonial period – the British, it must be admitted, could never run Singapore. Clenched fists and waving banners – the gestures of imperial seediness – were the signs of that time, now firmly allocated to the past. Then the present age dawned. A sort of rosy glow and warbling heavenly host ushered in poly-ethnic progress and harmony as the voice of Lee Kuan Yew, Prime Minister and architect of the Singapore state, descended from on high to intone a blessing and gently urge the young to work even harder.

We switched to the Malaysian channel. The old cricket ground in front of the Royal Selangor Club had been temporarily cleansed of its patrolling transvestites and equipped with an only capriciously functioning laser display. A promotional pop video extolled the government. Not funk here but West Coast warbling, every note bent and breathy with its weight of sincerity. Plenty of photo-opportunities for the Prime Minister to be viewed, smiling, against the backdrop of the year's successes, in the company of triumphant sportsmen and deferential foreign politicians. 'A year of economic development extends before us,' must be one of the all-time hard lines to warble like a love lyric. But they managed it.

*

'Here all is life and activity; it would be difficult to name a place on the face of the globe with brighter prospects or more pleasant satisfaction. In little more than three years it has risen from an insignificant fishing village to a large and prosperous town, containing at least ten thousand inhabitants of all nations actively engaged in commercial pursuits which afford to each and all a handsome livelihood and abundant profit. There are no complaints here of want of employment, no deficiency of rents, or dissatisfaction at taxes. Land is rapidly rising in value and in respect of the present number of inhabitants we have reason to expect that we shall have at least ten times as many before many years have passed. This may be considered as the simple but almost magic result of that perfect freedom of Trade which it has been my good fortune to establish . . .

I am at present engaged in establishing a constitution for Singapore, the principles of which will I hope ensure its prosperity . . . In Java I had to remodel and in doing so to remove the rubbish and encumbrances of two centuries of Dutch maladministration. Here I have an easier task and the task is new. In Java, I had to look principally to the agricultural interests, and the commercial only so far as they were concerned with them; here on the contrary commerce is everything, agriculture only in its infancy. The people are different as well as their pursuits.' – T. S. Raffles

*

The signs everywhere proclaimed Singapore to be twenty-five years old, a neater age, it is true, than 171. Granny was lying about her age, posing as a go-go dancer. Raffles was unmentioned, having been shifted with the rest of the clutter from history to pre-history. Singapore is depicted as rising clean and pure from the blood and ashes of the failed Malaysian Federation of the sixties, when the British tried to unite all their former colonies into a single state. But the Malays and the Chinese had warred on each other and the Chinese had been unwilling to be mere managers of another's emporium. To found your *own* shop is the Chinese way. So Singapore had been cut adrift and expected to founder. Instead it had floated ever higher.

In the streets was one vast party, amplified pop music throbbing like a huge heart. Singapore was young, esculently clean and wholesome, well-behaved and – yes – happy. In the main business area, amongst the teetering towers of Singapore's new prosperity, a crowd of some half a million were forgathered for this huge event of dancing and chaste frolic. They pursued each other in conga lines up and down Orchard Road, singing along with a song, 'I want to be rich/I feel sexy.'

In Britain there would have been drunkenness, muggings, deaths. Here the worst that happened was an outbreak of exuberant bottom-pinching and an overflowing of litter bins. Everywhere were Malay policemen, tokens of control, their Malayness the sign that they too were subject to a higher power. It is one of the Malay jokes of Singapore that all males have to report for military service. 'It just happens,' they explain, 'that the Chinese get taught to fly fighters, bombers and drive tanks, while all the Malays end up sitting in the local police station. There is no policy. It just happens.'

I wandered down to the government area, bottom unpinched, where Raffles is supposed to have first landed. The façade of the Raffles Hotel stood off to one side, interior ripped out by Japanese machines, a metaphor for the new profitable and sanitized nation that was emerging – a tropical Switzerland. A gleaming shopping-centre of teetering glass and brass, Raffles City comes complete with artificial waterfall and Chinese millionaires in white Rolls-Royces. The top floor is called Bengkulu and has copious pot plants. One of the windows has Muslim paraphernalia, Koranic texts etched on glass with a saccharine image of Mecca surrounding a clock. A Chinese girl was using her reflection in the Koran to frizz out her hair.

A towering temple to Mothercare and Habitat has been built on the sea bed, and traffic swoops out over the waves around it to be fed back through the new, efficient highways. On the Esplanade, a young Chinese sat eating a hamburger in the dark, crooning the latest political jingle and tapping his be-trainered foot, 'One people, *one* nation, *wu-hu-u-n* Si-i-in-gapore, Boom! boom!'

*

Farquar, British Resident at Malacca, had been chosen to nurse the infant Singapore. Raffles was quite often a poor judge of men and Farquar would prove himself arrogant, unconscientious, oversensitive to insult, in fact a reincarnation of Gillespie in Java. And as with Gillespie, there could be no compromise, but rather pettiness, peevishness and pique while Raffles demolished Farquar's Singapore and rebuilt it according to his own ideas, tipping hills into the sea, building a botanical garden, drawing the lines between the races, framing laws and ideology and finally dismissing Farquar – which he had no power to do. The administration of the colony became a thing of high farce, a rainshower of petulant memoranda as Farquar, his withdrawal often announced, doggedly refused to budge. Their disputes were sometimes on matters of weight, slavery for example, but more often about minor courtesies and quibbles of dress and protocol. In the end, Raffles had him marched off under escort.

In all this Raffles was no angel. Throughout his career he had been incapable of handling opposition. His authority with Europeans was tentative, as though it had no depth of root. They must love him or leave him. He was not above sneering at Farquar's Malay wife and the children by her he had acknowledged. 'The Malay connexion', he termed them archly. And throughout it all he still found time to correspond with the experts of the world about squirrels, mermaids and giant yams.

*

Levels beneath levels. By the harbour, buildings of colonial pomp cowered under the skyscraper offices of banks. Javanese migrant workers, with only a toe-hold in Singapore's prosperity, hung around under the pillars, looking like urban degenerates but really only behaving as harmlessly as in an Indonesian village square. They had come to build the Japanese-designed underground railway, and spoke of military structures secreted under the stations.

Across the road stood Raffles, a wallflower at the party, in duplicate. Two identical statues, one white, one black, milk and chocolate, a Manichaean universe. Take your choice, sir, madam. He was thin, urgent, reflective. Knee-breeches and a frock coat. As in Westminster Abbey, he trampled on papers, this time interpreted as the map of Singapore. The face was that of a decent schoolmaster with a certain simplicity of beliefs. The sculptor, of course, had never seen Raffles.

*

Singapore mushroomed. It rocketed with tropical exuberance, swiftly eclipsing Penang and Malacca. Its land was snapped up, warehouses built, labour flocked to the city even before the Company announced it would retain the settlement. That did not happen for another five years. Important in this was its status as a port of India. This meant that merchants could transship material from China at Singapore and so evade the Company's monopoly on direct trade between China and Europe. For once Raffles was able to take genuine delight in the figures he amassed, the hundreds of ships, the thousands of tons, the millions of dollars. Raffles termed it pathetically, 'almost my only child'. Yet there is an irony that spelt the end of this form of commercial imperialism. For all the fortunes Singapore would make and regardless of its net value to Britain, it seems that it still cost the Company money.

*

'We have lately built a small bungalow on Singapore Hill, where, though the height is inconsiderable, we find a great difference of climate. Nothing can be more interesting and beautiful than the view from this spot. I am happy to say the change has had a very beneficial effect on my health, which has been better the last fortnight than I have known it for two years before. The tombs of the Malay kings are however close at hand; and I have settled that if it is my fate to die here, I shall take my place among them; this will, at any rate, be better than leaving one's bones at Bencoolen.' – T. S. Raffles

There is a plan to rebuild that bungalow to mark the nation's anniversary. It will not, of course, be the same, but enhanced, a thing of solid mahogany floorboards with countersunk brass screws. Memorials were much in Raffles's mind at this time when he felt himself so near to death and the only reality was the pounding pain in his head, the slow growth of the hungry tumour that would ultimately kill him. So is Singapore that memorial? It does, after all, embody the spirit of free trade, the search for excellence, the faith that commerce is ennobling, the composite creed that Raffles held to. But is that enough? Raffles gives us the answer himself, in what is far and away the finest piece of writing he ever produced, a 10,000-word memoir on the founding of the Singapore Institution.

'If commerce brings wealth to our shores, it is the spirit of literature and philanthropy that teaches us how to employ it for the noblest purposes. It is this that has made Britain go forth among nations, strong in her native light, to dispense blessings to all around her. If the time shall come when her Empire shall have passed away, these monuments of her virtue will endure, when her triumphs shall have become an empty name. Let it still be the boast of Britain to write her name in characters of light; let her not be remembered as the tempest whose course was desolation, but as the gale of spring, reviving the slumbering seeds of mind, and calling them to life from the winter of ignorance and oppression. Let the Sun of Britain arise on these Islands, not to wither and scorch them in its fierceness but like that of her own genial skies whose mild and benignant influence is hailed and blessed by all who feel its beams.'

The Institution was to be the redemption of a pledge taken by Raffles, many years ago, when he visited a Koranic school in Malacca with Munchi Abdullah. The boys were screaming out their lesson in Arabic, as they still do today. Did no one teach them their own native Malay, asked Raffles, their own history and literature? The teacher testily said no one did. Raffles determined that one day this would be put right. It was the confrontation of two different definitions of education, the Islamic and the Western, and Raffles held that it was Western education that would lead the local people forward to a higher state of civilization, 'towards the light', and justify the British presence.

Nothing shows the admirable optimism of Raffles more than the local reaction to his purple prose. Munchi Abdullah gives us an account of the founding of the noble Institution at which the address was read:

> 'Now when Mr Raffles had announced that the East India Company would subscribe $4,000 and that he himself would give $2,000 on his own account he asked with a smile what the Sultan would give: shall it be $2,000 also? But he replied with a loud exclamation and a laugh that he was a poor man, so where would he get $2,000? To this Mr Raffles argued that he should give more than he gave, as the undertaking was of immediate utility to the Malays, and greatly more so than to the English; but let it be a thousand dollars.'

Within a very few years, Raffles's Institution was defunct, its building collapsing, its land and funding clawed back. Those who succeeded him lacked his sacerdotal awe of education. It is said that Crawfurd, the next Resident, revenged himself on Raffles's project for a bad review Raffles gave his book. There is no end to the malevolence of authors.

The Institution was not, it should be noted, an original idea. It was clearly based on the Fort William College founded by Lord Minto in India, an institution dedicated to the study of Indian language and culture. Raffles even published reports of its Speech Day in his *Government Java Gazette*. But original or not it survives, relaunched, rethought, transformed into – of all things – an English public school. The nobility of its purpose has somehow tunnelled through the vicissitudes of history and it stands now in a brand new building on Raffles Road – The Raffles Institution.

The first thing you see is Raffles's coat of arms, fifteen feet high, patinated with age, clearly moved from the old site. As you look at it, a polite schoolboy appears magically at your side.

'You are looking at the Raffles arms, sir? We wear it by our hearts.' He taps the pocket of his crisp white shirt. He glows with limpid Chinese youthfulness in a way that makes me feel seedy and dog-eared.

'See. That is the Eastern crown. That medallion and chain is the Order of the Golden Sword given him by the Sultan of Aceh.'

'What? What did you say?'

'The Golden Sword. That is the Golden Sword, sir.'

'I see.'

'And that . . .' he points, '. . . is the Founder's bust.' A new, modern bust, Raffles beetle-browed and granitic. 'We carry it into Hall on Founder's day and sing our Founder's song. Excuse me, sir. I must go to my duties.'

He bows in a courtly gesture and goes to the gate where very small boys with skinny arms and legs and one enormous Indian child with a pot belly are staggering in from a cross-country run in a state of collapse. He congratulates them, assists the weary off to the changing room, asks anxiously about stragglers and goes off to look for them. A model of responsibility. A prefect.

There is an office to one side. I go in.

'Excuse me. Could you tell me where to find the Head-master?'

The Eurasian woman shoots me a glance of disapproval.

'You must mean the Principal, isn'i'?'

'Yes, I suppose it is.'

Mr Wijeysingha is Indian, enthusiastic, a believer in his school. The boys, it was immediately clear, would call him V J. There would be sniggering in history lessons when the third form got to V J-day. The Institution, he tells me, has just been privatized. This means freedom to run things better, freedom to pursue excellence and cultivate leadership.

'Raffles would have understood that.' He points to a sketch

on the wall, Raffles in Bengkulu, hedgehog-haired and hunched. 'Raffles men may not own Singapore,' he quips, 'but they run it. Our Prime Minister is an old boy, most of our ministers and intellectuals. He gives us his support and contributes personally to R.I.'s funds. We have an endowment so poor but clever boys can come here. There is a competitive examination for entrance, then we allow some foreign boys in – Thais, Indonesians, that sort of thing.'

I am taken on a tour, whitewashed walls, red quarry tiles. Everything new and respected. The school has squash courts, laboratories, music-rooms.

'All the English traditions,' says the Principal with relish, 'we have them all. House spirit, army cadets, prefects, the brass band, scouts, rugby, cricket . . .', a litany of the foreigner's view of England. 'It is a pity you have come on a Saturday.' He worries at his glasses. 'The boys are not fully operational.'

Mr Wijeysingha flings open a door and a strange scene is frozen in bright light, rows and rows of Chinese boys in PT kit, baying like rugger hearties, one pursuing another over the seats with a rolled newspaper, raised to strike. They leap to their feet, faces blank like all boys in the presence of authority.

'Good morning, sirs,' they pipe. A prefect comes forward with an expression of radiant innocence and looks at me steadily, almost defying me to contradict such obvious virtue. The innocence is a border guard. You shall not, it says, go beyond this and see behind it.

'Please take a seat, sirs,' he says smoothly, 'and witness our colourful brass-band tradition.' Two seats are immediately vacant. There is dithering. Perhaps we should stay. Embarrassment of foreign visitor seeing odd habits, unpredictable foreign reaction. Perhaps we should go. We half crouch over proffered seats. As our buttocks commence their final descent, Mr Wijeysingha thinks better of it and hustles me out.

'Aha, yes. Traditions, traditions. Aha, yes, the boys in the band, you understand. They are good boys. Our chief problem here is *too great enthusiasm.*'

'Do you,' I ask, 'have racial quotas?'

'No, no. 84 per cent Chinese, 9 per cent Indian, 7 per cent Malay.'

'But no quotas?'

'No, no. It just works out that way.'

He reels off statistics: '96 per cent of Raffles boys go on to higher education. We have 1,640 pupils and 91 teachers. They take Cambridge Certificate, you know. All teaching in English, though we teach the other tongues of Singapore.' *That* would perhaps not have pleased Raffles, dedicated as he was to the knowledge of Malay.

'Raffles,' I ask, 'is he important?' Mr Wijeysingha stops dead and looks at me genuinely shocked.

'Important? Of course he is important. Did you not see his arms as you came in? Actually,' he confides, 'I personally decided to use them. Perhaps the College of Heralds would not agree, but . . .' He looks at me fiercely. 'Raffles *belongs* to us. The government, you know, have a sort of copyright on the name of Raffles – Raffles lighthouse, hotel etc. But nowadays you need government permission to use the name. If you go to our rugger matches, you will hear the boys calling out the name of Raffles, a sort of war-cry. We have a little ceremony for the making of prefects, where . . .' No, no more ceremonies, no . . . 'Raffles was unlike the common run of imperialists, so we preserve his name. Singapore is not like colonies where we have to pull down statues and change all the street names. Singapore was not *grabbed*, it was *built* by Raffles. We are proud of him.'

So perhaps here, at last, was to be found that love that Raffles craved, for jealous ownership has the lineaments of love, and institutional pride dwells fondly on the symbols of its own greatness.

We arrive back at the coat of arms. The Principal points to the motto.

'*Auspicium Melioris Aevi*. Do you know what that means?' How many tongue-tied little boys had he put through this on their first day at R.I.?

'Er . . . Ah . . . "A brighter future through more aggressive marketing"?' No. Wait. That was another place. 'Something like "Let us hope for better days."'

'Wrong,' snaps the Principal. 'Noun not verb. You will never get anywhere until you learn the difference between a noun and . . . That is to say, a better rendition would be: "The hope of a better age". *That* is what Singapore is all about. There is too much selfishness and aggression, too much pushing and shoving. "One people, one nation, one Singapore." You know the slogan? Hah. That too is what Singapore is all about.'

As I leave, the prefect is supervising boys who are picking up litter outside the school. He wishes me goodbye and sketches a bow, but lowering eyes spot a sweet wrapper at my feet. Instinctively he pounces on it, becomes confused at having to pull it from under my shoe, sees nowhere to put it and desperately stuffs the wrapper, blushing, into his top pocket. It is hard to be the hope of a better age, a noun and not a verb.

'Would that I could infuse into the Institution a portion of that spirit and soul by which I would have it animated as easily as I endow it with lands etc. It will be long in its infancy and to arrive at maturity will require all the aid of friends and constant support. It is my last public act and rise or fall, it will always be a satisfactory reflection that I have done my best towards it. I pray you befriend it . . .' – T. S. Raffles

*

'It is a criminal offence,' says the sign, 'not to flush the toilet after use. Fine $500.'

'They say,' offered the man as we performed the Hindu hand gesture of emptiness under the blow-dryer, 'that they have put cameras in some of the WCs to check. Also the lifts. They have hidden cameras to catch those who urinate in the lifts. It is good. People should not be dirty.'

You come out of the curry shop and try to cross the road. A sign reminds you that it is an offence to cross except at a light. Fine $500.

Across the legally uncrossable street is a huge banner. It urges you to go to night classes. Another offers exercise classes for the elderly. A poster entices with civil defence, warns against wasting water.

And then the penny drops. A school is not only Raffles's memorial, it has become the model for the whole of Singapore. The entire nation is a vast school. The residents are orderly pupils to be instructed and led, as Raffles would have said, 'towards the light'. Change is always improvement. Structure and regulation are good in themselves. Above it all is the Headmaster, or maybe Principal, a being of a different order, who always knows best. A little strict and old-fashioned, certainly benevolent, incorruptible and a little frightening. Discussion with authority is always possible but, like the school debating-society, it is not to be taken too seriously. It is the sound of children learning, learning to be good citizens who see how well-off they really are.

Is it a vision of government that would have appealed to Raffles, the reformer, the pedagogue? Did he merely prefigure Lee Kuan Yew and hand on to him the sputtering torch of rationality? In the course of his life, there is a development towards authoritarianism. In his Java days Raffles always believed that, other things being equal, people would make sensible choices and behave rationally. He found himself fighting oppressive exploitation and violent monopoly. So the task of authority was to make sure that other things were indeed equal and support human free-will as an almost metaphysical duty.

His experience at Bengkulu undermined such a belief and he drifted towards benevolent autocracy. This was further strengthened in Singapore where there was no question of respecting the many mutually incompatible cultural traditions of such a mixed population. He therefore returned to first principles and framed laws that reflected universal, i.e. British, common sense. One of his major reforms was the notion of trial by a jury to which natives would be admitted. So there is an increasing feeling that cultural differences are unimportant, that they must be made unimportant, that all are equal before – for example – the law. To some this seems progressive, to others crass cultural imperialism. Small wonder that long before he returned to Bengkulu to put his affairs in order for the return to England he was toying with the idea of attracting European settlers.

*

'Mr Raffles and his Lady embarked, followed by hundreds of people of all races, myself among the rest, as far as the ship: and when they had ascended the ship's side and the crew were raising the anchor Mr Raffles called me to him and I went into his cabin where I observed that his face was flushed as if he had been wiping his tears. He told me to return and not be distressed: "If it is to be I will see you again." His Lady now came and gave me twenty-five dollars, saying "I give these to your children in Malacca," and when I heard that my heart burned the more by this act of grace. I thanked her very much, clasping them by the hand in tears, and then descended to my sampan and when I had been off some distance I turned round and saw Mr Raffles looking out of the window when I again saluted him. He raised his hand to me. This was just as the sails were being hoisted; and the vessel sailed.

Such was my separation from Mr Raffles. I was not distressed about my livelihood or because of his greatness, or because of my losing him; but because of his noble bearing, his justness, modesty and respect to his fellow men. All these I remember to this day. There are many great men besides him, clever, rich and handsome, but in good disposition, amiability and gracefulness, Mr Raffles had not his equal, and were I to die and live again such a man I could never meet again, my love of him is so great.' – Munchi Abdullah, *Hikayat Abdullah*

18. Fame

Raffles sailed for Bengkulu, calling in at Jakarta to the great consternation of the Dutch. 'He is a Herostrate,' declared the Dutch plenipotentiary, Van Nagell, comparing him to the man whose thirst for renown was so great that he burnt down the Temple of Artemis at Ephesus simply to be famous.

The Editor gave birth yet again but the child did not live long. Mortality still raged in Bengkulu, gathering in friends and colleagues. The Editor herself was so ill Raffles despaired of her life. They scanned the horizon each anxious day, watching for a sign of the ship that was to take them back to England. They knew, if it did not come soon, they would never see their native shores again. 'We are daily treading on the edge of eternity,' wrote Raffles. The Editor was poisoned with laudanum, debilitated with thirty leeches and tortured with hot baths in the name of medicine. The ship was the *Fame*. Still it did not come.

It was to be three long months before the vessel finally appeared. Raffles and the Editor embarked thankfully. Their entire worldly goods and the collections of plants, animals and books that were the result of a lifetime's research took up a third of the ship. Four of their children they left behind in the Bengkulu graveyard.

'The ship was everything we could wish; and having closed my charge here much to my satisfaction, it was one of the happiest days of my life. We were, perhaps, too happy: for in the evening came a sad reverse. Sophia had just gone to bed, and I had thrown off half my clothes, when a cry of fire, fire! roused us from our calm content, and in five minutes the whole ship was in flames! I ran to examine whence the flames principally issued, and found that the fire had its origin immediately under our cabin. Down with the boats. Where is Sophia? – Here. The children? – Here. A rope to the side. Lower Lady Raffles. Give her to me, says one; I'll take her, says the Captain. Throw the gunpowder overboard. It cannot be got at; it is in the magazine close to the fire. Stand clear of the powder. Scuttle the water-casks. Water! water! Where's Sir Stamford? Come into the boat, Nilson! Nilson, come into the boat. Push off, push off. Stand clear of the after part of the ship . . .

We then hauled close to each other, and found the Captain fortunately had a compass but we had no light except from the ship. Our distance from Bencoolen we estimated to be about fifty miles in a south-west direction. There being no landing place to the southward of Bencoolen, our only chance was to regain that port. The Captain then undertook to lead, and we to follow in a N.N.E. course, as well as we could; no chance, no possibility being left, that we could again approach the ship; for she was now one splendid flame, fore and aft, and aloft, her masts and sails in a blaze, and rocking to and fro, threatening to fall in an instant. There goes her mizen mast! Pull away my boys! There goes the gunpowder! Thank God! Thank God!' – T. S. Raffles

They lost everything, clothes, money, the property of others for which Raffles had accepted responsibility. Yet the loss that Raffles felt most bitterly was that of his natural history collection. One hundred and twenty-two cases of 'curiosities' were destroyed as well as all Raffles's papers. It was enough to break most men. But, as always, his greatest comfort was the love shown by his former subjects. The morning after their return to Bengkulu he began to redraw the maps he had been working on for years and sent locals into the forests to begin collecting specimens anew.

'And when I heard this news I was breathless, remembering all the Malay books of ancient date collected from various countries – all these lost with the wonderful collection. As to his other property I do not care, for if his life was spared he could reinstate them. But the books could not be recovered for none of them were printed but in manuscript – they were so rare that one country might have two of them; that is what distressed me . . .' – Munchi Abdullah, *Hikayat Abdullah*

Ironically, Raffles's scholastic attention had dealt Malay literary studies the greatest blow it would ever receive.

*

When I got back to England, a letter was waiting on the mat, its stamp the portrait of the President, in miniature, that hangs on a hundred million Indonesian walls. The postmark was Bengkulu.

'You have perhaps forgotten me,' it said. 'My name is Yusuf. We met on a bus and talked and I asked for your address.' Yusuf? I remembered no Yusuf but then you meet so many people . . .

'I wanted to warn you about giving your address to just anyone who asks for it. You are kind and do not know how bad people here can be. If they have your address they have power over you.

'For example, there was a man in the market at Padang selling pills and showing pictures of you. They were not nice pictures. I asked my father about what you said about Bung Karno and Bengkulu people and I think you were wrong.

Bung Karno did not fight with Bengkulu people. He admired them for their piety so much that he built them a mosque and wanted to live in Bengkulu for ever but the Dutch made him leave.

'Raffles too was not a good man as you said. I have cousins in Bengkulu who all have blue eyes. Indonesian peoples do not have blue eyes. This must be from your Raffles. The fort there was built by Raffles to make Bengkulu people suffer and they had to grow crops in buffalo shit and were not paid for it. If you doubt this, you can go there and look for yourself but I think you would be afraid to. He did not even give them the buffalo shit.

'If you want to, you can send me a letter. You already have my address.'

I stared at it baffled. Yusuf? Then the penny dropped. Buffalo shit – bullshit. This must be Yet and May. Had I told them about all this? Probably. They were tweaking my tail. It was Minang humour again.

*

This time there would be no deliberate stopping on the way, no jaunts, no edifying visits to mines, but with relatives and festivities there were already delays enough. The Raffleses were in such a rush to get back to their one surviving child that the wheels of the carriage caught fire. On the trip home there had been no compromises. Raffles had worked out a timetable of self-improvement.

'Before breakfast – One hour mathematics or logic – one hour Latin, Greek or Hebrew.

After breakfast, from 10 to 11 – In committing to paper and arranging and reviewing what I studied before breakfast.

From 11 to 1 – Writing an account of my administration in the East.

From 2 to 4 – General reading and reading out to Sophia.

In the evening for one hour – Reading out a play of Shakespeare's, or other entertaining productions.

By this arrangement, I have, in the morning, by rising at 6, one hour of exercise before breakfast, and half an hour for the same after breakfast. One hour from 1 to 2 for tiffin and exercise, and after dinner from 5 to 7, two hours for exercise or relaxation in the cool of the evening. As the servants are always behindhand in furnishing the meals, I may freely trust to their affording me time for dressing by such delays . . .'

He was, we must try to remember, a man on his way to retirement on grounds of ill-health. His only plans were to become a farmer in a small way of business . . . or perhaps a magistrate . . . maybe even Parliament.

'I was enabled to see the Chairman and Deputy of the E.I. Company and most of my best friends. The feeling, I am glad to say, seems very general in my favour, and I trust that before Christmas something will be done by those in power to acknowledge my past Services and remunerate me for my losses.' – T. S. Raffles

Raffles worked away at a document that would be a justification for his entire life's work with the Company, but his health declined and he was plagued with crippling headaches that made work impossible even for him. Then Farquar began bickering in the Court of Directors over his conduct at Singapore. But Raffles was not too weary to embrace a new project of natural history, the establishment of London Zoo. It was both a joy and a national duty.

But wherever he was, Java, Bengkulu or Singapore, Raffles always contrived to move a little outside the main settlement into the country. In the present case, this meant Hendon, where he bought a small property next to that of the anti-slavery campaigner, William Wilberforce, and installed his family and his adopted nephew Charles. He knew he was *really* a gentleman farmer, just as Bung Karno was *really* a painter.

*

It was an incredibly hot spring day with thick, honeyed sunlight, the sort of day so rare in England it seems the exclusive preserve of glazed childhood memories. Almost the final ethnographic expedition I owed to Raffles, by underground train to Hendon Central, bursting out from the dark of the tunnels into brilliant sunshine with trees reaching out in benign English growth.

To travel to Hendon, as to Nias, involves not just space but time. There are the rounded shapes of London Underground standard architecture, known from childhood outings to that zoo founded by Raffles, a main street of red-brick shops from the fifties with the familiar names of suburbia. I need no map to find the church where Raffles lies. The unconscious rules of rural planning pin it firmly to the top of the hill, though recent motorways smash through the village like a fist.

The church is 'embosomed', as Raffles would have it, in greenery, also pubs, also Ford Cortinas slewn to the kerb's edge by traditional British lager louts. They sit in the sunshine, swilling, bare-torsoed, wattles of pink flab lavishly on display. I enter the churchyard and walk through the gravestones naming those who have 'fallen asleep' and 'gone to rest', but the building is locked. Of course. This is London.

Round the back are a couple grunting in oral passion, as in the Penang fort. Further on, in the midst of the tombs, sits a man on a deck-chair, in shorts, two cans of lager at his feet. He grips a third and swigs mechanically, turning the pages of a magazine devoted to second-hand sports cars. Can this, I wonder, be the vicar? In the Church of England anything is possible. I pause and wait until he looks up peevishly.

'Excuse me,' I ask, 'are you anything to do with the church?' (or possibly, 'Church?')

'Nah, mate. But I knows me way around.'

'I'm trying to get in.'

'Well, it's locked innit. This is London. And it's Sundee. The assistant vic lives in the house by the gate. I should try there if I was you.' I do. He returns, sated of discourse, to study an article on wire wheels.

'The curate is away teaching his Scottish dancing.' Forget it. I go to the museum next door.

The bell on the door brings out the custodian, a long-haired, busily spectacled man, used to repelling bousculant youth. A whiff of something stronger than Sunday mouthwash is in the air. I greet, I sniff around. Upstairs is an exhibition of English batik, tamed to the production of dressing-gowns and 'art'. Raffles would have approved of that. I hit my head twice on low beams.

Downstairs I launch into my curatorial solidarity act, ask about the church, Raffles.

'Highwood House,' he says. 'You can walk across the fields from here. It's been through the mill since Raffles lived there, nursing home, private school. Everyone's had a go at it. In a decent country, it would be a Raffles museum but there you are. Church? Well, I'm not supposed to but I've got the key. Take you round if you can hang on a bit. He's got no tomb, of course. Just a bit of a plaque they put up later. The vicar had shares in a West Indies plantation and seeing as how Raffles opposed slavery, they didn't get on.'

The inside of the church is the familiar mix of cold stone and warm colour. Most of the memorials seem to celebrate feats of competitive campanology. Raffles is reduced to a little square of brass, the sort of thing you might screw to your gate, saying 'No Hawkers' or 'Beware of the Dog'.

'I farm the ground, 111 acres, myself, and Sophia takes charge
of the Poultry and Pigs. We brew our own beer and bake our
own bread and lead an entire Country life. The change of air,
scene and interest have already worked an amendment in my
health, and as this is the first point to be attended to I devote
my time almost exclusively to the farm and grounds . . .' –
T. S. Raffles

It is a verdant haunch of English countryside, nibbled at by
trim suburban villas. The air zithers with heat, muting sound
like snow. It is thick, a medium in its own right, like the water
in an aquarium. Time is particularly slow today. It takes an
eternity to raise your hand to wipe the sweat off your forehead.

Parks make the greenery practical, and Singaporean poly-
ethnicity has come home to visit Raffles, a world reversed,
like English batik. The cold realities of England buckle and
melt in the heat. The cricket teams treading the soft grass are
all black, while Indians and Chinese dominate the tennis
courts. A Tamil family eat a picnic, the parents withdrawing
under a tree, dipping languidly into dishes with their fingers,
the children baring their flesh redundantly to darkening sunshine, ears plugged with Walkmans. In the streets, paunched
Pakistanis whisper past in fat-tyred Mercedes.

Up the hill, may, bluebells and cow-parsley are all in riotous
growth, the whole impoverished herbarium of the townie. As I
pick my way through the trees there is a crackle of twigs, the
whiplash of branches as some great beast moves through the
glade. A deer perhaps, as in the park at Bogor. No – a lurking,
fat flasher performing his austerities in the undergrowth, who
waves his slack, pink slug at me in a token fashion, without –
it is implied – personal relish or rancour. A duty paid to the
mere name of concupiscence. Or perhaps he is waving it at
Nature, some sort of besotted ecologist. He looks dispirited,

driven by joyless devils. It is hard to believe this is happening. The English way seems to be to insist it isn't and intimidate with my lack of belief. Help thou my unbelief.

'The East India Company are now talking of taking up my case and granting me an annuity, but I fear it will be very moderate, and £500 a year is the largest amount I hear of. This, had I the means of living independent of them, I should not be inclined to accept, but necessity and consideration of my family must predominate and I must e'en be content with what I can get. I have unfortunately been a considerable loser by the cession [to the Dutch] of Bencoolen – some thousands. My Bankers have failed here and altogether my prospects are not as comfortable as they were.' – T. S. Raffles

At the top of the rise is Mill Hill School, with immaculately mannered Indian boys, conversing in cut-glass English accents as they wait for their parents to call and take them to tea. A cricketing pullover lies on the path. I pick it up. The woven nametape reads 'Ahmed Akbar – fourth form'. Surely I saw that willowy Chinese prefect, now playing croquet, at the Raffles Institution? An absurd 'gate of honour' stands outside the school – massively shut – but, like a sacred principle, with plenty of space to skirt round it in everyday life. It is impossible not to create in your head silly rituals that would be played out there, perhaps even colourful brass-band ceremonies.

*

Life never tired of hitting Raffles when he was down. Having destroyed his family it now completed the rout of his modest fortune. Late in 1826 Raffles's Javanese bankers went bankrupt, stripping him of most of his small remaining capital. The extraordinary thing is that he showed no signs of bitterness, though the incompetence of his friend and banker,

McQuoid, seems to have been largely responsible. Friends began to notice his speech had become thick and inarticulate. Life was paring him down for the final blow. It came in the form of a reply to his many years of petitioning the Company for justice in their judgement of his Java administration. They grudgingly approved much but still referred, ponderously, to the land sale as a 'questionable proceeding'. Attached to the judgement was not the pension whose meagreness he confidently deplored, but a bill for over £20,000 in repayment of accounting quibbles going back nearly ten years, charged with interest. The unkindest cut of all was to demand repayment of expenses involved in the founding of Singapore. On the same day Raffles became first president of the Zoological Society. They would put a bust of him in the Lion House in memory of Singapore, the Lion City. He was to have more busts than children.

*

There it was, Highwood House, a good, serviceable house, a reduced, middle-class mockery of the classical, but very far from the sprawling splendours of Buitenzorg. 'Unpretending but very convenient', it had been termed. A blue plaque, attached curiously to the gate, recalls the founding of Singapore. Here Raffles exhibited some of his Eastern 'curiosities', dusted no doubt by the Editor. Poverty had reduced them to buying in nothing but wine and fish, a reversion to the subsistence economy of their Bengkulu estate. Yet still no bitterness poisoned Raffles's life. At the end he was reduced to doing his own haymaking, the sort of task that pleased him best, though he complained a little of the heat. He had become a marhaenist.

To one side stood a pub, doubtless the one Raffles had bought with the estate. I looked at the sign – The Rising Sun. I had to smile. It was as if I could feel keys turning and tumblers clicking in my head. That, after all, had been the name of the Masonic lodge in Bengkulu, Raffles's lodge. I remembered a comment he had laughingly made. 'Wilberforce has the "Crown" and I the "Rising Sun".' He had delighted in the absurdity of it. Was there here some great secret revealed? Should I look for obelisks or other signs of Masonic conspiracy in the car-park? I thought not. After all, the rising sun was the symbol of Edward III and, I was sure, old maps would show the pub had that name long before Raffles. It was the last in a line of serendipities, and clearly amused Raffles himself.

'When I was a small child, maybe two years old, Mother pronounced a benediction on me. She had risen before sunrise and was sitting motionless in the dark on the verandah of our little house, doing nothing, saying nothing, just looking toward the East and patiently watching the break of day.

I, too, got up and came to her. She stretched forth her arms and, gathering me to her bosom, she hugged me silently. Moments later, she turned me around so that I, too, faced the East. Then she said softly, "Son, you are looking at the sunrise. And you, my son, will be a man of glory, a great leader of his people, because your mother gave birth to you at dawn. We Javanese believe that one born at the moment of sunrise is predestined. Never, never forget you are a child of the dawn."'
– C. Adams, *Soekarno: An Autobiography*

*

'The poor dear fellow [Raffles] got up and left his room at five o'clock and at six was a corpse, found seated upon the stairs after life had fled. Sir Everard Home who was attached, I believe sincerely, came to High Wood, and under his superintendence the body was opened and his report stands a striking proof how little the best medical opinions are to be depended upon. For years I had witnessed the sufferings of my friend and whenever medical aid was called in, whether in India or in Europe, no notice was ever taken of the sufferings of the head but as they said to denote disease of stomach or liver. Yet on dissection, it was found that liver and stomach were quite perfect and sound in every respect, whilst the head gave the clearest proofs of long continued disease. And the opinion was that if death had not occurred, idiocy or madness must have soon appeared, an opinion that reconciled his best friends to his early death, for he was only forty-five years of age.' – Captain R. Travers

Confusion was to dog Raffles to the end. As well as two sets of names, he has two ages and dates of death. Being born at sea on 5 July is the same as being born on land on the 6th, since in those days the nautical day ran from noon to noon and the land day from midnight to midnight. Since he died on the morning of 5 July he was, in fact, still forty-four.

The East India Company were incredulous when probate revealed how little the total goods and property of Sir Stamford Raffles, forty-four, were worth. Normally, anyone who had enjoyed such high office in the Company would have devoted himself avidly to feathering his own nest. Raffles had been unusual in spending freely on science and learning and had never stinted on creature comforts and hospitality, signs not of love of luxury but rather largeness of spirit. The Company was therefore grudgingly obliged to reduce its claims on his estate and settle for £10,000 in cash, contenting itself with thus stripping the Editor of all her capital.

Another wave of mortality engulfed the Editor, taking her sister and father, as if in mockery of Bengkulu. But her first duty was to clear her husband's name of all the insinuations of the Company. She sat in the lonely house on the hill, surrounded by signs of former greatness and Raffles's schoolboy treasures – worthless from a purely pecuniary point of view – and began to gather the materials for her *Memoir*, to transmute personal experience into history and so, perhaps, lay it to rest.

*

It was cool and quiet in the Abbey. The notion of paying to enter a church troubled Yet, transported to London by the dark ways of the academic mafia. It was clearly wrong if you were a Christian, and if a Muslim it smacked troublesomely of sloppy offering at the wrong address. He was not happy with all these images and reacted like an Ulsterman in the face of high Popery. He edged nervously past them, taking care not to touch.

'It is,' I said, 'like the Taman Prastasi, in Jakarta, just memorials. Here there are not even bodies.'

We paused before Raffles, myself saying nothing, waiting to see how he would respond. With what I had learned of the many griefs of Raffles's life, the enigmatic smile now looked less like patrician serenity and more like a pale European version of the Javanese shit-eating grin. He had been no child of the dawn – rather, one of the setting sun. Yet paused, smiled, looked up and read.

'Wah! Someone from Indonesia! So this is why we came here. What does it mean, gone to the place where only his harmonies are surpassed?'

'No,' I corrected. 'That's not Raff-lesh, that's another one, Purcell, a musician. They put it over his head because there was no room.' He looked blank. 'Too many great men.'

'Oh.' He ran his hand over Raffles's foot in a gesture that looked like affection. 'The foot,' he alleged, 'has been broken and mended.' He sounded like an appraiser about to deliver a low valuation.

I looked. He was right.

'Perhaps,' he twinkled, 'if I pray to Raffles, he will mend my sore feet as Bung Karno's well-water mended yours.'

I pouted sceptically.

He peered at the date. 'Today is his birthday.' I had not noticed.

'Happy Birthday to you/You belong in a zoo.'

Yet grinned. 'Ah yes. It is like our *lanjut umurnya*. You sing it for birthdays. But why was Raff-lesh so important?'

It was hard to know where to begin. Should I speak concretely of Singapore, the pearl of the Eastern Empire, or abstractly of social justice, the ending of slavery, freedom of trade and the duty to govern for the good of the governed? Crawfurd had written, with an author's bitchiness, that Raffles was not an original thinker. There was some truth in that. After all, neither the Javanese land reform nor the Singapore Institution had been entirely new. But what would have been grandiloquent Empire-building in others seemed in Raffles to rest upon human sympathy. He never lost the ability to see himself in his subjects. Sukarno wrote somewhere that revolutionaries were either destroyers or builders. He, he pointed out, had been trained as an architect, therefore had the soul of an architect. Well, Raffles had the soul of one too. Not knowing which of these to speak of, I spoke of them all. Some Japanese, true children of the dawn, gathered, whispering, to listen.

'Wrong,' said Yet.

'Wrong?'

'Wrong. I see the importance of Raff-lesh every time I walk down the street. We drive on the left. The Dutch drove on the right. That is Raff-lesh. He bothered to work out the traffic regulations. The Dutch didn't. So, Malaysia, Thailand, Indonesia, Philippines, we all drive on the left.'

There came an angry poking at my elbow.

'Oi, you. Can't you read?' It was a uniformed attendant, red of face, indicating a 'No lecturing' sign, puffing outrage. The sign was a nice piece of work of polished wood, lettered in gold, firmly jointed. 'You're causing a blockage. Move on. If I catch you again, I'll have you removed.'

Yet was delighted. 'Where shall we go now? But please, no tombs, no bodies, no Raff-lesh.'

Good Lord Minto was further along there somewhere, lurking undiscovered in the shadows, but perhaps Yet was right. Too much necrophilia.

'It's a nice day,' I observed innocently. 'Too nice to be indoors. Let's go to the zoo. They have lions.'

A Bibliographical Note

The most complete study of Stamford Raffles is C. E. Wurtz-burg's *Raffles of the Eastern Isles* (Hodder and Stoughton 1954, OUP paperback 1986). Raffles's papers have become widely scattered as the result of his prodigious correspondence and Wurtzburg, a former Singapore shipper, did more than anyone else to bring them together. The book, pruned down for publication after Wurtzburg's death, has all the virtues of an archive, but somehow loses the sense of Raffles as a person.

The bedrock of all Raffles studies must be Demetrius Boulger's monumental *The Life of Sir Stamford Raffles* (London 1897). Boulger came to the subject after meeting a member of the Raffles family in a London fever-hospital and making his own vow to the deity to write such a book if spared. It is clear that he had access to family material now lost, but the work is hopelessly biased in favour of 'Raffles as Hero'. It is biography as penitential, memorial architecture.

Best by far of the 'lightweights' is Emily Hahn's *Raffles of Singapore* (Doubleday, New York 1946). It is lively, chatty and speculative, while drawing on important Dutch published material that is ignored by most academic biographers. It homes in on 'Raffles the Man'. As an American Singaporean, Hahn brings a welcome breath of fresh air to a subject heavy with colonial piety. Since Hahn, Raffles has attracted several popular biographers, but none has anything to add to her.

A Bibliographical Note

For contemporary insights into Raffles we rely heavily on Sophia, Lady Raffles, the Editor. Her *Memoir of the Life and Public Services of Sir Thomas Stamford Raffles : F.R.S.:&c.* (London 1830) is the original source of many later interpretative works. Unfortunately, she sticks almost entirely to 'Raffles as Public Figure', steering clear of exactly that priceless personal information only she could have given. It is largely through this work that we know her, as she piquantly describes the erratic and eccentric life foisted on her by a man she clearly adored, in formal, costive, slightly puzzled prose.

The foremost scholar on British involvement in the East Indies is John Bastin, who has brought together a number of invaluable sources that shed light on Raffles and the era in which he worked. *Memoirs of the Raffles Museum, 4, 1957* contains the journal of Raffles's assistant T. Travers. *The Native Policies of Sir Thomas Stamford Raffles in Java and Sumatra* (Clarendon Press, Oxford 1957) and *The British in West Sumatra* (University of Malaya Press, Kuala Lumpur 1965) are fundamental to any assessment of Raffles as administrator. Also, J. Bastin and M. Archer's *The Raffles Drawings in the India Office Library London* (OUP, Kuala Lumpur 1978) and J. Bastin and P. Rohatgi's *Prints of Southeast Asia in the India Office Library* (HMSO, London 1979) contain useful pictures of many of the places he visited.

The indispensable work of Raffles himself is his *History of Java* (London 1817), an amazing jumble of miscellaneous knowledge. It shows us a man of omnivorous learning but little time, with an eighteenth-century faith that it is possible to learn *everything*. Through what he holds to be facts, Raffles shows us some of his most strongly held opinions. Many of these were shaped by Lord Minto, who is most usefully represented by his own letters home from India, collected as *Lord Minto in India: Life and Letters of Gilbert Elliot* (London 1880) and published by his wife, the Countess of Minto.

The East India Company is such obvious thesis fodder that a small library has been written on it. The most useful introduction is perhaps H. Furber's *John Company at Work. A study of European expansion in India in the late eighteenth century* (Harvard UP, Cambridge, Mass. 1948).

Sukarno has attracted a large literature of vilification and hagiography, much of it in Dutch. Wearily complete as a political record is G. Penders's *The Life and Times of Sukarno* (Sidgwick and Jackson, London 1974). Set against this is the highly journalistic *Soekarno: An Autobiography* (Bobbs-Merrill, New York 1965), actually written by the American, Cindy Adams. The subsequent *My Friend the Dictator* (Bobbs-Merrill, New York 1967) sheds valuable light on the circumstances of the production of this work, a book that still grossly embarrasses Indonesian officialdom.

Important Dates in the Life of Stamford Raffles

1781 born
1795 enters East India Company as a clerk
1805 Assistant Secretary to Governor of Penang; marries Olivia
1807, 1808 visits Malacca
1810 to Calcutta
1811 invasion of Java; Raffles appointed Lieutenant-Governor
1812 land reform in Java
1813 death of Olivia
1815 dismissed
1816 returns to England
1817 *History of Java*; knighted; marries Sophia
1818 to Bengkulu
1819 founds Singapore
1820 death of son
1822 deaths of two other children
1823 death of infant daughter
1824 fire on *Fame*
1826 dies in England

Index

Abdullah bin Abdul Kadir, Munshi: on
English in Malacca, 36; on Malacca Fort,
26; on Minto, 40, 148; and Raffles, 244;
on Raffles, 29–30, 212–13, 251–2; on
Raffles Institution, 245; Raffles's Malay
manuscripts, 255
Aceh, 210–11
Agus: author and, 45–6, 48; in Ancol, 54;
Bandung wedding, 150, 153; in Batavia,
62–3; becomes Westernized, 46; his friends,
47–8; his granny and the telephone, 84–5;
in Tanjung Priok, 49–51
Alvarez, Alfonso, 33–6
Aneke: ghosts, 139; her home, 139; oranges,
137; physician, 140–41; rice, 134–5, 136,
137
author, the, see Barley, Nigel

Bali: Amplapura, 206–7; author in, 196–209;
drought breaks, 203; hotel building, 197–
8; Raffles, 142; Raffles on Balinese, 197,
199; Tampaksiring, 202–3; University
football team, 160, 161–4, 177–9, 180
Bandung, wedding, 150–53; rainman, 153
Bangka, 100, 108
Bannerman, John Alexander, 238
Barley, Nigel: at Bandung wedding, 150–53;
bus journey to Minangkabau, 182–4;
magic knocking, 71–4; malaria, 173–5,
177–9
    and people: Agus, 45–6, 48, 62–3, 84,
150; Aneka, 134–5, 136–7, 140–41; Bali
University football team, 160–64, 173–4,
177–9; becak driver, 125–6; Javanese

noodle-seller, 1–4, Ketuk, 204–6, 208–9;
Lukas, 98–102, 112–14, 116–17, 118, 122–
5; Marwan, 56; the minister, 4–5; Nyoman,
199–200, 203–4; Pak Suyono, 126–8; pedlar
of aphrodisiac capsules, 230; Yet and May,
185–92 passim, 256, 266
    and places: Bali, 196–209; Batavia, 62–
8; Bengkulu, 161, 171–2, 180–81; Bogor,
Great Garden, 87–9; Bogor, National
Palace, 77–81; Borobodur temple, 121–2;
Hendon, 258–61, 262; Jakarta, 135, 143–4;
Malacca, 27–8, 31, 33–9 passim; Nias,
222–3, 225–6; Parangtritis, 122–5; Penang,
11, 14–15, 19, 22, 24; Raffles Institution,
245–9; Si Pitung's house, 51; Singapore, 11,
232–3, 236–7, 240–41, 250; Singapore
Airlines office, 41; Solo, 92–5; Westminster
Abbey, 5–9, 265–7; Yogya, 98–102, 109
Bataks, 217
Batavia (see also Jakarta), 47, 57, 60–63
passim
becaks, 92–5
Bengkulu: author in, 161; author on the
beach, 180–81; author ill in, 173–5, 177–9;
author's bus journey from, 182–3; Bung
Karno in, 168–9; convicts, 161;
disadvantages, 158–9; East India Company
and, 235; Freemasonry, 165; graveyard
253; obelisks, 165; population, 160;
Raffles's house, 232–3; Raffles's journeys
through, 172–3, 175–6, 179;
transmigration, 171; under Raffles, 161;
vaccination, 225
Bogor: author in, 77–81; Great Garden, 75,

Index

87–9, 138; National Palace, 75, 77–80; Raffles's residence, 71; Tanah Abang cemetery, 66–8

Borobodur, 116, 117, 121

Boulger, D. C., 7

British Museum, Raffles Collection, 54–5, 150, 221

Buitenzorg, *see* Bogor

Bung Karno, *see* Sukarno

Chinese, the: East India Company and trade with, 59, 243; joggers, 27–8; karaoke, 181–2, 184; Marwan and, 56; Probolingo currency, 60; Stockdale on, 55–6

Crawfurd, John, 91, 213, 245, 266

Daendels, Herman Willem: death, 88; drill square, 86; and Freemasonry, 85; remembered, 127, 149; reputation, 65

Dick (the Papuan boy), 145

Dion (the Indonesian), 38–41

Dutch, the: assault on Yogya, 103, 108; Batavia, 49; Borobodur temple, 117; corruption, 53; intern Sukarno, 108; Java, 64, 90, 140, 144; and Malay archipelago, 210; Nagasaki factory, 119, 120; National Palace, Bogor, 75; Probolingo currency, 60; and Raffles, 30, 133, 170–71, 204, 261; and rhinoceros, 203; and Singapore, 237; slavery, 131; torture, 55; trade, 53, 58

East India Company: administration, 110; agents in Bengkulu, 158; dissimulation, 120; incompetent builders, 23; and Java, 32; and Malacca, 26; and Malays, 10; monopolistic, 59; and opium, 132; and Padang, 192; in Penang, 13–14; and Raffles, 138, 210, 261, 262, 264; Raffles joins, 17; and Singapore, 237, 243; and Singapore Institution, 245; slavery, 161

Farquar, William, 241–2

Francis Xavier, St, 30–31

Freemasonry, 85–7, 117–18, 136, 165

Gillespie, Sir Robert Rollo: assault on Cornelis, 48; Farquar likened to, 241;

Mason, 85; reduces Palembang, 100; and Raffles, 102, 107, 135, 136, 138

Hahn, E., 7; *Raffles of Singapore*, 57, 61, 62, 166–7

Hastings, 1st Marquess of, *see* Moira, 2nd Earl of

Hendon, 257–61

Horsefield, Thomas, 91

Ito (Japanese surfer), 222–3

Jakarta (*see also* Batavia): art show, 143; author in, 64–6, 71–4; clothes, 114; kite-flying, 69–70; 'magic knocking', 71–4; Masonic meeting house, 85

Janssens, Johann Willem, 60

Japan, 119–20, 138

Java: blockade, 39; British government and, 138; British victory, 47, 48, 53; buffalo/tiger fights, 111; elephant returned to, 120; Raffles Lt-Governor, 48; Raffles's reforms, 63–4, 224–5; Raffles's work in, 239; spice trade, 39, 59; Tanjung Priok, 46, 49; transmigration, 171; under Dutch, 53, 58–9

Javanese noodle-seller, 1–4

Joseph, George, 154

Ketut (Balinese mechanic): and author, 204–6, 208–9

Klaten, 96

Krakatoa, 218

Lee Kuan Yew, 238

Leyden, John: Bitara, 147; burial place, 139; at Cilincing, 45; death of, 47; Minto on, 44; and Raffles, 43–4, 119; scholar, 43; tomb lost, 67–8

Light, Francis, 10, 12–14

Loro Kidul (South Seas goddess), 122–3, 128–30

Lukas: and author, 98–102; batik paintings, 102; at Borobodur, 121; and boy with condoms, 104–6; at circus 112–14; motorbike, 116–17, 118, 124, 125; at

Lukas (cont.)
   Parangtritis, 122–4; and Tunjong Segara, 128

Malacca: author in, 31, 37–9; cemeteries, 27–8, 31–2; English in, 36; fortifications, 25–6, 30; harbour, 37; hotel, 28; Koranic school, 244; the Portuguese, 33–6; Raffles in, 33; Raffles on, 26; Singapore Airlines office, 41; 'song and lumier', 31
Marwan (the Javanese boy), 56
May (the Minang), 185–6, 187, 189–91, 192, 256
Minang people, 187–9
Minangkabau, 184, 191
Minangs: author with Yet and May, 184–94 *passim*
Minto, 1st Earl of: Abdullah on, 40; abolition of torture, 55; on assault on Cornelis citadel, 48; on Batavia, 57; on Batavian mulatto women, 61; death, 139; eponym, 100; Fort William College, 245; free trade, 58; Freemasonry, 85; Java, 36, 52, 53; on Leyden, 44; *Modeste*, 37; and Moira, 136; portrait, 155; Raffles and, 26, 33, 42–3, 52, 136; and Raffles's sisters, 23; slave children, 114–16; tomb, 267
Moira, 2nd Earl of, later 1st Marquess of Hastings: and colonization of Singapore, 237, 238; Governor-General, 136, 137; and Raffles, 137–8, 158, 194–5, 210
Muntinghe, Hermann Warner, 85, 132

Napoleon I, Emperor, 148–9
Nias Island: author in, 222–3, 225–6; characteristics of the people, 218–19; Gunungsitoli, 215, 217; Lagundi, 219–20; religion, 221; slaves, 216; Telukdalam, 218; tourists, 215
Nyoman (the Balinese footballer): author and, 199–200; introduces author to Ketut, 203–4; money from God, 200–201; at temple, 202; university fees, 178, 196

Padang, 192
Pageruyong: architecture, 186–7; author, Yet and May at, 189–91

Pak Suyono, 126–8
Paku Alam, the, 127, 128
Palembang, Sultan of, 100
Parangtritis, 122–4
Parr, Thomas, 164, 166–7
pedlar of aphrodisiac capsules, 229–31
Pelabuhan Ratu, 128–30
Penang: author in, 11, 14–15, 22, 24; East India Company and, 26; Fort Cornwallis, 23–4; Independence Day in, ll; Light and, 10; Love Lane, 14, 17, 19; population, 17; Raffles in, 21–2

Raden Rana Dipura, 145, 150, 160
Raffles Collection, 54–5, 150, 221
Raffles Institution, 245–9
Raffles, Lady (Sophia): and Abdullah, 251; adopts slave girl, 161; after Raffles's death, 264–5; in Bengkulu, 172, 253; botany, 212; to Calcutta, 194; *Memoir*, 7, 179–80, 226, 228–9, 233; and Olivia, 7, 114
Raffles, Leopold, 212, 231
Raffles, Olivia: Leyden and, 44, 139; marriage, 20; monument, 89; in Penang, 24; question of children, 114; tomb, 67, 139–40
Raffles, Sir Thomas Stamford: Bengkulu, 158–9, 164, 167–8, 172–3, 175–6, 253; Buleleng, 205; *History of Java*, 90, 111, 154–5, 197, 199, 203; and Japan, 8, 119–20; Java, 32–3, 36, 52, 53; Malacca, 25–6, 33; naval route to Java, 39–40; National Palace, 75; and Penang, 12, 21–3, 24; Philippines, 138; trade, 41, 58
   character: attitude to 'little people', 133; benevolence, 146, 149; courtesy, 29; good nature, 66; happiness and unhappiness, 44–5; hospitality, 21, 60; inability to handle opposition, 242; industry, 76; intellectual honesty, 147; lack of bitterness, 261, 262; largeness of spirit, 264; longing for recognition, 157; naïveté, 54, 147; need to be loved, 136; optimism, 147; paternalism, 146; scholarship, 76, 142–3, 144; studiousness, 17–18
   and colleagues: Crawfurd, 91; Farquar, 241–2; Gillespie, 48, 135–6; Horsefield, 91;

Index

Leyden, 43–4, 47; Minto, 42–3, 52, 54, 85; Moira, 137–8, 194–5, 210

homes: Bogor (Buitenzorg), 71, 75, 76–7; Highwood House, 259, 262; Permatang Balam country plantation, 227; Singapore bungalow, 243

interests: ancient architecture, 117; Freemasonry, 85–7, 117; literature, 143; mineralogy, 182; natural history, 30, 88, 158, 175, 211–12, 232, 242, 254; science, 142; Zoological Society, 257, 262

Lieutenant-Governor: abolition of torture, 55; administration, 81–2; Bangka, 100; dismissed, 144; and the Dutch, 170–71; gambling, 131, 161; hospitality, 60–61, 63, 102; and Indian plot, 118; Java, 48, 63–4, 90–91, 131–4, 140; knighthood, 53, 154; land reform, 81–2, 132, 133; medical care, 172, 224–5; monument to, 5–9 *passim*; opium, 132; and Paku Alam, 127, 128; his philosophy of government, 146–7, 250–51; protocol, 68, 95; reputation, 100; Singapore, 12, 212–14, 234–5, 243; Singapore Institution, 244, 245; slavery, 76, 131–2, 161; statues, 242, 246; and Sultan of Yoga, 102; trade, 59, 100, 119; in Yoga, 95, 100

private life: appearance, 28–9, 154; attitude to education, 18, 244; attitude to religion, 86–7; in Bencoolen, 228–9; Borobodur temple, 117, 118, 121; buys land, 138; children, 114, 116, 124, 130, 228–9, 231–2, 253; death, 263–4; durian, 135; in England, 153–4; finances, 261–2; Freemason, 85; health, 23, 140, 146, 154, 231–2, 243, 257–60; Hendon, 257–8, 259–60; impoverished childhood, 17–18; linguisitc ability, 17, 21, 22; Malay manuscripts, 255; marriages, 20, 156; name, 16–17; and Napoleon, 148–9; nicknames, 157; portraits, 154, 155, 246–7; return journeys to England, 145, 253–4, 256–7; statues and busts, 242, 246, 262; writer, 14

quoted on: Javanese and Balinese religion, 203; Minangkabau, 184, 191; natives of Bali, 197, 199; Nias, 216, 223; shame among Malayans, 207–8; Singapore, 239

quotations on Raffles by: Abdullah, 29–30; Addison, 66; Colburn, 20; Lady Raffles, 179; Travers, 21–2, 75; Wurtzburg, 76–7, 96

Rafflesia arnoldii, 88, 175

Regent, Prince, *later* King George IV, 53, 157

Si Pitung, 50–51

Singapore: architecture, 19; contemporary city, 236; 238–41; economy, 235; founding, 212, 237; gambling and slavery, 131; and Malacca, 37; mixed population, 236; Raffles founds, 12; Raffles Institution, 245–9; Raffles on, 239; Raffles's administration, 234–5; Singapore Institution, 244, 245

slavery: convict labour, 235; East India Company, 161; gambling and, 131; Gillespie, 135; Nias, 216, 218; Raffles and, 53, 76, 131–2

Solo, 90, 130: author in, 92–5

Sukarno: artist, 80–81, 258; batik portrait, 102; bicycle, 169–70; birth at dawn, 263; drought breaks, 203; and the Dutch, 176; Dutch attack on Yogya, 103; exile in Bungkarno, 168; house, 168–9; as *ingénue*, 42; interned, 108; Javanese noodle-seller and, 2–3, 4; and Loro Kidul, 129–30; Marhaenism, 82–3; marraige, 20–21, 168; name, 16; National Palace, 75, 78, 79, 80; Nusantara, 147; Pelabuhan Ratu hotel, 128, 129; philosophy, 87; President, 15; and revolutionaries, 266; Tampaksiring, 202–3

Sumatra, 191, 210

Surabaya, battle of, 151

Tanjung Priok, 48–50

Tengku Long, Sultan, 212–13

trade: Bengkulu, 160; China/Europe, 243; Dutch and, 58–9; East India Company, 110; Japan, 119–20; pepper, 161; Raffles's objective, 213; spice, 39, 59, 235

Travers, T., 145, 165, 264: *Journal*, 21–2, 71, 75

Westminister Abbey, Raffles's tomb, 5–9 *passim*, 265–6

Wijeysingha, Mr (the Indian schoolmaster), 246–9
Wilberforce, William, 258
Wurtzburg, C., 7: Raffles of the Eastern Isles, 76–7, 136

Yet (the Minang): author and, 185, 187, 256; in London, 265–6; and Minang social

system, 192–4; at Pageruyung palace, 189–91
Yogya: author in, 98–106 *passim*; author at the palace, 125–8; British take, 107; Crawfurd in, 91; Dutch attack, 103, 107–8; and European dominance, 91–2; Raffles, 95, 100; Sultan, 91, 102